Closing the Gold Window

DOMESTIC POLITICS AND THE END OF BRETTON WOODS

JOANNE GOWA

CORNELL UNIVERSITY PRESS

Ithaca and London

First published 1983 by Cornell University Press.
Published in the United Kingdom by Cornell University Press, Ltd., London.

International Standard Book Number 0-8014-1622-1
Library of Congress Catalog Card Number 83-7184
Printed in the United States of America
Librarians: Library of Congress cataloging information
appears on the last page of the book.

The paper in this book is acid-free and meets the guidelines for permanence and durability of the Committee on Production Guidelines for Book Longevity of the Council on Library Resources.

Closing the Gold Window

Cornell Studies in
Political Economy

EDITED BY

PETER J. KATZENSTEIN

To Andy and Katie

Contents

Preface

In this book I explain the domestic political influences that contributed to the Nixon administration's decision on August 15, 1971, to end the dollar's convertibility into gold, a decision that effectively brought to an end the Bretton Woods regime that had governed postwar international monetary relations. This book is, as a consequence, simultaneously a case study of foreign economic policy making and one of international regime transformation.

In attempting to fill the explanatory gaps left by and acknowledged in system-level analyses of international regime change, I focus on the internal politics of the key currency state of the Bretton Woods regime, the United States. I argue that, within the context of domestic politics, the mid-1971 decision can be explained in terms of two factors. First, the Nixon administration emphasized the primacy of national autonomy over regime maintenance, an emphasis that accurately reflected the preferences of society at large and the structure of the U.S. economy. Second, the U.S. government was organized for the conduct of international monetary policy in such a way as to award a position of preeminence to the Department of the Treasury.

Although cautiously, because the analysis is based on a single case, I conclude that international regimes influence state behavior less than some other authors have assumed. I also contend that bureaucratic politics explanations of the foreign-policy decision-making process are less useful at the core than at the margins of that process. Within the context of ongoing debates about the nature of the state, I argue that a conception of the American state as a "weak" or constrained state best fits this case.

Without the support and encouragement extended to me, in different ways and at different times, by a substantial number of people, I could not have written this book.

I owe much more than I can gracefully express to Robert G. Gilpin, Jr., Eisenhower Professor of International Affairs at Princeton University. I am profoundly grateful for Professor Gilpin's rare ability to be both relentlessly critical and unfailingly supportive over an extended period of time.

I am grateful, as well, to several colleagues from different disciplines who offered comments, criticisms, and suggestions on the manuscript at various stages. Fred Block, Benjamin J. Cohen, Frederick W. Frey, Peter J. Katzenstein, Robert O. Keohane, Stephen D. Krasner, John S. Odell, Daniel Ounjian, Robert F. Rich, John Gerard Ruggie, Marc Trachtenberg, and Richard H. Ullman enabled the manuscript to become a better book by raising perceptive questions that forced me to rethink several sections.

Almost without exception, the twenty-three former Nixon administration officials who subjected themselves to interviews responded generously to questions about the decision-making process that must occasionally have seemed to them wholly unrelated to their experience in government. Their gifts of knowledge and time were, in some cases, extraordinary and, in all cases, very much appreciated.

I also thank my research assistant, Sandra L. Levy, who not only aided admirably in the process of substantive research but who also spent countless hours tracking down obscure citations. The Department of Political Science at the University of Pennsylvania is owed a debt of gratitude as well for its financial support of this project, as are Marla I. Chazin and Christine M. Quinn, who transformed the manuscript into a legible state.

A unique contribution to my work was that of my husband and daughter, to whom this book is dedicated. Without their love, laughter, and reminders that there was life outside Bretton Woods, the book would have been even harder to write.

JOANNE GOWA

Philadelphia, Pennsylvania

Closing the Gold Window

CHAPTER ONE

Introduction

On August 15, 1971, President Richard M. Nixon delivered the *coup de grâce* to the postwar international monetary regime. In a twenty-minute address to the nation and the world, he made the *de facto, de jure*: henceforth, he declared, the dollar would not be convertible into gold or other primary reserve assets. In thus "closing the gold window" he abruptly ended one of the crucial fictions that had allowed the system constructed at Bretton Woods in 1944 to stagger along beyond its natural life span. As Robert O. Keohane and Joseph S. Nye later observed, "August 15, 1971, marked the end of an international monetary regime as clearly as did 1914 [the end of the gold standard] or 1931 [the collapse of the gold-exchange standard]."[1]

In this book I explain the domestic political processes that led the Nixon administration to close the gold window. I argue that the dominant domestic political influence on the August decision was the consensus within the Nixon administration on the primacy of national autonomy over regime maintenance. That consensus was deeply embedded not only within the administration but within the fabric of domestic society as well. I also maintain that the structure and process of international monetary policy making in Nixon's administration played an important supporting role in the decision that ended the Bretton Woods system.

[1] Robert O. Keohane and Joseph S. Nye, *Power and Interdependence: World Politics in Transition* (Boston: Little, Brown, 1977), p. 83.

In short, the Nixon administration's emphasis on national autonomy and the structure of its international monetary policy making, given contemporaneous developments in the monetary regime itself, led ineluctably to the August decision. This argument diverges considerably from other interpretations of that decision cast at the same level of analysis.[2] It also suggests, implicitly throughout and explicitly in the conclusion, that international regimes influence state behavior less than is sometimes assumed;[3] that bureaucratic politics models of decision making in foreign policy are powerful at the margins but weaken toward the core of that process;[4] and that U.S. international monetary policy is the product of a relationship between "state and society," between public and private sectors, much more complex than has previously been assumed.[5]

Before elaborating on these conclusions, I explain why what is

[2] It disagrees, for example, with the contention that "the August 1971 decision is another negative example of royal-court decision making" (see Wilfrid L. Kohl, "The Nixon Foreign Policy System and U.S.-European Relations: Patterns of Policy-Making," *World Politics* 28 [October 1975]: 20); and with the argument that the decision is a "classic example" of the "presidential fiat" model of decision making (see Stephen D. Cohen, *The Making of United States International Economic Policy: Principles, Problems and Proposals for Reform* [New York: Praeger, 1977], pp. 80, 81). It also places much more emphasis on domestic politics than does the section of John S. Odell's book that deals specifically with the unit-level variables implicated in the 1971 decision (see Odell, *U.S. International Monetary Policy: Markets, Power, and Ideas as Sources of Change* [Princeton: Princeton University Press, 1982], chap. 4.) I discuss the differences—and similarities—among explanations of the decision at greater length in Chapter Seven.

[3] For a discussion of the differences among scholars that illustrates the strength that some attribute to international regimes, see Stephen D. Krasner, "Structural Causes and Regime Consequences: Regimes as Intervening Variables," *International Organization* 36 (Spring 1982): 189-94.

[4] For a statement of the bureaucratic politics model, see Graham T. Allison, *Essence of Decision: Explaining the Cuban Missile Crisis* (Boston: Little, Brown, 1971), or Morton H. Halperin et al., *Bureaucratic Politics and Foreign Policy* (Washington, D.C.: Brookings, 1974).

[5] The distinction between state and society has been employed recently in *Between Power and Plenty*, edited by Peter J. Katzenstein, to explain the formation of foreign economic policies in the advanced industrialized states. The key independent variable in the essays in that volume is differences among the "domestic structures" of the advanced states, differences that are analyzed "using the traditional distinction between 'state' and 'society' " (p. 16). That definition refers to the difference between the public and private sectors, although Katzenstein then goes on to argue that "the distinction between state and society connotes a gap between the private and public sector which exists today in no advanced industrial state" (p. 17). Relations between

essentially a study of international regime change is focused on the domestic political processes of a single state—on what the international relations literature more formally labels unit-level or intrastate variables. I will also explicitly acknowledge the limits to explanation that such a focus tends, almost inevitably, to impose.

INTERNATIONAL REGIME CHANGE AND THE GOLD WINDOW DECISION

In this book I equate the closing of the gold window with the breakdown of the postwar international monetary regime. This equation commands considerable but by no means universal con-

---

state and society do differ among states, however; Katzenstein maintains that "state power [is] . . . stronger in some countries, such as Japan or France, than in others . . . " (p. 20). See Katzenstein, ed., *Between Power and Plenty: Foreign Economic Policies of Advanced Industrialized States* (Madison: University of Wisconsin Press, 1978). Also in that volume, Stephen D. Krasner argues that the United States, in the field of international monetary policy, has had, in effect, a strong state, contending that "United States leaders have had a relatively free hand" in international monetary policy decision making, because of the arenas in which decisions have been made (p. 66). The locus of decision making for money, unlike that for trade, according to Krasner, has been in "the White House, the Treasury Department, and the Federal Reserve Board, arenas that are well insulated from particular societal pressures" (p. 65). See Krasner, "US Commercial and Monetary Policy," in ibid., pp. 51-88. Janet Kelly assumes a perspective broadly similar to Krasner's, arguing that the structure of politics within "today's democratic societies" relevant to the formulation of international monetary policy is one in which the state acts independently of societal pressures. Kelly maintains, "The politics of monetary interdependence are . . . of a special kind. Trade policy, energy policy, agricultural policy—all of these instantly call to mind specific constituencies within countries which will react quickly to foreign events affecting their welfare. These are highly charged questions which in today's societies soon become politicized. Domestic constraints act to limit the autonomous exercise of state power. Yet the monetary system does not bring to mind any particular group whose vital interests are at stake. . . . All of these considerations make the nature of international monetary relations a rarified area of politics. The international monetary system remains largely in the sphere of elite politics. . . . Central bankers and finance ministers still meet secretly over weekends, priding themselves on their ability to avoid leaks to the public." See Kelly, "International Monetary Systems and National Security," in *Economic Issues and National Security*, ed. Klaus Knorr and Frank Trager (Lawrence: Regents Press of Kansas, 1977), p. 240.

sensus among analysts of that regime.[6] Among the dissenters are some who contend that Bretton Woods died not in 1971 but in 1973 (with the advent of widespread currency floating)[7] and others who argue that Bretton Woods still lives.[8] This divergence in perspectives arises as a result of an inherently unresolvable academic debate about appropriate definitions of regime change as well as of the untidy way in which the Bretton Woods regime unraveled.[9] There is ultimately no impregnable interpretation of whether and when Bretton Woods died.

I follow Keohane and Nye in distinguishing "regimes from one another on the basis of their formal or de facto rules and norms governing the behavior of major actors" and in defining international monetary regime periods "in terms of the behavior of the key currency countries—Great Britain until 1931 and the United

[6]Those in agreement include, among others, David A. Walker, "Some Underlying Problems for International Monetary Reform," in *The United States and Western Europe: Political, Economic and Strategic Perspectives*, ed. Wolfram F. Hanrieder (Cambridge, Mass.: Winthrop, 1974), p. 166; Marina v. N. Whitman, *Reflections of Interdependence: Issues for Economic Theory and U.S. Policy* (Pittsburgh: University of Pittsburgh Press, 1979), p. 199; Keohane and Nye, *Power and Interdependence*, p. 83; W. M. Scammell, *The International Economy since 1945* (New York: St. Martin's, 1980), p. 109.

[7]See, for example, Alfred E. Eckes, *A Search for Solvency: Bretton Woods and the International Monetary System, 1941-1971* (Austin: University of Texas Press, 1975), pp. 265, 267; Fred L. Block, *The Origins of International Economic Disorder: A Study of U.S. International Monetary Policy from World War II to the Present* (Berkeley: University of California Press, 1977), pp. 199, 203; Thomas D. Willett, *Floating Exchange Rates and International Monetary Reform* (Washington, D.C.: American Enterprise Institute, 1977), p. 1; Odell, *U.S. International Monetary Policy*, chap. 4.

[8]See, for example, John Gerard Ruggie, "International Regimes, Transactions, and Change: Embedded Liberalism in the Postwar Economic Order," *International Organization* 36 (Spring 1982): 379-416.

[9]On regime change, Krasner, for example, argues that only changes in norms and principles constitute changes of regime (see Krasner, "Structural Causes and Regime Consequences," p. 186). Oran Young contends that regime transformation refers "to significant alterations in a regime's structures of rights and rules, the character of its social choice mechanisms, and the nature of its compliance mechanisms," while observing that the whole issue of when a regime disappears reminds him of "the well-known query posed by philosophers: how many Chevrolet parts added to a Ford automobile would it take to transform the vehicle from a Ford into a Chevrolet?" (see Young, "Regime Dynamics: The Rise and Fall of International Regimes," *International Organization* 36 [Spring 1982]: 291). Keohane and Nye focus on changes in rules and norms (see Keohane and Nye, *Power and Interdependence*, p. 73).

States thereafter."[10] The United States was the key currency country of the Bretton Woods regime, because the dollar served as the reserve, intervention, and vehicle currency of the postwar regime;[11] the closing of the gold window violated the regime's rule that the United States maintain a stable value for its currency; and the action violated the regime norm that the United States remain passive with respect to the exchange rate of the dollar. August 15 can thus be defensibly interpreted as the end of Bretton Woods and, therefore, as an instance of regime transformation. As such, its explanation both benefits from and contributes to the expanding literature on international political economy in general and on international regimes in particular.

Implicit or explicit in the variety of available definitions of international regimes is the assumption that international regimes influence the behavior of states and thereby influence outcomes in international politics. International regimes have been defined, for example, as the "networks of rules, norms, and procedures that regularize international behavior and control its effects";[12] as "social institutions" that govern "actions of those interested in specifiable activities (or meaningful sets of activities)";[13] and as "sets of implicit or explicit principles, norms, rules, and decision-making procedures around which actors' expectations converge in a given area of international relations."[14] The monetary regime specifically has been defined by Richard N. Cooper as "the rules and conventions that govern financial relations between countries."[15]

The transformations of regimes, arguably the most important topic in the entire literature on international regimes, have at-

[10]Keohane and Nye, *Power and Interdependence*, p. 73.

[11]A reserve currency is defined as a currency used by states "as an asset in their international reserves"; a vehicle currency is one "used for settlement of international commercial or financial transactions"; an intervention currency is used to defend an exchange rate in international markets (see Susan Strange, *Sterling and British Policy: A Political Study of an International Currency in Decline* [London: Oxford University Press, 1971], p. 202).

[12]Keohane and Nye, *Power and Interdependence*, p. 19.

[13]Oran R. Young, "International Regimes: Problems of Concept Formation," *World Politics* 32 (April 1980): 232.

[14]Krasner, "Structural Causes and Regime Consequences," p. 186.

[15]Richard N. Cooper, "Prolegomena to the Choice of an International Monetary System," in *International Economics and International Politics*, ed. C. Fred Bergsten and Lawrence B. Krause (Washington, D.C.: Brookings, 1975), p. 63.

tracted the interest of political scientists not only because of their intrinsic importance but also because an understanding of regime dynamics may yield invaluable insights into the ways in which international systems change. An international system is what, as Kenneth N. Waltz put it, "intervenes between interacting units and the results that their acts and interactions produce."[16] To date, most theorists of international systems have been preoccupied with explaining continuities in international politics: they have concentrated on defining systems, delineating the effects of a system on its constituent units, and identifying the mechanisms that serve to perpetuate a system's existence. As several prominent systems theorists themselves have agreed, current theories of international systems are theories of comparative statics;[17] theories of systems change, changes of rather than within a system, are notable largely by virtue of their absence.[18] In their effort to explain the profound continuities that characterize international politics, scholars have neglected the forces that can undermine and transform a system.

Studies of regime transformations can begin to fill this lacuna in our understanding of international relations although they cannot, by their nature, do so completely. International regimes are, by definition, constituent elements of the international system; they regulate aspects of political and economic processes within the larger system. Transformations of international regimes, therefore, are changes in, but not of, international systems. They influence the patterns of interactions among units within the system but they do not change the system itself. Nonetheless, because international regimes exist in spheres of activity critically important to the course

[16]Kenneth N. Waltz, *Theory of International Politics* (Reading, Mass.: Addison-Wesley, 1979), p. 79.

[17]At the panel "Systemic Theories of Change" (Robert G. Gilpin, Jr., Robert O. Keohane, Kenneth N. Waltz) of the annual meeting of the American Political Science Association, New York, September 3-6, 1981. See also Dina A. Zinnes's comments that "the number of studies that analyze international systems is relatively small" and that "those studies that have appeared, with only a few exceptions, are largely static. Most studies of international systems concentrate on identifying and describing types of systems" (in Zinnes, "Prerequisites for the Study of System Transformation," in *Change in the International System*, ed. Ole R. Holsti, Randolph M. Siverson, and Alexander L. George [Boulder, Col.: Westview, 1980], p. 3).

[18]For exceptions, see the various articles in Holsti, Siverson, and George, *Change in the International System*; and Robert G. Gilpin, *War and Change in International Politics* (New York: Cambridge University Press, 1981).

of international politics, transformations of international regimes can suggest variables of importance to any understanding of systems change. This is why, as Keohane remarked recently, "if we could understand how international regimes change—and why— we would have made significant progress in the theory of international relations. We would have identified major features of international politics."[19]

This analysis of the Nixon administration's decision to close the gold window was undertaken with a view to understanding the influence of international regimes and the processes of regime transformation. That I focus on the domestic politics of Bretton Woods's demise does not imply that systemic variables were unimportant in that process; indeed, I explicitly presuppose that such variables are integral to any adequate explanation of the collapse of the postwar monetary regime. That collapse cannot be understood if the critically important roles played by systemic constraints and incentives are ignored.

Nor, however, can it be understood without some knowledge of the domestic political processes of the regime's leading state. This statement is applicable not only to the transformation of the postwar international monetary regime but to that of other regimes as well. As their proponents themselves attest, system-level analyses of international regimes do not adequately explain the dynamics of regime change, for system-level variables alone do not possess sufficient leverage to reveal the forces that contribute to the transformations of regimes. As a result, proponents of system-level explanations themselves maintain that an adequate understanding of regime dynamics requires the incorporation of unit-level variables. In a wry commentary on their own efforts to explain a variety of regime changes at the systems level, Keohane and Nye, for example, remarked: "Policy conceived as if the world consisted of billiard-ball states guided by philosopher-kings is not very useful. For international regimes to govern situations of complex interdependence successfully they must be congruent with the interests of powerfully placed domestic groups within major states, as well

[19]Robert O. Keohane, "The Study of Transnational Relations Reconsidered," address to the British International Studies Association, Warwick University, December 1976, p. 5.

as with the structure of power among states."[20] Stephen D. Krasner's investigation of changes in international regimes led him to a similar conclusion.[21]

This book, therefore, serves as a complement rather than as an alternative to the extensive analyses of the breakdown of Bretton Woods that have already been completed from a system-level perspective. Its raison d'être is to explain the dynamics of domestic politics in the key currency country, which contributed to the ending of the dollar's convertibility into gold. System-level analyses by definition neglect these dynamics, but they are critical elements of any attempt to specify the causes of state action in the international system.

In the case of the breakdown of Bretton Woods, a unit-level analysis is particularly appropriate because it reveals a very different perspective on the sources of U.S. action on August 15, 1971, than do systemic accounts. The latter tend to posit generally, and in this case specifically, that the national interests of states are determined by their positions in the international system and that the core national interest of every state is to maintain or enhance its power in that system.[22] With respect to the Bretton Woods regime, for example, a systemic analysis locates the source of the August 1971 decision in the growing disjunction between power as defined by the regime and more fundamental measures of, particularly, U.S. power.[23] Determined to realize its national interest in en-

[20]Keohane and Nye, *Power and Interdependence*, p. 226.

[21]Krasner's study of the relationship between the distribution of power among states and the structure of the international trading order led him to conclude that "for a fully adequate analysis, it is necessary to amend a state-power argument to take account of the impact of past state decisions on domestic social structures as well as on international economic ones" (Krasner, "State Power and the Structure of International Trade," *World Politics* 28 [April 1976]: 318).

[22]See, for example, Keohane's discussion of realist theory in his "Theory of World Politics: Structural Realism and Beyond," paper prepared for the 1982 annual meeting of the American Political Science Association, Denver, Colorado, September 2-5, 1982.

[23]See Keohane and Nye, *Power and Interdependence*, pp. 139-43. Also see the more recent article by Keohane, "The Theory of Hegemonic Stability and Changes in International Economic Regimes," in Holsti, Siverson, and George, *Change in the International System*, pp. 131-62 (despite its title, the article employs not an eroding hegemony but essentially an issue-structural or what is called a "differentiated, issue-specific version" of the overall hegemonic model). Keohane concludes there that "the hegemonic stability theory is helpful in accounting for the collapse of the

hancing its international power, the United States closed the gold window in order to "throw off the regime's constraints on the exercise of American economic power to influence international monetary politics."[24]

The evidence suggests, however, that redressing its position in international monetary politics was much less important to the United States in 1971 than was its desire to enhance its control over its domestic economy, a control that *was* threatened by the rules of the Bretton Woods game. Systemic explanations, in other words, are eminently accurate in emphasizing the desire of the United States to abrogate constraints imposed by the rules of Bretton Woods. They do not, however, locate the dynamics of the August decision correctly because they assume, as do all realist analyses, that the national interest underlying the U.S. action was that of enhancing its position in the international system. In this analysis I contend that the national interest at stake in the August 15 decision derived from and was·directed to a greater extent toward the relationship between, to borrow (and bend somewhat) Charles E. Lindblom's phrase, "politics and markets" in the United States than it was from or toward the U.S. position in the international system.[25] Thus, realists are correct in assuming that the U.S. interest in the break-down of Bretton Woods can be treated as a constant and the proximate source of change found at the systemic level; they err, however, in assuming that the interest at stake had its roots in international rather than in domestic structure.

Analysts who attribute explanatory power to contradictions inherent in the structure of the Bretton Woods regime itself run afoul of the evidence presented here in a different way.[26] They argue, in brief, that by August 1971 the logjam in international

---

Bretton Woods regime, and its proposition linking potential power resources to regime outcomes is not disconfirmed by events. Yet the causal sequences it suggests are not adequate; one has to take into account the symbolic nature of power resources, direct effects of U.S. policy, and the dual nature of the U.S. power position in 1971" (p. 151).

[24]Keohane and Nye, *Power and Interdependence*, p. 140.

[25]Charles E. Lindblom, *Politics and Markets: The World's Political-Economic Systems* (New York: Basic, 1977).

[26]See John H. Williamson, *The Failure of World Monetary Reform, 1971-74* (New York: New York University Press, 1977), chap. 2; Scammell, *The International Economy since 1945*, chap. 12.

monetary relations created as a consequence of the Bretton Woods regime's failure to resolve the intertwined problems of liquidity and adjustment left the Nixon administration no choice but to close the gold window. This argument does not explain, however, why the Nixon administration made so few attempts between 1969 and 1971 to avoid the highly predictable denouement that eventually occurred on August 15. I argue that that inaction is attributable in part to external constraints. But it is also attributable to the influence of unit-level variables: the strength of the Nixon administration's consensus on the primacy of national autonomy and the organization of the government for the making of international monetary policy.

In this book I do not in any way intend to deny that system-level variables are crucial elements of any adequate explanation of the closing of the gold window. I do maintain, however, that these variables do not by themselves satisfactorily explain that event.[27] I focus, therefore, on the unit-level or domestic political variables that also played a role in the decision to suspend the convertibility of the dollar into gold. Inevitably, such a focus has a tendency to imply that other influences were of significantly less consequence; although this may be the effect, it is not my intent.

THE GOLD WINDOW AND U.S. POLITICS

From the perspective of politics within the United States, the single most important factor explaining the breakdown of Bretton Woods was the prevalence within the monetary regime's most powerful country of a nationalist outlook on the appropriate relationship between the United States and the international monetary system.[28] In the view dominant within the United States, the in-

---

[27]A "satisfactory" explanation, from my perspective, requires an identification of the actual causes of state behavior.

[28]I use the term "nationalist" here in consonance with K. J. Holsti's definition of the term to connote attempts to contain the impact of external influences on the ability of a particular country to control its own affairs. In his words, nationalism is reflected in "governmental policies that are designed to control, reduce, or eliminate a wide range of foreign influences and transnational processes on a society. . . . Such policies reflect a search for autonomy in a world of interdependence, amalgamation, and homogenization" (Holsti, "Change in the International System: Interdependence, Integration, and Fragmentation," in Holsti, Siverson, and George, *Change in the International System*, p. 24).

ternational monetary system existed to serve the interests of the United States in maintaining both a healthy domestic economy and a foreign policy calculated to meet its security needs as it alone defined them. As a consequence, the monetary system would be supported only as long as it did not infringe more than marginally on U.S. autonomy—on the country's freedom to set domestic economic and foreign security policy independently of either's impact on the U.S. balance of payments or on the Bretton Woods regime. Once that boundary was crossed, a withdrawal of U.S. support for the system was highly probable.

The demise of the postwar monetary regime, then, can be attributed in part to the incompatibility that developed between its demands and the consensus that prevailed within the United States on the importance of regime maintenance relative to that assigned to other objectives of the nation. The regime's survival depended upon a degree of subordination of national to internationally agreed upon goals; the consensus within the United States, however, implied a profound unwillingness to adjust national objectives in any significant way to the maintenance of an established network of economic interdependence. It is, of course, true that the imperatives of international regime maintenance and the implications of the American domestic political consensus on the importance of international monetary policy had been incompatible in both theory and practice for a substantial period of time before the Nixon administration assumed office in 1969. However, it was only in mid-1971 that a critical impasse demanded a resolution of the underlying incongruity. That the incongruity would be resolved in favor of the nation's rather than the regime's priorities should not have come as a surprise to any observer familiar with the perspective that had long shaped the U.S. relationship to the Bretton Woods system.

That U.S. perspective effectively relegated the survival of the postwar international monetary regime to a distant third in the priorities of the United States, lagging far behind the goals of maintaining a prosperous domestic economy and ensuring the achievement of U.S. security objectives.[29] Domestic economic and

[29]This statement is not inconsistent with the tenets of theories of hegemonic stability, which posit that the dominant power of an international monetary system will sustain short-run economic costs in the interest of establishing a stable monetary

foreign security policy goals imposed substantial costs on the Bretton Woods regime. But these costs were heavily discounted as a result of the strength of the domestic consensus on the ranking of values involved in any effort to preserve the postwar monetary system. The sources of that consensus, however, differed: the strength of the consensus behind the primacy of domestic economic policy derived from different forces than did that behind the priority accorded to foreign security policy.

The Primacy of the Domestic Economy

Both U.S. balance-of-payments policy and its policy on questions relevant to the structure of the Bretton Woods regime itself were a residual of domestic economic policy. There was no question, either within or outside the preserve of those government officials specifically charged with the making of U.S. international monetary policy, that domestic economic policy should be given precedence, without much more than symbolic regard for the impact on or consequences for the postwar monetary regime.

In part, this consensus on priorities can be attributed to the fact that there was no sensible alternative to the established ordering of values that governed the conduct of domestic economic and international monetary policy. To have shaped the domestic economic policy of a relatively closed economy (i.e., an economy in which the traded goods sector is relatively small in proportion to national income) to the demands of the international monetary system would have exacted an exorbitant toll on domestic economic activity. It would also have been somewhat self-defeating, both in terms of its effects on the U.S. payments accounts and, for some time, in terms of its effects on the monetary system as well.

Not unrelated to the relatively closed structure of the domestic

system that it expects will return to it long-run economic and political benefits. My thesis is that the U.S. interest in the Bretton Woods regime was subordinated to its long-run, more broadly defined, political interests and that the economic costs the United States bore as a consequence of the Bretton Woods regime, although increasingly severe in terms of particular industrial sectors, did not exert a strong influence on the course of the overall economy. (For the classic statement of the hegemonic thesis, see Charles P. Kindleberger, *The World in Depression, 1929-1939* [Berkeley: University of California Press, 1973], particularly chaps. 1 and 14.)

economy was a political component of the perspective that pervaded U.S. decision making regarding the Bretton Woods system and the domestic economy. Given the relatively low dependence of the U.S. economy as a whole on exports and imports, there was no significant political constituency within the United States that would support suppressing the American economy to the end of reducing the U.S. balance-of-payments deficit and thereby improving the long-term prospects of the Bretton Woods regime. The idea of increasing domestic unemployment in order to preserve the monetary regime commanded no political following either within or outside the executive branch. Even those corporations and financial institutions with an especially strong stake in the preservation of a stable international financial system could not be expected to lend their support to policies that threatened the prosperity of the economy from which the bulk of their profits derived.[30]

As a consequence, domestic economic policy was considered virtually sacrosanct, very largely immune from the conduct of U.S. balance-of-payments or international monetary policy. The latter was, instead, the residue of domestic economic policy, reflecting the primacy of national policy over the demands of the international monetary regime. That the two did not collide irreconcilably before 1971 was a result partly of the noninflationary course U.S. domestic macroeconomic policy adhered to until the mid-1960s, partly of the vigorous demand for U.S. dollars abroad in the early years of the Bretton Woods system, and partly of the more recent series of ad hoc arrangements concluded between the United States and other governments to insulate the monetary system from the effects of a long series of U.S. payments deficits.

In mid-1971, however, the conflict between autonomy in domestic economic management and the preservation of the international monetary regime became unavoidably acute. By August 1971, the future of the Bretton Woods regime appeared extremely tenuous: international financial markets had been shaken by currency floats and revaluations, the announcement of an impending annual deficit on U.S. merchandise trade, and the report of a congressional subcommittee urging the United States to seek a

---

[30]See the figures cited for American multinational corporations in Waltz, *Theory of International Politics*, p. 148.

depreciation of the dollar.[31] Market participants seemed poised to initiate a massive run against the dollar at any sign of a weakening in U.S. resolve to defend its currency. By precipitating a wave of gold conversions, a speculative run against the dollar would force the United States to end convertibility and thereby bring the Bretton Woods system to an end.

At the same time, the Nixon administration was confronting a domestic environment in which demands for an expansion of the domestic economy were becoming irresistibly strong. A positive response by the administration to demands from its domestic constituents would be very likely to trigger the collapse of the Bretton Woods system: as the U.S. deficit increased as a consequence of domestic expansion, market participants, anticipating a dollar devaluation, would be very likely to sell dollars on a scale sufficient to precipitate a run on U.S. gold stocks.

As a result, officials in the Nixon administration confronted a stark choice. They could preserve U.S. autonomy in making domestic economic policy or they could try to preserve an established network of economic relationships that had returned substantial, albeit diminishing, benefits to the United States. That they would choose to preserve national autonomy was eminently predictable from the strong domestic consensus on the desirability of insulating domestic economic policy from what was considered to be the extraneous influence of developments in the network of international financial relationships.

This argument obviously differs from analyses that attribute a high degree of freedom to government officials in their conduct of U.S. international monetary policy. It resonates closely instead with conceptions of the United States as a system in which the autonomy of public officials is limited by the existence of what Stephen L. Elkin has described as "the division of labor between market and state," a division that compels elected officials, if they expect to remain in office, to respond to domestic economic imperatives.[32] Given the structure of the economy and the polity,

[31] U.S., Congress, Joint Economic Committee, *Action Now to Strengthen the U.S. Dollar*, 92d Cong., 1st sess., August 1971.

[32] Stephen L. Elkin, "State and Regime in the American Republic," paper prepared for the 1981 annual meeting of the American Political Science Association, New York, September 3-6, 1981, p. 1. He argues that American officials, because their tenure in office and public revenues depend on the performance of an economy

public officials could not, even had they so desired, have given pride of place to international monetary policy. My analysis, there-fore, diverges considerably from existing interpretations of the United States as a "strong" state (i.e., a state or public sector rel-atively impermeable to societal or private pressures) in the arena of international monetary policy.[33]

The Primacy of Foreign Policy

A second secular trend evident in U.S. international monetary policy is integral to an explanation of the Nixon administration's decision to abandon the postwar monetary regime. Successive U.S. presidents had insisted adamantly that American foreign policy should be conducted without considering its effects on the U.S. balance of payments and on the international monetary regime. In the pursuit of U.S. security interests, expansively defined, only very marginal, if any, attention was to be paid to the burdens imposed on the U.S. balance-of-payments accounts and, as the Bretton Woods regime aged, on the monetary system itself.

The "low politics" of money were, in short, not to affect the "high politics" of security.[34] Focused on the political-military aspects of state power in the international system, presidents have tended to ignore the international economic components of power. They have instead pursued a definition of American security interests abroad that, by virtue of its enormous costs in terms of foreign exchange and its alienation of U.S. allies, eventually weakened the ability of the United States to order the international monetary system in accord with its interests. American presidents, however, have never found power to shape the international monetary system as im-pressive as political-military power. U.S. international monetary

---

that is largely privately owned, must be highly responsive to business demands although not uniformly so across all sectors of public activity (p. 26). Government officials, as a result, are not autonomous actors.

[33]See fn. 5 above.

[34]The distinction between high politics and low politics (essentially the difference between issues of high and issues of low political salience, which engage corre-spondingly large or small amounts of top-level attention) was drawn by Cooper in an effort to suggest that trade issues were, in fact, high politics issues (see Richard N. Cooper, "Trade Policy Is Foreign Policy," *Foreign Policy*, no. 9 [Winter 1972-73], pp. 18-37).

policy, therefore, became the stepchild not only of domestic economic policy but of foreign security policy as well.

Presidential emphasis on the high politics of security, even at substantial cost to the low politics of money, derived from what Morton H. Halperin has called the "shared images" of Washington policy makers in the postwar period. Policy makers have tended to view the world as an arena of conflict between the Soviet Union and the United States. They have believed that military power was the primary component of national power and that the Third World was a critical focus of struggle.[35] The politics of money were not salient among these dominant images of the world and of the role the United States played in that world.

In the absence of any significant domestic dissent from its definition of what constituted primary and secondary areas of foreign-policy concern, the administration would support the continued existence of the Bretton Woods system only as long as that system did not unduly constrain its ability to conduct its security policy. Indeed, as the Bretton Woods regime increasingly evolved into a gold-dollar exchange system, the United States had good reason to prolong the system's life span. The dollar's multiple roles in the Bretton Woods system in effect enabled the United States to finance the payments deficits that were in part the concomitants of its expansively defined security interests without having to exchange either goods or gold in return. Thus, it was the U.S. Department of the Treasury that itself devised a number of life-support systems for the gold-dollar regime and opposed any fundamental reform that might threaten to diminish the role of the dollar.

U.S. support for the postwar monetary regime was likely to erode, however, when the system's members threatened to exercise their power to restrain U.S. spending abroad—a threat that would, in turn, compromise the ability of the United States to pursue its perceived security objectives. That such a threat would at some point materialize was a virtually inevitable consequence of the structure of the Bretton Woods system and of the changes in world politics during the 1960s. The Europeans perceived an asymmetrical distribution of privileges and burdens as inherent in the structure of the Bretton Woods system. They believed the system enabled

[35]Halperin, *Bureaucratic Politics and Foreign Policy*, chap. 1.

the United States to continue to play the role of imperium within the alleged Atlantic alliance and elsewhere. They would tolerate this situation only as long as they perceived the supply of dollars generated by U.S. deficits as beneficial rather than as burdensome, or they believed that the United States played a critical role in ensuring European security. This role could be endangered were the Europeans to object to the structure of the monetary regime.

The phrase "dollar glut" gained popularity in the late 1950s and early 1960s as it became clear that U.S. deficits were becoming burdensome. With the advent of Soviet-American detente the Cold War unmistakably waned later in the 1960s. As East-West tensions receded, the Europeans expressed ever more loudly their resentment at a monetary system that, they alleged, facilitated U.S. adventures abroad, particularly, of course, in Vietnam. The United States responded less to the substance than to the form of European restiveness, escalating efforts to persuade the Europeans and the Japanese to hold dollars rather than reining in its foreign policy.

By mid-1971, however, the United States had exhausted its supply of palliatives capable of protecting its gold stocks without seriously impinging on its freedom to spend abroad. By August of that year, participants in both private and official foreign-exchange markets were showing signs that they would no longer give credence to U.S. protestations that it would maintain the convertibility of the dollar into gold; a run on U.S. gold stocks appeared imminent. The U.S. government would choose to protect what was, in effect, its ability to determine foreign policy autonomously rather than to preserve the postwar monetary regime, and the choice was consistent with U.S. policy making on international monetary affairs.

It is difficult and, perhaps, even impossible to determine conclusively the genesis of the shared images that dominated U.S. foreign policy[36] and that relegated international monetary policy to the realm of low politics. However, this difficulty does not impair the validity of the observation that U.S. officials have been less autonomous in their conduct of international monetary policy than

---

[36]See the valiant attempt of Krasner to do so, for example, and Ruggie's pointed criticism of that attempt (Stephen D. Krasner, *Defending the National Interest: Raw Materials Investment and U.S. Foreign Policy* [Princeton: Princeton University Press, 1978] and John Gerard Ruggie's review in *American Political Science Review* 74 [March 1980]: 296-99).

some have assumed. The difficulty in identifying the determinants of those images bars only a stronger statement about the influence of the division between politics and markets on U.S. international monetary policy; it does nothing to negate the importance of the relationship already identified.

The Gold Window and the Nixon Administration

This hierarchy of domestic economic, foreign security, and international monetary policy suggests that the Nixon administration's decision to close the gold window can, given concurrent developments in the monetary regime itself, be understood simply as the inevitable result of a long tradition in American foreign policy. Yet no administration before that of President Nixon had confronted the need to choose among those priorities: each had instead managed to preserve national autonomy in the making of domestic economic and foreign security policy and the Bretton Woods system simultaneously. None had been forced to decide whether it was prepared to sacrifice internationally agreed upon rules of the game in an extremely important sphere of interstate relations in order to uphold the sanctity of U.S. freedom of action. It is, therefore, impossible to know whether any administration, Democratic or Republican, would have adhered to or deviated from the established order of priorities when actually required to choose between national autonomy and the monetary regime. The Johnson administration, which came closest to such a decision, imposed what appeared to be drastic controls on the activities of American corporations abroad rather than close the gold window. The Nixon administration, in a similar although admittedly much more difficult situation than that which confronted its predecessor, chose differently: it suspended the convertibility of the dollar. It had decided to do so in a sense, moreover, months in advance of the international financial crisis of August 1971.

Why and how the Nixon administration did so is the central focus of this book. As I argue at greater length in Chapter Three, an important element in explaining the Nixon administration's choice was its officials' explicit concurrence in the priorities governing domestic economic, foreign security, and international monetary policy that guided their predecessors in office. That concurrence excluded from the Nixon administration's long-range planning for international monetary policy several courses of action that might have staved off the collapse of the Bretton Woods regime. Deflation, foreign policy restraints, and dollar devaluation were all consigned to the realm of "nondecisions" because the Nixon administration's policy makers, across all agencies and at all levels, emphasized the primacy of national autonomy.

Capital controls and international monetary reform were also excluded as possible responses to the monetary regime's difficulties, however, and their exclusion can not be explained solely by reference to traditional patterns of thought and behavior. They must instead be explained in terms unique to the Nixon administration. A consensus within the Nixon administration excluded capital controls, albeit a consensus of a kind different from that which centered on the goal of autonomy. Administration officials agreed that capital controls had become an anachronism: given President Nixon's aversion to controls and the increasing ineffectiveness of the controls themselves in stemming the flow of capital abroad, the option of expanding the system of selective correctives garnered little support within the administration.

As I argue in Chapter Four, the only remaining alternative to a deathwatch over the Bretton Woods regime—international monetary reform—was consigned to oblivion by a different process than were the other options considered by Nixon administration officials. Consensus governed most of the Nixon administration's international monetary policy making in the dying days of the Bretton Woods regime but heated controversy erupted over the issue of international monetary reform. Displaying all the classic marks of bureaucratic politics, the controversy over reform was eventually resolved as a consequence of the structure of power that governed the making of international monetary policy within the Nixon administration.

That structure, unaffected by individual or agency-based sources of influence, gave to the Department of the Treasury the lion's share of power over the making and implementing of U.S. international monetary policy. Because the Treasury, for a variety of reasons, opposed vigorous U.S. advocacy of regime reform and because the president did not interfere with his administration's conduct of international monetary policy (as Chapter Five will explain), the Nixon administration moved inexorably toward the crisis of August 1971 in which it had no real alternative but to close the gold window.

Thus the way the Nixon administration made international monetary policy was another domestic political influence that led to the decision, and the bureaucratic politics model of explanation, while imperfect, nonetheless serves nicely to elucidate the struggle on monetary reform within the administration. Yet the debate itself was much less important than the breadth and depth of consensus within the Nixon administration on the primacy of national autonomy. Thus the explanatory power of the bureaucratic politics model in this case is limited, more applicable at the margins than at the core.

The recollections of officials involved in Nixon administration international monetary policy making[37] and documents previously classified or otherwise unavailable have made it possible to reconstruct the domestic politics of the decision to close the gold window. But an understanding of both the history and structure of the Bretton Woods system and of the U.S. role in that system is essential to an explanation of the U.S. decision to end the dollar's convertibility into gold. That history is an appropriate place to begin this book; Chapter Two briefly reviews it.

[37]For a list of these officials, see the Appendix. Officials granted interviews on the general understanding that their comments were not for attribution.

CHAPTER TWO

The Bretton Woods Regime
and the United States

Certain "rules and conventions" were intended to govern the conduct of postwar international monetary relations; the rules of the game as it actually came to be played were somewhat different.[1] In this brief review I accord particular emphasis to the accommodations made by the United States to the operative rules of the Bretton Woods regime, not only because the actions of the United States are the focus of this book but also because the United States came to assume a central role in the operation of the regime.

Because my focus in this chapter is primarily on the problems that were besetting the regime by 1969 and the U.S. role in and responses to those problems, I pay less attention to the accomplishments of the regime than might seem appropriate. Particularly neglected is the extent to which the Bretton Woods regime, despite all its problems, encouraged more than a decade of expansion in international trade and finance. Concerned less with what went right than with what went wrong with the postwar monetary re-

---

[1]For comprehensive treatments of the origins and history of the Bretton Woods regime, see, inter alia, Richard N. Gardner, *Sterling-Dollar Diplomacy: The Origins and Prospects of Our International Economic Order*, rev. ed. (New York: McGraw-Hill, 1969); Eckes, *A Search for Solvency*; Susan Strange, *International Monetary Relations. International Economic Relations of the Western World, 1959-1971* (London: Oxford University Press, 1976), vol. 2; and Margaret Garritsen deVries, *The International Monetary Fund, 1966-1971: The System under Stress* (Washington, D.C.: International Monetary Fund, 1976), vol. 1.

gime, I attend in this chapter largely to the departures of states from the rules and norms to which, implicitly or explicitly, they were expected to adhere.[2] Thus, I concentrate on the failure of states to adjust their exchange rates and their concomitant failure to assume the burdens of responsibility of adjusting to payments imbalances—an individual and systemic failing that would contribute significantly to the undermining of the regime itself. I pay special attention to the departures by the United States from the norms attached to its center-country status.

THE BRETTON WOODS REGIME: THE CHARTER AND THE REALITY

Designed largely by Harry Dexter White, then an assistant to Secretary of the Treasury Henry Morgenthau, and John Maynard Keynes, then a consultant to the British Treasury, the original blueprints for the Bretton Woods regime specified rules and norms regarding both exchange rates and the supply of international liquidity (essentially, international money or financial assets acceptable for the settlement of international imbalances).[3] During the actual operation of the postwar monetary regime, however, departures from those carefully constructed blueprints would occur in both realms. These departures, in turn, would create unique privileges and special problems for the United States, as well as critical problems for the regime as a whole.

Exchange rates were originally to be established, maintained, and changed according to the precepts of an adjustable peg mechanism. Requiring that exchange rates be fixed but adjustable when fundamental payments disequilibria so dictated, the adjustable peg was a compromise between fixed and floating rates, both of which were regarded as incompatible with a viable international monetary sys-

[2]Rules are "specific prescriptions or proscriptions for action" (see Krasner, "Structural Causes and Regime Consequences," p. 186); norms are "standards of behavior defined in terms of rights and obligations" (ibid.).

[3]Both White and Keynes, of course, were heavily influenced by international and domestic political and economic considerations (see, for example, Block, *The Origins of International Economic Disorder*, particularly chaps. 2-4).

tem in a Keynesian world. Fixed rates (i.e., unalterable exchange rates set by governments) were excluded because they required, at least in theory, that domestic economies bear the entire burden of adjustment to payments disequilibria, an anachronism in a Keynesian age. Floating rates (i.e., exchange rates set by and changed in accord with market forces) were excluded because, although they theoretically insulated domestic economies from payments imbalances, economists at the time associated them with an instability inimical to orderly international monetary relations.[4]

Although White and Keynes initially disagreed over exactly how to allocate the burden of adjustment to a payments imbalance between the exchange rate and the domestic economy, they eventually agreed that an exchange rate could be changed only in cases of "fundamental" disequilibrium (a term left undefined) and, after a one-time adjustment not to exceed 10 percent, only with the approval of the International Monetary Fund.[5] Otherwise, exchange-rate stability was to be achieved by the declaration by each member country of the Fund of a par value for its currency, which that country would maintain either by intervening in exchange markets to keep its currency within a range of one percent above or below its par value or by exchanging its currency for gold at a fixed exchange rate.

The United States was the only country to opt to buy and sell gold, at the rate of $35 per ounce, to fulfill its obligation to maintain the stability of its exchange rate. It did so, among other reasons,[6] because the system could not function unless one country remained out of the foreign-exchange markets, passive with respect to the level of its exchange rate.[7] Maintaining what was known as an "open

[4]See Willett's reference to the "distrust of freely floating rates by informed economists of the time" in his *Floating Exchange Rates*, p. 3.

[5]See Eckes, *A Search for Solvency*, p. 130.

[6]Among those reasons were that the United States wanted gold to retain a central role in the system, in part because the United States held 60 percent of the world's gold stocks at the end of World War II (the figure is from Charles A. Coombs, *The Arena of International Finance* [New York: John Wiley, 1976], p. 6), and that the United States, as a relatively closed economy, could best afford to abandon control of its exchange rate.

[7]As Scammell explains, "in a world of *n* countries, as long as one currency acts as *numeraire* [the currency against which all other currency values are set], only (*n* − 1) exchange rates can be independently determined, the *n*th is implicit in the others" (Scammell, *The International Economy since 1945*, p. 180).

gold window" became, as a result, the way in which the United States adhered to the regime's rule regarding exchange-rate stability; maintaining a laissez-faire attitude with respect to the exchange rate of its currency became, in turn, one of the norms or standards of behavior to which the United States was expected to adhere.

To complement the adjustable peg system, the Bretton Woods architects constructed a system in which liquidity consisted of drawing rights at the International Monetary Fund and gold, although both sterling and dollars were already and would continue to be prominent reserve assets. Keynes's arguments that countries temporarily in deficit should have unconditional access to borrowed reserve assets and that an international central bank (an "International Clearing Union") should issue international reserve assets ("bancors") were overridden;[8] countries were eventually granted largely conditional access to Fund resources and gold "(with a little equivocating) was enshrined as the ultimate reserve asset of the system, . . . [while] newly mined gold was expected to provide for needed growth in reserves."[9]

The system that the Bretton Woods architects constructed in 1944 to govern postwar international financial relations, then, was one in which the burden of adjustment to a payments imbalance was to be divided between the domestic economy and the exchange rate. In cases of fundamental disequilibrium in their balance-of-payments accounts, states were to be permitted to alter their currency's par values in accord with the provisions of the Articles of Agreement. Otherwise, participants in the regime were to intervene in foreign-exchange markets to stabilize their rates at the agreed upon values with their own or borrowed reserve assets. Borrowed assets, in turn, were to be supplied by the International Monetary Fund under specified conditions, while the secular increase in the supply of international reserve assets thought necessary to support an expanding volume of international trade was to be provided for by newly available gold.

[8]"Bancor" is a contraction of bank and "or," the French word for gold (Eckes, *A Search for Solvency*, p. 76).

[9]Lawrence B. Krause, *Sequel to Bretton Woods: A Proposal to Reform the World Monetary System* (Washington, D.C.: Brookings, 1971), p. 10.

The system that actually prevailed during the period in which the Bretton Woods regime operated, however, bore relatively little resemblance to that so laboriously designed during World War II. Shortly after the Western European states resumed current-account convertibility in 1958 and the Bretton Woods provisions actually went into effect, the adjustable peg was transformed into a system of virtually fixed exchange rates among the major countries and the International Monetary Fund and gold were overwhelmed by the magnitude of the demand for international liquidity. Over time, the member states of the Bretton Woods regime came to rely not only on the Fund and gold but also on a variety of ad hoc arrangements and, increasingly, on U.S. payments deficits for supplies of international liquidity. Thus, the system evolved into a full-fledged gold-dollar standard; the United States was its key currency country. That evolution imposed upon the United States an obligation to act "responsibly" (in particular, not to inflate unduly) and in the interests of the system as a whole. The obligation became increasingly difficult to meet because of the other interests of the United States and the general failure of states in the system to fulfill their responsibilities in the process of adjustment.

The transformation of the adjustable peg mechanism into a regime of virtually fixed exchange rates among the major countries was the product of domestic politics within the countries concerned as well as of international pressures. Several changes in rates occurred not long after 1958: in 1961, for example, Germany revalued the deutsche mark and the Netherlands, the guilder; the Canadian dollar had been floating since 1950 and would not be repegged until 1962. As John H. Williamson has observed, "there then followed a period when exchange rate changes were relegated to the status of confessions that the adjustment process had failed, and an attempt was made to operate a fixed rate system."[10] For more than five years, between 1962 and 1967, not a single major country altered its currency's parity.[11]

Indeed, devaluations became politically untouchable. They were perceived to be symbols of a government's inability to manage successfully the domestic economy. Political resignations or elec-

[10]Williamson, *The Failure of World Monetary Reform*, p. 6.
[11]Ibid.

toral defeats could be expected to follow a devaluation. Because the political leadership was assigned the blame for shortcomings in the domestic economy, a rate of inflation sufficient to induce a payments deficit was punishable at the polls. To compound that problem by the clear admission of defeat signaled by a devaluation was to be avoided in spite of the costs thereby incurred. The political onus of rate changes was also, in part, a consequence of official efforts to dampen speculative attacks that could force a change in a currency's value. Trying "to ward off speculative capital flows, national officials would tend to offer assurances that changes in the rate would not be made, thus converting maintenance of the rate to an important political objective of the officials who had made such promises."[12]

An equally effective deterrent to exchange-rate devaluations was the real cost imposed on any country opting to devalue. A devaluation would result in higher prices for imports and increased demand for exports, representing a contraction in the real buying power of the devaluing country. If that contraction were met by an expansionary fiscal or monetary policy, the devaluation would be futile: inflation would overwhelm the devaluation's original effect on prices and incomes. If domestic demand were suppressed, however, the governing political coalition would be likely to suffer. As a result, no government, as long as it had some alternative, was eager to incur the political risks attendant on a devaluation; devaluations, therefore, became scarce despite the provisions in the Articles of Agreement for such changes.

For different reasons, revaluations met a similar fate. In West Germany and Japan, the two countries most persistently in surplus during the Bretton Woods era, political coalitions were constructed around particular par values. In both countries, as Robert M. Dunn observes, "an important part of the existing capital stock was put in place at times when investment decisions were significantly biased toward traded goods by a combination of exchange rates that undervalued the local currencies and macroeconomic policies that protected the domestic economies from most of the potential inflationary effects of payments surpluses."[13] Politically powerful ex-

[12]Willett, *Floating Exchange Rates*, p. 14.

[13]Robert M. Dunn, Jr., *Exchange-Rate Rigidity, Investment Distortions, and the Failure of Bretton Woods*, Essays in International Finance, no. 97 (Princeton: Princeton University, International Finance Section, February 1973), p. 4.

port and import-competing industries in Germany and Japan opposed revaluation and were "successful in forestalling parity adjustments for some time."[14]

Most countries experienced strong indigenous opposition to exchange-rate changes, and the known antipathy of the United States to par value alterations reinforced the tendency. Of particular concern to the United States were devaluations, which, it was feared, would hurt the competitive position of the United States in world markets, force its payments accounts into even deeper deficit, and ultimately catalyze a speculative run on the dollar that would result in the collapse of the Bretton Woods system.[15] Among the currencies that were potential candidates for devaluations it was sterling that aroused the most concern within the U.S. government. It feared that a British devaluation would suggest to exchange-market participants that if one reserve currency could be devalued, the other could be devalued as well.

The United States, however, was not unreservedly enthusiastic about currency revaluations either. Although revaluations would ease the strain on the U.S. payments deficit by increasing the competitiveness of U.S. exports, they might also precipitate a wholesale dumping of dollars by market participants who anticipated a further rise in the revalued currency and who were also confident that the dollar would not rise. These potentially contradictory effects left U.S. officials with, at best, an ambivalent attitude toward revaluations.[16]

While political and economic factors acted in concert to reinforce resistance to rate changes, however, the attempt to hold rates stable became increasingly difficult as time went on. As participants in foreign-exchange markets became increasingly sophisticated, payments imbalances persisted, and the Eurodollar markets grew, speculative onslaughts increased in scale and threatened to overwhelm the ability of central banks to defend a given parity. Funds that

[14]Ibid., p. 6.

[15]This does not apply, of course, to the wave of European devaluations that occurred, with U.S. encouragement, in 1949, when the Bretton Woods regime was in suspended animation.

[16]See Martin Mayer's account in his *The Fate of the Dollar* (New York: Truman Talley, 1980), p. 90. Interviews confirm that this ambivalence plagued some high-level officials well into the Nixon administration (see below, Chapter Five).

could be and were mobilized in anticipation of movements in parities expanded steadily as the Bretton Woods system aged, eroding the ability and willingness of government officials to support currencies under attack and, as a result, undermining an important part of the Bretton Woods regime itself.[17]

Entrenched official resistance to changes in exchange rates and increasing short-term capital mobility swamped, in turn, the facilities for the supply of liquidity designed in the 1940s. The result was a mixture of supplementary, ad hoc mechanisms to supply assets for the defense of par values. The International Monetary Fund's lending capacity was limited to the supply of internationally acceptable currencies paid during the subscription of national quotas. It was soon supplemented by cooperation among the central bankers of the industrialized nations, meeting at the Bank for International Settlements in Basle; by the organization of a "swap" or short-term credit network among the advanced countries; and by the agreement of what became known as the "Group of Ten" countries to supplement Fund resources through the General Arrangements to Borrow.[18]

None of these arrangements, however, adequately responded to the need of the system for a secular growth in international reserve assets. Under the arrangements concluded at Bretton Woods, as noted earlier, an expanding supply of gold to international markets was to foster increases in international trade. Gold, however, proved to be a capricious source of liquidity. Its supply was dependent on the financing needs of the Soviet and South African governments and was not, therefore, keyed to the needs of the international monetary system. The price of gold, moreover, fluctuated in response to the demands of industrial consumers and gold speculators, and it required continued governmental attention until 1968,

---

[17]In the 1960 gold crisis, for example, $300 million in funds moved into Swiss francs in four days; in 1971, $3.7 billion in funds moved into European currencies within the same period (see the table in Robert Russell, "Crisis Management in the International Monetary System, 1960-1973," paper presented at the March 1973 meeting of the International Studies Association, New York [reprinted in Willett, *Floating Exchange Rates*, p. 17]).

[18]For a detailed description of these developments, see Strange, *International Monetary Relations*, pp. 82-89, 105-16, and 136-37.

when the private and the official gold markets were severed.

Increasingly, the dollar came to play the role assigned to gold at Bretton Woods. The extensive use of the dollar in the international monetary and trading systems followed logically from the size of the U.S. economy and the extent of the country's involvement in international economic exchanges. With the largest share in world trade and the most highly developed capital markets of any industrialized country, the United States became the single most influential actor in both trade and finance. The dollar became the primary vehicle currency and the primary intervention currency, acquiring its role as reserve currency by logical extension. Because of the role of the dollar as the *numéraire* of the Bretton Woods system (the currency in terms of which all other parities were set), the passive exchange-rate role of the United States, and the steady, noninflationary growth of the United States (at least until the mid-1960s), most countries assumed that the capital value of dollar assets would remain stable. The desirability of holding dollars in lieu of gold was enhanced by the fact that the United States paid interest on dollar balances whereas gold offered no such guaranteed return. In addition, unlike gold, the dollar was in ample supply, the consequence of a long series of U.S. balance-of-payments deficits.[19]

---

[19]The overall U.S. balance of payments is depicted for the years 1958-1971 in the list on the following page, which shows three different measurements of that account: the basic balance, the net liquidity balance, and the official settlements balance (in billion U.S. dollars; data from U.S., White House, *International Economic Report of the President*, March 1973, pp. 82, 86). Since 1966, the United States has used both the official settlements and the liquidity balances as measures of its payments position. The measures differ as to what they consider to be "autonomous" transactions (those "undertaken for their own sake") and placed above the line and what they consider "accommodating" transactions (those that "take place . . . because the other items are such as to leave a gap to be filled") and are placed below the line.

The basic balance regards only current-account transactions and long-term capital movements as autonomous flows; it treats short-term capital flows, errors and omissions, and official reserve transactions as accommodating flows. The official settlements balance places only official reserve transactions in the category of accommodating flows. The liquidity balance places both official reserve transactions and changes in liquid liabilities to private foreigners below the line. There are objections that can be made to the validity and utility of each of the measures (see Benjamin J. Cohen, *Balance-of-Payments Policy* [Baltimore, Md.: Penguin, 1970], pp. 39-55, from which this discussion is drawn; quotations from p. 40).

Thus, the Bretton Woods regime became a gold-exchange standard and the United States became the key currency country of the regime. The evolution of the Bretton Woods regime into a gold-exchange standard compensated for shortfalls in the regime's liquidity as well as, to some extent, in its exchange-rate mechanism. It was also and inevitably accompanied by all the problems incident upon such a standard.

THE GOLD-DOLLAR SYSTEM

Problems and Stakes

Inherent in the structure of a gold-exchange system are technical problems and political problems. A gold-exchange standard is intrinsically unstable: it depends for its existence on market confidence in the stability of the rate of exchange between its reserve assets while simultaneously depending on an increasing supply of foreign exchange to satisfy its need for increases in liquidity. As Robert Triffin pointed out in 1959, the Bretton Woods system was doomed to succumb at some point if the United States continued to run deficits of a magnitude that threatened its ability to convert dollars into gold.[20] Were a crisis of confidence to develop about the convertibility of the dollar, a run on U.S. gold stocks could

	Basic balance	Net liquidity balance	Official settlements balances
1958	− 3.5		
1959	− 4.3		
1960	− 1.2	− 3.7	− 3.4
1961	Negl.	− 2.3	− 1.3
1962	− 1.0	− 2.9	− 2.6
1963	− 1.3	− 2.7	− 1.9
1964	− Negl.	− 2.7	− 1.5
1965	− 1.8	− 2.5	− 1.3
1966	− 1.7	− 2.2	.2
1967	− 3.3	− 4.7	− 3.4
1968	− 1.4	− 1.6	1.6
1969	− 3.0	− 6.1	2.7
1970	− 3.1	− 4.7	− 10.7
1971	− 9.3	− 22.7	− 30.5

[20]Triffin testified before Congress in 1959 on what later became known as the Triffin dilemma, expanding on his views in his *Gold and the Dollar Crisis* (New Haven: Yale University Press, 1961).

ensue that would force the United States to float the dollar, thus terminating the Bretton Woods system. If, on the other hand, the United States controlled its deficits to avoid a crisis of confidence, the international monetary system would be deprived of a vital source of reserves, nations would be deterred from engaging in trade and financial exchanges, and the international economic system would suffer enormous damage. The only solution, Triffin argued, was to supplant the dollar and gold with an internationally created and controlled reserve asset, the equivalent of Keynes's bancor and International Clearing Union. The Bretton Woods system was, as Triffin argued, resting on a time bomb.

The political flaws in the gold-dollar standard stemmed from the privileges other states thought accrued only to the United States as a result of the system. In the early years of the Bretton Woods regime, expressions of this dissatisfaction were constrained by the dollar shortage and by international political tensions. The U.S. role in strengthening Western Europe against the Soviet threat, the foreign-exchange costs incurred as a result of that effort, and the need for dollars abroad muted protests against U.S. privileges in the Bretton Woods system. Opposition began to be expressed more freely as the 1960s progressed, however, as the perceived threat from the Soviet Union faded, opposition to the U.S. role in Vietnam increased, the dollar shortage turned into a dollar glut, and the United States showed no signs of reducing its deficit.

The French, in particular, argued vociferously that the willingness of other countries to hold dollars as reserves relieved the United States from a discipline that all other countries experienced when their expenditures exceeded their supply of reserves. While other countries could theoretically exert discipline on the United States by converting their surplus dollars into gold at the U.S. Treasury, most—France was a notable exception—were unwilling to run the risk that the United States would respond to a depletion of its gold stock by suspending convertibility rather than by restraining its deficit.

The reserve currency role of the dollar aroused contention as well, because Europeans believed that it permitted American citizens to acquire control over European industries more cheaply and easily than would otherwise have been possible. The Europeans also argued that the excessive American demand represented by the U.S. deficit imparted an inflationary bias to the rest of the world, threatening the stability of economies that were relatively much more open to foreign influences than was the American economy.

The French argued along with Triffin that inequities inherent in the operation of the Bretton Woods system would be significantly alleviated only when the U.S. deficit was under control and the system itself reformed so as to end the dollar's key role in the system. In an effort to achieve both objectives, the French in the mid-1960s announced that they would increase their monthly demands on U.S. gold stocks and began to campaign for a fundamental reform of the monetary system.

The French indictment of the United States and the Bretton Woods regime was not without merit, although it understated the costs the United States incurred as a consequence of the regime's evolution. With respect to the merits of the French case, there is no question but that the role of the dollar in the postwar monetary regime extended unique and significant advantages to the United States. These advantages included, as Williamson noted, "the ability to borrow cheaply to finance past deficits, as analysed in the literature on seigniorage;[21] the ability to finance future deficits without first stockpiling low yielding reserve assets, as neglected in the literature on seigniorage; the freedom in foreign policy (and especially its military extension) conferred by this lack of financial constraint of the customary type; the ability to avoid adopting costly adjustment measures; and the political influence given by an unconstrained ability to lend to other countries suffering a run on their currency."[22] Moreover, as Williamson also points out, the United States, because of the role of the dollar as the intervention currency and the de facto inconvertibility of the dollar, did not suffer reserve changes as a result of speculation on the dollar.[23]

The role of the dollar in the postwar monetary regime, in short, conferred upon the United States a greater degree of freedom in

[21]Seigniorage refers to the "gain of real resources, over and above costs of production and administration, associated with the creation and issue of any kind of money—including also international money" (Benjamin J. Cohen, *Organizing the World's Money: The Political Economy of International Monetary Relations* [New York: Basic, 1977], p. 67).

[22]Williamson, *The Failure of World Monetary Reform*, p. 78.

[23]Ibid.

domestic economic and foreign security policy than was available to other states participating in the regime; a measure of real financial gain, although the amount of that gain remains the subject of dispute;[24] and both tangible and intangible increases in its power resources. Beyond enhancing U.S. power because it enabled the United States to extend financing to or withhold it from countries in deficit, the dollar's status as the reserve currency also enabled the United States to escape the conditions imposed, for example, on Britain and France when they turned to the International Monetary Fund for financing in 1956 and 1957-58, respectively.[25] It also extended to the United States alone the prestige traditionally attached to the key currency country of an international monetary system.

The European indictment of the postwar monetary regime tended to ignore, however, the costs that attended the role of the United States and the dollar in the Bretton Woods regime. Most importantly, because of its passive position in exchange markets, the United States was unable to control directly the exchange rate of its currency; the status of the dollar relegated the determination of its value to the net effect of the operations of all other participants in the system in the exchange market. In a world where, the U.S. government believed, most countries were intent on accumulating payments surpluses, the dollar was doomed to be overvalued; the U.S. deficit was, from the government's perspective, a demand-determined deficit.[26] The overvaluation of the dollar, in turn, officials in Washington came to believe in the late 1960s, exacted costs from the United States in terms of exports and jobs foregone.[27] It also, however, returned some significant advantages to the United States.[28]

[24]For a discussion of the seigniorage issue, see C. Fred Bergsten, *The Dilemmas of the Dollar: The Economics and Politics of United States International Monetary Policy* (New York: New York University Press, 1975), pp. 209-20.

[25]Robert Solomon, *The International Monetary System, 1945-1976: An Insider's View* (New York: Harper & Row, 1977), p. 24.

[26]Based on interviews.

[27]Different methods of calculating the dollar's value resulted in estimates of appreciation during the 1960s of between 1.15 and 4.7 percent (see Bergsten's survey in *The Dilemmas of the Dollar*, p. 308).

[28]As Bergsten points out, the dollar's overvaluation, because it increased imports, decreased exports, and encouraged American direct investment abroad, reduced inflationary pressures in the United States economy (see C. Fred Bergsten, "New

The critics of the Bretton Woods regime tended to neglect, in addition, the benefits they received from the regime. The trading regime that was the counterpart of the Bretton Woods regime accorded preferential treatment to both the European Community and the Japanese. Furthermore, the gold-dollar system also afforded most member states of the regime an extended period of expanding trade and prosperity at relatively low cost. The original Bretton Woods arrangements, as David P. Calleo and Benjamin M. Rowland point out, required "rather firm domestic discipline and occasional adjustments in parities."[29] Neither, however, as Calleo and Rowland add, "proved as significant as had been imagined." Instead, "with America's lavish and continuing deficits greatly increasing the world's supply of international money, . . . everyone else found it relatively easy to run a surplus. With their share of the surplus dollars, nearly all developed countries had ample monetary reserves. Hence, once popular recovery got underway, the developed Atlantic countries maintained convertibility without frequent devaluations, stern domestic discipline, protectionism, or tight exchange controls. It was, in short, economic liberalism without tears."[30]

United States Responses

The United States, in its own calculus of costs and benefits stemming from its role in the postwar monetary regime, for a long time weighted the benefits more heavily than it did the costs. For, as Calleo and Rowland also observe, "If the dollar's role as a reserve currency was a cross, it was one we had embraced with alacrity and fought fiercely to retain. For it was the dollar's position as a reserve currency that allowed the United States to run deficits. And it was these deficits that financed 'world responsibilities' without forcing cutbacks in the private outflow."[31]

Urgency for International Monetary Reform," *Foreign Policy*, no. 19 [Summer 1975], p. 81).

[29]David P. Calleo and Benjamin M. Rowland, *America and the World Political Economy: Atlantic Dreams and National Realities* (Bloomington: Indiana University Press, 1973), p. 89.

[30]Ibid. As Calleo and Rowland themselves point out, however, both Britain and, to a lesser extent, France are exceptions to this generalization about ample liquidity (see ibid., p. 283, n. 6).

[31]Ibid., p. 165.

Determined to maintain intact the privileges derived from the effective rules of the Bretton Woods game, the United States responded vigorously and ingeniously to the form but not to the substance of grievances expressed about the operation of the postwar monetary regime. Through a series of seemingly never-ending ad hoc adjustments at the margins of the system, the United States attempted to extend the life span of the system without affecting its own privileged position within it. It attempted to do so, moreover, without sacrificing in the process either its domestic economic or its foreign security policy.

Thus, absent from the long series of U.S. efforts to restrain its balance of payments and preserve the postwar monetary regime is any serious or consistent compromise of the objectives of domestic macroeconomic policy or foreign security policy. While the United States clearly had an interest in preserving the monetary regime, that interest did not supersede the importance of maintaining autonomy of action in these two policy areas. Its hierarchy of objectives was clear and consistent: ranked above the survival of Bretton Woods was the U.S. ability to respond freely to the perceived needs of its domestic economy and its foreign policy.

As a result, the "shared images" at the core of postwar American foreign policy consistently dominated the conduct of U.S. international monetary policy. In the service of containing the Soviet Union and communism, for example, the liberalism enshrined in the Bretton Woods charter was shelved as the United States encouraged the formation of the European Payments Union in 1950, although a return to currency convertibility and the principles of the Bretton Woods regime was envisioned as the result of the European reconstruction of which the payments union was a part. Although the Union and later, of course, the European Community discriminated against American exports—although not against American investments—both were perceived as critical building blocks in an integrated Western alliance designed to contain communist expansion.

As Benjamin J. Cohen has pointed out, there were other security benefits perceived in the European (and Japanese) arrangements that more than outweighed what the U.S. government hoped would be short-term costs to American exporters. Implicit in those arrangements, Cohen argues, was a bargain between the United States and its allies. The bargain allowed the United States, as the world's central banker, to expend dollars abroad as freely as it deemed necessary in pursuit of its grand foreign policy schemes. In exchange, its allies received trade and monetary allowances. As Cohen puts it, "Implicitly, a bargain was struck. The Europeans acquiesced in a system which accorded the United States special privileges to act abroad unilaterally to promote U.S. interests. The United States, in turn, condoned Europe's use of the system to promote its own regional economic prosperity, even if this happened to come largely at the expense of the United States. . . . The potential cost to the United States was considered to be a quite tolerable trade-off for the broader advantages to be gained for the overall U.S. foreign policy design."[32]

Throughout the history of the Bretton Woods regime, the United States continued to subordinate balance-of-payments considerations to the conduct of its security policy. In the pursuit of reductions in the U.S. deficit that might stabilize the regime, the United States altered its foreign policy in only very marginal ways. Spurred into action by the gold crisis of 1960 the Eisenhower administration, for example, ordered military units overseas to "buy American" where possible and restricted the number of dependents who could accompany U.S. military personnel abroad.[33] Eisenhower and the Department of Defense also began to attack the largest single item accounting for the deficit on government account, the cost of stationing American troops overseas. Most of these were in West Germany: in late 1960 military offset negotiations with the Federal Republic began, later to be pursued by both the Kennedy and the Johnson administrations.[34] All three U.S. administrations also tied

[32]Benjamin J. Cohen, "The Revolution in Atlantic Economic Relations: A Bargain Comes Unstuck," in Hanrieder, *The United States and Western Europe: Political, Economic and Strategic Perspectives*, p. 118.

[33]A policy Kennedy reversed when he entered office, concerned about its adverse effect on troop morale (see Theodore C. Sorensen, *Kennedy* [New York: Harper & Row, 1965], p. 407).

[34]For a detailed account of the substantive issues involved in the offset negotiaitons and the intense interagency battles in the United States that accompanied them, see Gregory F. Treverton, *The Dollar Drain and American Forces in Germany: Managing the Political Economies of Alliance* (Athens: Ohio University Press, 1978).

foreign aid to the purchase of goods manufactured in the United States.

The core of an expansive and extremely expensive U.S. foreign policy was not touched, however, throughout the history of the Bretton Woods regime.[35] As Henry C. Wallich observed of the Eisenhower administration, for example, "balance-of-payments considerations were not given priority . . . over the recognized need to continue and expand aid to less developed countries. The President's proposals for foreign aid consistently remained at a high level, though they were cut back just as consistently by Congress." Wallich notes that "even in the second half of 1960, when concern over the balance of payments was intense, plans for a Latin American fund of $600 million were announced and substantial aid prospects held out to the countries of Africa."[36] Official American spending abroad was not susceptible to influence by considerations that related to the U.S. payments deficit or the Bretton Woods regime itself. As was true in particular of the prosecution of the war in Vietnam,[37] the demands of American foreign policy gen-

[35]Government expenditures overseas between 1958 and 1971 (U.S. balance on government account) are as follows (in billion U.S. dollars; from *International Economic Report of the President*, [1973], p. 83):

	Military	Foreign aid	Total
1958	−3.1	−2.6	−5.7
1959	−2.8	−2.2	−5.0
1960	−2.8	−2.6	−5.4
1961	−2.6	−2.8	−5.4
1962	−2.4	−2.8	−5.2
1963	−2.3	−3.1	−5.3
1964	−2.1	−3.2	−5.3
1965	−2.1	−3.3	−5.4
1966	−2.9	−3.3	−6.3
1967	−3.1	−3.4	−7.3
1968	−3.1	−3.9	−7.0
1969	−3.3	−3.6	−6.9
1970	−3.4	−3.8	−7.2
1971	−2.9	−4.4	−7.3

[36]Henry C. Wallich, "Government Action," in *The Dollar in Crisis*, ed. Seymour E. Harris (New York: Harcourt, Brace & World, 1961), p. 100.

[37]As Odell points out, "economic officials were not major participants in decisions regarding Vietnam"; the Council of Economic Advisers was not asked to estimate the impact of the war on the domestic economy until 1968; and "Treasury Secretary [Henry H.] Fowler was a particularly firm adherent of the view that the United States should not constrain its security policies to any fundamental degree because

erally superseded whatever costs policy imposed on the monetary regime.

Macroeconomic policy in the United States displayed much the same indifference to payments considerations and the status of the Bretton Woods regime. As Willett observes, "U.S. monetary and fiscal policy over the postwar period has been dominated by domestic macroeconomic objectives."[38] On the basis of an empirical study of the relationship between U.S. macroeconomic policy and the course of its balance of payments between 1958 and 1966, Michael Michaely concurs, concluding that "the hypothesis that comprehensive monetary or budgetary variables responded, from 1958 onwards, to balance-of-payments improvements or deteriorations cannot be sustained."[39]

Departures from this pattern occurred rarely. The Federal Reserve did, in the early 1960s, apparently attempt to raise and keep short-term interest rates high ("Operation Twist") in order to prevent a deterioration of the balance of payments. Yet, even then, the Federal Reserve's action did not disturb its basically accommodating stance during the period. As Arthur M. Okun later observed of the years between 1961 and 1965, "basically, monetary policy was accommodative while fiscal policy was the active partner.

---

of balance of payments considerations" (Odell, *U.S. International Monetary Policy*, p. 170). Odell adds, however, that the gold crisis of 1967-68 "probably affected" Vietnam policy (p. 177). The important question is, though, *how much* of a role the gold crisis played in Johnson's March 1968 decision to deescalate the war. Leslie H. Gelb's recent analysis of that decision assigns major explanatory roles to changing opinion within the government, to the opinions of the "Wise Men," to increasing public sentiment against the war, and to the "awesome costs" that the troop increases then under consideration would impose. Most influential among those costs, according to Gelb, was the "need to put the country on a 'real' wartime footing by mobilizing reserves or instituting economic controls and heavy taxes. It was no longer possible to avoid these measures and still follow the course of escalation" (p. 177). Added to these costs, Gelb notes, was the burden that would be imposed on the dollar, as well as the creation of an international financial crisis (p. 179). The major explanatory variables in Johnson's decision, however, clearly lay elsewhere than in the situation of the dollar (see Leslie H. Gelb, with Richard K. Betts, *The Irony of Vietnam: The System Worked* [Washington, D.C.: Brookings, 1979], pp. 170-78).

[38]Thomas D. Willett, *International Liquidity Issues* (Washington, D.C.: American Enterprise Institute, 1980), p. 23.

[39]Michael Michaely, *The Responsiveness of Demand Policies to Balance of Payments: Postwar Patterns* (New York: National Bureau of Economic Research, 1971), p. 264.

The Federal Reserve allowed the demand for liquidity and credit generated by a rapidly expanding economy to be met at stable interest rates."[40]

It is sometimes contended that both the Eisenhower and the Kennedy administrations' fiscal policies were restrained by the state of the U.S. balance of payments.[41] To refute this contention conclusively may not be possible, given the nature of the available evidence, but it does not stand up well under close scrutiny. At most, the available evidence suggests that balance-of-payments considerations played a secondary role in the making of both administrations' fiscal policies—the drive against inflation and the public's alleged addiction to a balanced budget assumed the leading roles. As Herbert Stein observes of the Eisenhower administration's making of policy in 1959 and 1960, for example, "Considerations of growth and the balance of payments were influential in the administration's drive for a surplus. But the main, continuing argument was the argument about inflation. The President and his chief economic advisers came out of the 1958 recession more convinced than ever that inflation was *the* great problem, and that a budget surplus was the necessary condition for solving the problem, if not the solution itself."[42]

The balance of payments occupied a similar position in the Kennedy administration, despite Kennedy's apparently well-founded reputation as the postwar president most concerned about the status of the dollar and its link to gold. Theodore C. Sorensen, special counsel to President Kennedy, maintains, for example, that "the payments 'club' . . . hung over . . . [the president's] head, limiting the size of his domestic economic program." Sorensen then goes

[40]Arthur M. Okun, *The Political Economy of Prosperity* (New York: W. W. Norton, 1970), p. 53.

[41]Cooper, for example, has argued that "the United States did take deflationary measures in the severe budget of 1959, largely as a result of balance-of-payments considerations. The Kennedy administration was basically out of sympathy with that approach, but it nonetheless refrained from reflating as rapidly as might have been possible. Balance-of-payments considerations—and public attitudes toward 'gold losses'—played a major role in the caution with which the administration moved toward more aggressive expansion" (see Cooper, "Comment," *Journal of Political Economy* 25 [August 1962]: 542).

[42]Herbert Stein, *The Fiscal Revolution in America* (Chicago: University of Chicago Press, 1969), p. 354.

on to state, however, "but even had there been no balance of payments pressure, the President would not have felt free to unbalance the Federal Budget by as much as his liberal critics would have liked. . . . [H]is political judgment told him that a period of gradual re-education would be required before the country and Congress, accustomed to nearly sixteen years of White House homilies on the wickedness of government deficits, would approve of an administration deliberately and severely unbalancing the Budget."[43]

Insulated from balance-of-payments concerns, U.S. domestic macroeconomic policy would not become inconsistent with the center country's implicit obligation to keep domestic inflation within tolerable bounds until the mid-1960s. Beginning in 1965, however, as Lyndon Johnson attempted to finance both his Great Society and the Vietnam war simultaneously without imposing a tax increase on the U.S. public, inflation would begin to accelerate at a pace dangerous for the domestic economy and for the international monetary system.[44]

The nature of U.S. domestic macroeconomic and foreign security policy meant that, in responding to the problems that persistent U.S. deficits created for the Bretton Woods regime, the United States would rely on a variety of tactical devices designed to calm gold markets and preclude foreign central banks from converting dollars into gold. It would also rely on a series of measures designed to reduce, if only temporarily, the size of U.S. payments imbalances; the executive branch's freedom to maneuver would, however, be limited by the resistance of Congress and private industry.

Because it was interested in preserving the privileges it derived from the operation of the Bretton Woods regime, the United States would not, however, condone a structural reform of the regime as a solution to the Triffin dilemma and U.S. deficits until it became clear that the intended reform did not profoundly threaten the continued preeminence of the dollar. Instead, the United States

[43]Sorensen, *Kennedy*, pp. 412, 413.

[44]"At bottom," as Cohen notes, "the Bretton Woods system rested on one simple assumption—that economic policy in the United States would be stabilizing . . . and indeed, before 1965, the assumption did seem quite justified. . . . After 1965, however, the situation reversed itself, as a direct consequence of the escalation of hostilities in Vietnam. America's economy began to overheat and inflation began to gain momentum" (Cohen, *Organizing the World's Money*, pp. 103-4).

relied largely on a series of tactical expedients to preserve the Bretton Woods regime and its own role within the regime.

The measures undertaken to relieve potential pressure on U.S. gold stocks via a rise in the market price of gold included in 1960 a bilateral and then in 1961 a multilateral gold pool among eight industrialized countries to supply gold to the London market when the price began to rise.[45] In March 1968, when pressure on the London market became intense in the wake of a devaluation of sterling, the United States persuaded the other members of the Gold Pool to accept what became known as the Two Tier Agreement.[46] Confronted with a threat by William McC. Martin, then chairman of the Federal Reserve Board of Governors, to close the gold window unless agreement were reached, central bankers agreed to stay out of the private market and to deal in gold only among themselves.[47]

With the severance of the private and official markets, calm returned to the London market. The U.S. obligation to exchange dollars for gold when requested to do so by foreign monetary officials remained formally unchanged. It was understood, however, that any attempt to convert a substantial amount of dollars into gold would result in a closing of the gold window. The dollar had thus become in practical terms inconvertible by the time the Johnson administration left office.[48]

In addition to the series of measures necessitated by the existence of a private market in gold, the United States used its political and economic power to restrain foreign central banks from exercising their legal right of access to U.S. gold stocks. The most blatant

[45]For a detailed description of the gold pools, see Strange, *International Monetary Relations*, pp. 65-79. France, one of the original eight members of the 1961 Gold Pool, later dropped out.

[46]See ibid., pp. 292-95, for details on the Two Tier Agreement.

[47]Interview.

[48]For an expression of this view, see Calleo and Rowland, *America and the World Political Economy*, p. 284, n. 9. Cooper contends that the view that the dollar was de facto inconvertible between 1969-1971 is "not strictly true," (p. 79) pointing out that in 1970 more than sixty countries exchanged $630 million for gold at the U.S. Treasury. Cooper adds, however, that it was true that large holders of gold were aware that large conversions would threaten the United States ability to maintain an open gold window (p. 80) (see Richard N. Cooper, "The Future of the Dollar," in *A Reordered World: Emerging International Economic Problems*, ed. Cooper [Washington, D.C.: Potomac Associates, 1973], pp. 75-91).

example of the use of U.S. political-military power to gain economic ends—what might be called the translation of high politics into low—was what has become widely known as the "Blessing letter." In that 1967 letter, Karl Blessing, then president of the Bundesbank (the West German central bank), pledged that Germany would abstain from increasing the gold content of its reserves despite anxiety about the exchange value of its ever-growing dollar reserves. The letter responded to an apparent threat by the U.S. government that further conversions would endanger the future of American troops stationed in Germany. As Fred Hirsch and Michael W. Doyle have observed, the Blessing letter "amounted to underwriting, as far as Germany was concerned, an inconvertible dollar."[49]

No other surplus country was quite so vulnerable as West Germany to political pressure aimed at securing the U.S. gold stock. The U.S.-Japanese security relationship, for example, was more symmetrical than that between the United States and Germany; in the latter 1960s, the United States depended on access to bases in Japan to prosecute the war in Vietnam. Japan resembled Canada, however, in its vulnerability to the application of economic pressure by the United States, because both Tokyo and Ottawa depended heavily on access to American capital markets to finance their domestic investments. When controls were imposed on the outflow of capital from the United States, Japan was exempted in return, apparently, for Tokyo's commitment to continue holding its reserves largely in dollars; Canada was also exempted in exchange for its agreement not to allow excessive reserve accumulation.[50]

The United States also resorted to economic incentives to preclude the conversion of surplus dollars into gold. The Federal Reserve, with the concurrence of the Treasury, offered guarantees of exchange value for the dollars accumulating in foreign reserves through "swap" agreements, which served other purposes as well. Robert V. Roosa, under secretary for monetary affairs in the Kennedy and Johnson Treasuries, also conceived of the idea of offering

[49]Fred Hirsch and Michael W. Doyle, "Politicization in the World Economy: Necessary Conditions for an International Economic Order," in *Alternatives to Monetary Disorder*, ed. Hirsch, Doyle, and Edward L. Morse (New York: McGraw-Hill, 1977), p. 41.
[50]Block, *The Origins of International Economic Disorder*, p. 184.

Treasury securities—liquid instruments denominated in foreign currencies and offering interest payments—to absorb foreign reserves of dollars. Such securities became known as "Roosa bonds."

Each administration from Eisenhower's through Johnson's also devoted highly publicized attention to the payments accounts, voiced its determination to reduce the deficit, and imposed a variety of correctives to improve, at least temporarily, the appearance of those accounts. There is little indication that any administration believed that the various measures taken would extirpate the deficit and thus firmly reestablish confidence in the dollar; rather, the hope seems to have been that the deficit would eventually be eliminated through other, more fundamental processes of adjustment. Thus temporary, relatively painless measures were all that were necessary. While a plausible hypothesis in the early years, this became an increasingly unrealistic proposition as Vietnam sowed inflation deeply into the U.S. economy and Western Europe and Japan scored economic gains unmatched by the United States.

The number and variety of expedients tried, however, was impressive, even if their effect was not. The Eisenhower administration initiated what would become a decade-long effort to bolster confidence in the dollar by reducing the foreign exchange costs of U.S. military and economic commitments abroad. Its measures included, as noted earlier, the pursuit of offset negotiations with West Germany, the tying of foreign aid, and a short-lived restriction on the number of American military dependents living abroad.

President Kennedy's administration was the first to act directly on the capital account in an effort to retard the outflows of funds that contributed to general fears about the dollar manifest in the first real gold crisis of 1960. Developed in the U.S. Treasury, proposed to Congress in July 1963, and authorized in August 1964, the Interest Equalization Tax imposed a 1 percent tax on foreign security issues in the United States in an attempt to equalize the cost of borrowing in the United States and Europe without raising long-term interest rates for domestic borrowers.

In its efforts to reduce U.S. payments deficits by maneuvers even at the margins of the domestic economy, the Kennedy administration provoked the ire of both Congress and some in private industry. The administration's proposed tax on foreign investment in securities issued within the United States encountered strong opposition by investment bankers and stock brokers as well as by Republican Congressmen, some of whom suggested that government expenditures abroad were a more appropriate target for restraint than was private enterprise. Nevertheless, the Interest Equalization Tax passed Congress in 1964, although one hundred forty Republican and two Democratic Representatives opposed it in the House and no Republican in the Senate voted for the bill.[51]

The Johnson administration extended the efforts of its predecessor to restrain capital outflows. It expanded the types of loans covered by the Interest Equalization Tax and also gave it a longer lease on life than Kennedy had intended. In 1965, the Johnson administration introduced the Voluntary Foreign Credit Restraint program, asking corporations and banks not to increase their export of funds by more than 5 percent above the levels outstanding as of December 31, 1964. Its administration assigned to the Federal Reserve Board of Governors, the voluntary restraint program also encouraged exports and discouraged capital transfers to foreign subsidiaries of American corporations. In the same year, President Johnson asked the Department of Commerce to oversee the repatriation of funds from American investment abroad. Although purely exhortatory, Johnson's Voluntary Foreign Credit Restraint program succeeded in reducing the deficit by over one billion dollars in 1965.[52]

In 1968, the chaos in the gold market that would eventually result in the Two Tier Agreement impelled the Johnson administration to take more severe measures for the restraint of capital outflows, as well as other outflows recorded in the balance of payments. The policy measures announced by President Johnson "at the time . . . looked remarkably draconian" and included a ban on any further investment in Western Europe, sharp cuts in investment allotments for other areas, tighter restraints on bank lending, and recommendations to curb American travel and the foreign exchange costs of military expenditures abroad.[53]

---

[51] For an account of the Interest Equalization Tax's reception in Congress, see the *Congressional Quarterly Almanac*, 88th Cong., 1st sess., 1963, vol. 19 (Washington, D.C.: Congressional Quarterly Service, 1963): 587 and ibid., 88th Cong., 2d sess., 1964, vol. 20 (Washington, D.C.: Congressional Quarterly Service, 1965): 545-48.

[52] Solomon, *The International Monetary System*, p. 46.

[53] Strange, *International Monetary Relations*, pp. 288-89.

Congress was no more enthusiastic about the Johnson administration's proposals than it had been about the Kennedy administration's. Although the imposition of capital controls was a fait
accompli, not susceptible to congressional veto because it fell within
the president's authority under the Banking Act,[54] both the U.S.
Chamber of Commerce and the National Association of Manufac-
turers registered objections to the controls. Under pressure from
the travel industry, Congress did reject Johnson's proposals to tax
U.S. citizens traveling abroad, to tax airline tickets for travel abroad,
and to decrease the dollar value of duty-free goods tourists could
bring home with them from trips abroad.[55] It had earlier agreed,
though, to an extension and increase of the Interest Equalization
Tax. With the exception of some episodic activity within the Joint
Economic Committee, however, the administration's initiatives (or
lack thereof) with respect to the structure of the international monetary system per se received scant congressional attention.[56]

Despite the appearance of the Johnson administration's capital
controls, they did not represent a departure from the expediency
that had characterized its and previous administrations' refusals to
reverse radically and permanently the deficits on the U.S. payments
accounts. Capital controls tend to have an immediate effect on
private capital outflows but that effect fades over time, as corporations become more adept at concealing the transfer of funds
abroad. In the interim, corporate activity overseas tends to continue

[54] 12 United States Code Section 95a.

[55] For a discussion of congressional and industry reactions to Johnson's proposals,
see the *Congressional Quarterly Almanac*, 90th Cong., 2d sess., 1968, vol. 24 (Washington, D.C.: Congressional Quarterly Service, 1968): 717-28.

[56] The Subcommittee on International Exchange and Payments of the Joint Economic Committee (JEC) was the locus of whatever concern existed within Congress
on the issue of the U.S. relationship to and the structure of the Bretton Woods
regime per se. In 1962, for example, the JEC was advocating the creation of a new
method of supplying international reserves; in July 1965, the JEC subcommittee
issued a report with twelve recommendations for improving the international monetary system—advocating a study of the possibility of increasing the limits of exchange rate flexibility and recommending the creation of a new international reserve
asset that would supplement the role of the dollar (see U.S., Congress, Joint Economic Committee, Subcommittee on International Exchange and Payments, *Guidelines for Improving the International Monetary System*, 89th Cong., 1st sess., September
9, 1965). In 1971, the Subcommittee would call for a unilateral depreciation of the
dollar if negotiations were not successful in achieving that goal (see *Action Now to
Strengthen the Dollar*).

as planned, albeit at a higher cost, as corporations shift their borrowing to capital markets abroad. Thus the Johnson administration measures could not affect the deficit on anything other than a temporary basis. As Calleo and Rowland observed in 1973, "at the heart of our failure to end the deficit lay an obstinate refusal to do anything serious about its causes."[57]

It was, of course, true that any American effort that successfully dealt with the U.S. payments deficit would have compromised the international monetary system, in accordance with the tenets of the Triffin dilemma. It was also true, though, that a reduction in the U.S. deficit and the viability of the monetary system could have been pursued simultaneously, had the U.S. government so desired, by some reform of the Bretton Woods system that would have introduced an international reserve asset. The United States was intent, however, on preserving, not destroying, the role of the dollar and its concomitant ability to spend abroad. Until, therefore, it became convinced that the creation of an international reserve asset would not compromise the role of the dollar as a reserve currency, the United States firmly resisted the efforts of other governments to create such as asset.[58] Only when it became clear that the reserve role of the dollar was not in fundamental danger and that the proposed new asset might provide additional flexibility in financing the U.S. deficit did the United States, in 1965, extend its enthusiastic support to negotiations that would eventually result in the agreement on special drawing rights.[59]

The Nixon administration's legacy from its predecessors in office included commitments both to the sanctity of domestic macroeconomic and foreign security policy and to the preservation of the Bretton Woods regime. They had successfully reconciled these commitments by a series of tactical maneuvers designed to reduce

[57]Calleo and Rowland, *America and the World Political Economy*, p. 94.

[58]For accounts of the U.S. position on the special drawing right that support this interpretation, see Block, *The Origins of International Economic Disorder*, p. 191, and David P. Calleo, *The Imperious Economy* (Cambridge: Harvard University Press, 1982), pp. 52-53, 88-89. For a different perspective—emphasizing the role played by changing intellectual influences—see Odell, *U.S. International Monetary Policy*, chap. 3.

[59]For a detailed account of the special drawing right's history, see Stephen P. Cohen, *International Monetary Reform, 1964-69: The Political Dimension* (New York: Praeger, 1970).

pressures on U.S. gold stocks and to suppress temporarily the magnitude of U.S. payments deficits. Nixon's administration also inherited a monetary regime that was being progressively undermined by its failure to resolve the critical issue of distributing, equitably and effectively, responsibilities for adjustment; by domestic politics within its member states that reinforced the effects of the system-wide problem of adjustment; by U.S. deficits that soared to $3.4 billion in 1967;[60] and by the increasing mobility of short-term capital. It was not, in short, likely to be a particularly durable legacy.

[60]On the official settlements basis of accounting; deficits of $4.7 billion on net liquidity and $3.3 billion on basic balance (*International Economic Report of the President* [1973], pp. 82, 86).

CHAPTER THREE

The Influence of Consensus

By 1969, it was clear to many informed observers that the Bretton Woods regime was in serious trouble. Yet, although many of its officials concurred in that diagnosis, the Nixon administration made few attempts between its inauguration and its decision to close the gold window to alleviate the problems besetting the postwar monetary regime.[1] Neither vigorous unilateral initiatives nor multilateral initiatives designed to prolong the life span of Bretton Woods came from the Nixon administration during its two years in office before the August 1971 suspension of gold convertibility.

The absence of such initiatives can be attributed partly to the respite a confluence of circumstances afforded the Bretton Woods regime in 1969 and early 1970 and to external constraints on U.S. action. It is also attributable, however, to the consensus within the Nixon administration's policy councils on issues of profound importance to the future of the international monetary system and to the structure of power that governed that administration's making of international monetary policy. In different ways and with disparate effects, both the solid core of agreement among officials

---

[1] The Volcker Group's June 23, 1969, report to the president, for example, observed that "the current tensions in the international financial area . . . point to the urgent need for constructive change. . . " (U.S., Department of the Treasury, "Basic Options in International Monetary Affairs," June 23, 1969, p. 13, document released by the Department of the Treasury under a Freedom of Information Act [FOIA] request).

and the structure regulating policy making consigned the Nixon administration to a policy of "muddling through," a policy that was destined in the long run to be little more than a deathwatch over the Bretton Woods regime.

Despite the particularly severe crises that had beset the monetary system in 1968 and the underlying contradictions within the system that promised crises of a similar magnitude at some point in the near future, the Nixon administration did not adopt any of a series of measures that, by limiting the future outflow of dollars abroad, might have alleviated the problems plaguing the Bretton Woods regime. It refused to deflate the domestic economy, reduce the scope of American foreign policy, devalue the dollar, and intensify or expand the system of capital controls employed by previous administrations. It also did not pursue vigorously an alternative route to resolving the problems of the postwar monetary system: international monetary reform.

In the three chapters that follow, I explain why and how the administration remained largely motionless despite the high probability of an impending collapse of the postwar monetary regime. By examining the fate of various options considered either ephemerally or seriously by Nixon administration officials at the subcabinet level, this chapter and the next will make clear the influential roles in limiting the administration's freedom of movement played by shared values and by structure. In Chapter Five I consider the role of the president in the decision-making process, demonstrating that, because the president simply ratified the recommendations forwarded to him by his subcabinet-level advisers, the power of values and structure ultimately extended to the implementation of policy as well.

THE ROLE OF SHARED VALUES

Contrary to the predictions of the bureaucratic politics school of analysis, the process by which the Nixon administration made international monetary policy was to a very large extent characterized not by controversy and conflict but by a high degree of consensus. Sorting out options for administration policy in the sphere of international monetary relations occurred largely at the subcabinet level, within an interagency unit known as the Volcker Group.[2] The process was not one in which, for the most part, outcomes were determined, in Graham T. Allison's words, "by the pulling and hauling that is politics."[3] In stark contrast to Allison's image, it was one in which the dominant influence on outcomes was the extent and depth of agreement among participants on the appropriate relationship of the United States to the international monetary system, as well as on several related issues.

The members of the Volcker Group had various agency affiliations, including the Department of the Treasury, the Federal Reserve, the Council of Economic Advisers, the Department of State, and the staff of the Assistant for National Security Affairs. They were, however, united by a common assessment of the appropriate ordering of priorities among domestic economic policy, foreign security policy, and the international monetary regime. They shared, in short, a nationalist perspective on the nature of relations between states and the international financial system—a belief that national interests in the spheres of domestic economic and foreign security policy took precedence over the preservation of the international monetary system. The power over policy outcomes of this consensus on the hierarchy of priorities was substantial: it eliminated deflation, constraints on foreign policy, and devaluation as genuine options for U.S. policy. It also affected the administration's evaluation of another option: the immediate ending of gold convertibility.

Influential in its impact on the fate of capital controls and other "selective correctives" was the antipathy that members of the Volcker Group shared toward the various measures previous administrations had adopted to restrain capital outflows. This component of the dominant consensus had several sources, including the philosophical convictions of the members of the group, their knowledge of President Nixon's and private industry's aversion to controls, and the decreasing effectiveness of the controls themselves.

Thus, a solid foundation of common values, images, and expec-

[2]Paul A. Volcker, the under secretary for monetary affairs in the Nixon Treasury, led the group. The same group had existed during the Johnson administration and was then known as the Deming Group after Frederick L. Deming, the under secretary during much (1965-1969) of that administration.

[3]Allison, *Essence of Decision*, p. 144.

tations marked the process by which the Nixon administration made international monetary policy. That foundation exercised a profound influence over the determination of both the agenda and, of at least equal significance, the "nonagenda" of policy making in the administration that was eventually to preside over the breakdown of the postwar monetary regime.

THE POWER OF NATIONALISM AND THE DEMAND FOR AUTONOMY

The most important influence on the composition of the agenda and the nonagenda was the context within which the administration viewed the balance of payments and the international monetary regime as a whole. That context, referred to earlier as the "shared images" that dominate within policy making councils and create a sometimes unrecognized consensus on goals,[4] subordinated policy issues arising out of the Bretton Woods system to the demands of the domestic economy and to those of foreign policy.

Indeed, the Volcker Group's search for a viable international monetary policy explicitly presupposed that any such policy would be designed so as to permit the "retention of substantial flexibility for the United States both in terms of domestic economic policy and foreign spending."[5] Flexibility, in the opinion of the group, had been the major advantage that accrued specifically to the United States as a consequence of the Bretton Woods system. As the options paper eventually produced by the Volcker Group noted, "The present system has permitted financing some 70 percent of our cumulative balance of payments deficits (on the liquidity basis) of $24 billion over the past decade with increased foreign official and private liquid dollar holdings. . . . The available financing for our deficits has permitted the United States to carry out heavy overseas military expenditures and to undertake other foreign commitments, and to retain substantial flexibility in domestic economic policy."[6]

[4]See Chapter One.
[5]"Basic Options in International Monetary Affairs," p. 12.
[6]Ibid., p. 7.

The Fate of Deflation

In accord with this overriding consensus, deflation of the American economy for balance-of-payments reasons was so little considered in the economic policy councils of the Nixon administration that to say it was the recipient of even fleeting attention would be to exaggerate. Although the U.S. balance of payments was, at least on one measure, in surplus in both 1968 and 1969,[7] in part because of the restraints then being applied to the domestic economy to contain inflation,[8] Nixon administration officials foresaw the re-emergence of sizeable U.S. payments deficits as early as 1969.[9] Despite the strains that those deficits were likely to impose on an already overburdened international monetary regime, Nixon administration officials were not prepared to recommend the continuation of deflationary measures beyond what was considered desirable on domestic grounds alone.

This reflex exclusion of deflation as a balance-of-payments option made eminent economic and political sense to administration officials, at least in part because it was congruent with the larger structure of the American economy and polity within which they were operating. Restraining the American economy in order to aid the Bretton Woods regime was not an option either economically or politically consonant with the domestic structure of the United States. That the United States was a relatively closed economy, for example, militated against the adoption of deflation to contain the payments deficits that were expected to reappear as macroeconomic policy eased after 1969. Economists have long equated deflating

[7] On the official settlements basis, the U.S. surplus was $1.6 billion in 1968 and $2.7 billion in 1969. The net liquidity and basic balances registered deficits, however, in both years: the net liquidity deficit was $1.6 billion in 1968 and $6.1 billion in 1969; the basic balance deficit was $1.4 billion in 1968 and $3.0 billion in 1969 (see *International Economic Report of the President* [1973], pp. 82, 86).

[8] The U.S. inflation rate stood at 4.2 percent in 1968 and at 5.4 percent in 1969 (see Ronald I. McKinnon, *Money in International Exchange: The Convertible Currency System* [New York: Oxford University Press, 1979], p. 262).

[9] As the Volcker Group noted in mid-1969, "the dollar has been relatively strong on the exchange markets in recent months. However, this strength is accounted for mainly by unsustainably large short-term capital inflows induced by increasingly tight money in this country. We are," added the Volcker Group, "headed for a record deficit measured on the liquidity basis" ("Basic Options in International Monetary Affairs," p. 16).

the U.S. economy for the sole purpose of correcting a payments deficit with "the tail's wagging the dog." Conventional economic wisdom held, and still holds, that the toll imposed on the domestic economy by an attempt to improve the U.S. payments position through generalized deflation is excessive. The traded goods sector of the U.S. economy—9 percent of gross national product in 1970[10]—is simply too small to justify by itself the imposition of a penalty on the overall economy.

Moreover, that the United States was a relatively large economy also argued in favor of rejecting deflation as a balance-of-payments option. Because of the substantial impact of the United States on the world economy, any effort by the United States to correct its payments imbalance by deflating its own economy was likely to prove self-defeating: the reduction in aggregate demand in the United States would reduce the level of U.S. imports, thereby reducing the income of other countries. That reduction, in turn, would lower demand for U.S. exports, partially counteracting the positive effect on the U.S. payments accounts of the original decrease in imports.

There was some disagreement as to the magnitude of these so-called "feedback effects." According to one estimate, U.S. exports fell by approximately 40 percent of any decrease in American imports.[11] A 1969 U.S. government analysis suggested that "a $1 reduction in United States imports distributed proportionately among all United States suppliers results in as much as a $.70 offsetting reduction in United States exports on the average."[12] The feedback effects of domestic deflation were not insubstantial, however, even at the lower end of the estimated range where, as C. Fred Bergsten has observed, "most U.S. measures would [still] have to aim at improving . . . [the] trade balance initially by about double the targeted net gain."[13]

The economic contradictions implicit in a macroeconomic ap-

---

[10]Calleo and Rowland, *America and the World Political Economy*, p. 113.

[11]Bergsten, *The Dilemmas of the Dollar*, pp. 276-77.

[12]U.S. , Federal Reserve Board, Division of International Finance, "Balance-of-Payments and International Financial Policies for the United States: A Review of the Choices," June 30, 1969, p. 54, document released by the Federal Reserve Board under an FOIA request

[13]Bergsten, *The Dilemmas of the Dollar*, p. 277.

proach to U.S. international monetary policy were obvious to the Nixon administration's officials. None, as a consequence, dissented from the eminently reasonable objective of, in effect, letting the "dog wag the tail." It was, as a Federal Reserve staff member wrote in mid-1969, "abundantly clear . . . that it would be enormously costly and ultimately self-defeating for the United States to attempt to improve its balance of payments by deflating aggregate demand significantly below what is justifiable on domestic grounds."[14]

The politics attendant, in part, on the structure of the U.S. economy had equally obvious implications for the relationship between domestic macroeconomic policy and international monetary policy.[15] In an economy in which the traded goods sector represented only a relatively small proportion of overall national income, there was little compelling political support among the public at large, in Congress, or among private industry for a policy that would subordinate the demands of the domestic economy to those emanating from the postwar international monetary regime.

The American public generally has not manifested any strong interest in the conduct of U.S. international monetary policy. "International finance," as Richard Cooper has observed, "is an arcane subject and normally attracts little attention. . . . The public, at least in the United States, is likely to accept any reasonable sounding proposal, unlike in the area of foreign trade policy where much more is at stake for particularistic interests."[16] It is also true, however, as Cooper adds, that "precisely because the public does not perceive much at stake in the international monetary system, it will

[14]"Balance-of-Payments and International Financial Policies," p. 56.

[15]In view of the fact that domestic political opinion, even in open economies, has sometimes resisted the subordination of domestic macroeconomic policies to the demands of the monetary regime, the presence of a similar pattern in the United States cannot very likely be attributed solely to the fact that the United States is a relatively closed economy (see Cooper, "Prolegomena to the Choice," p. 92, for a brief commentary on the domestic political resistance in "most major countries" to conforming domestic to international policy); see Michaely, *The Responsiveness of Demand Policies*, p. 64, for a suggestive listing of factors other than economic structure that might account for the disparities among industrialized countries in their macroeconomic reactions to payments imbalances.

[16]Cooper, "Prolegomena to the Choice," p. 92.

not be willing to make many sacrifices to preserve it once its dictates conflict sharply with the requirements of domestic economic policy."[17]

Congress and private industry reflected similar sentiments, ignoring, for the most part, the executive's conduct of international monetary policy until that conduct threatened to impinge on the freedom of private actors in the United States. As illustrated in the last chapter, Congress has been relatively unconcerned with the course of U.S. international monetary policy but it has objected to specific measures designed to contain the U.S. payments deficit when those measures infringed on domestic economic activity, even at the margins.[18] Suppressing the entire economy for international monetary reasons would exceed the limits of congressional tolerance.

In the case of private industry, even those multinational corporations and banks with an especially strong stake in the maintenance of a stable, open international economic order would not support domestic deflation as a means to restrain U.S. payments deficits and thereby to enhance the viability of the postwar monetary regime. Most of their profits derive from domestic operations; the illogicality of depressing the U.S. economy, given its negative feedback effects on the payments accounts, was as evident to them as it was to members of the Volcker Group. As a consequence, even multinational corporations and international banks, while opposing the various measures proposed by successive administrations to control the U.S. payments deficits, have demonstrated virtually no support for the alternative of controlling that deficit by restraining the domestic economy.[19]

Reflecting the dominant opinion in the United States, the task force that the 1968 Nixon campaign team assembled on the balance of payments concurred in refusing to shape the domestic economy in order to save the Bretton Woods regime. Composed of academic and private-sector economists and chaired by Gottfried Haberler, then a professor of economics at Harvard University, the task force

[17]Ibid.
[18]See Chapter Two, pp. 55-57.
[19]For a summary of that opposition in 1968, for example, see *Congressional Quarterly Almanac* (1968), pp. 717-28.

met in several day-long sessions during the autumn of 1968.[20] It eventually submitted a 35-page analysis of and recommendations on the U.S. balance-of-payments problem and the international monetary system to the president-elect.[21] Although its influence, if any, on the Nixon administration's policy making is unclear, the Haberler task force report, while expressing the opinion that the U.S. deficit ought to be reduced, also stated firmly that "this goal must be achieved without violating major objectives of domestic economic policy, in particular the objective of maintaining a high level of employment and a rapid rate of growth at stable prices."[22]

Nor did President Nixon show any inclination to swim against the prevailing current of political opinion. According higher priority to international than to domestic considerations in the making of domestic macroeconomic policy threatened serious political consequences. This was particularly true when international problems would call for recessionary policies, policies to which President Nixon was strongly averse. Vice-president when Eisenhower insisted on budgetary restraint, Nixon attributed to the resulting recession the poor Republican showing in subsequent elections, including his own campaign for the presidency in 1960. In early 1969, President Nixon reminded his Cabinet Committee on Economic Policy of his predilections: "I remember 1958," he said; "we cooled off the economy and cooled off 15 senators and 60 congressmen at the same time."[23] Increasing domestic unemployment in an attempt to preserve the international monetary regime was not palatable for the president.

There was, in short, no political constituency within or outside the executive branch that would lend its support to suppressing the American economy in order to restrain the country's balance-

[20]The members of the task force included three banking-sector economists, Tilford Gaines, Walter E. Hoadley, and Herbert V. Prochnow; five academic economists in addition to the chairman, Hendrik S. Houthakker, William J. Fellner, Wilson E. Schmidt, Henry C. Wallich, and Thomas D. Willett; and an attorney, Arthur M. Becker.

[21]"Report of the Task Force on United States Balance of Payments Policies to the President-elect" (n.d.), document in the files of Gottfried Haberler, Washington, D.C.

[22]Ibid., p. 1.

[23]"Report on the Cabinet Committee on Economic Policy," April 10, 1969, p. 6, document in the files of William Safire, Chevy Chase, Md.

of-payments deficit and thereby ease the strain on the international monetary regime. The economic costs, moreover, of any such policy were considered to be prohibitively high. The Nixon administration's officials, as a consequence, took the primacy of the domestic economy as given. They consigned to the realm of nondecisions the option of deflation as a partial remedy for the ills besetting the Bretton Woods regime. Autonomy in domestic economic policy making was far more important than the survival of the postwar monetary regime in the calculus of the Nixon adminstration.

The Fate of Foreign-policy Constraints

The isolation of foreign policy from balance-of-payments and international monetary concerns also rested on a strong foundation of consensus within the Nixon administration. The note sounded in the Volcker Group's assertion that one "basic aim" of changes in the monetary system is "to free . . . foreign policy from constraints imposed by weaknesses in the financial system" was echoed in a long study concluded by the Federal Reserve Board staff in mid-1969.[24] It stated unequivocally that "it is one of the proximate objectives of United States balance of payments policy . . . to be able to carry out government overseas operations at levels determined entirely (that is, with no concern for the balance of payments as such) by the extent to which they are thought to promote basic United States objectives such as international peace and security."[25]

This consensus accurately reflected the priorities of the president himself, as well as those of his top advisors. That President Nixon chose to rely on a National Security Assistant who had no interest or expertise in the area of international finance; that he was preoccupied in his first several years in office by foreign-policy issues whose resolution was not at all influenced by payments considerations; and that he refused even to sanction the continuation of pressure on West Germany to extract foreign-exchange concessions because he valued German-U.S. ties more highly than he did the payments accounts[26]—all testify to the president's hierarchy of concerns.

[24]The quotation is from "Basic Options in International Monetary Affairs," p. 48.
[25]"Balance-of-Payments and International Financial Policies," p. 75.
[26]Interview.

President Nixon's sentiments were echoed at high levels in his State Department, as is evident in the comment of one of the department's highest-ranking economic officials: any international monetary system, he observed, ought to be judged from the perspective of "the political system you want to run, or from the United States' point of view, the foreign policy that we propose to carry out. That monetary system which is most compatible with our foreign policy is the one I favor as an American. To tell me that we have to adjust our foreign policy . . . to a particular monetary system or economic consideration I just don't believe is a correct approach."[27] The Nixon administration's philosophy was expressed even more succinctly by a member of its Council of Economic Advisers: discussing alternative balance-of-payments policies, he abruptly dismissed the notion of reshaping foreign policy, stating bluntly that "we didn't like the idea of bringing our troops home or that kind of stuff."[28]

Unlike the consensus on domestic economic policy, the intragovernmental consensus that foreign policy was sacrosanct and ought to remain immune from balance-of-payments concerns did not command a universal following outside the adminstration. The Haberler task force report, for example, asserted that, among the policies "which should have some favorable effect on our balance of payments and are worthy of pursuit for their own sake," would be a careful review of "United States Government economic and military commitments . . . from the standpoint of a new set of national priorities geared to the realities of the limits on our capacity to honor commitments. Broader sharing of the costs of defending the free world should be a high priority objective, and future overcommitments by the United States should be avoided."[29]

The opinions expressed in the task force report were evident in Congress as well. Resentment against the Europeans would in 1971 lead to some Senate support for the Mansfield amendment, which proposed to reduce the number of U.S. troops stationed in Western Europe in part because of their cost to the U.S. balance of payments. Moreover, in congressional debates over the years that responded

[27]Interview.
[28]Interview.
[29]"Report of the [Haberler] Task Force," pp. 20-22.

to administration initiatives with respect to the payments deficit, it was not unusual to hear industry representatives as well as individual Representatives and Senators suggest that cuts in government spending abroad would be both a more appropriate and a more efficient remedy than capital controls.[30] That an obvious concomitant of those cuts would be a redefinition of American foreign policy seems to have been of little concern to those suggesting the reductions.

Recommendations that restraints on government spending abroad should supplant or supplement those imposed on private industry, however, never gained a significant following in Congress, in private industry, or among nongovernmental foreign-policy elites. Given that the decade in which efforts to control the deficit through the use of capital controls coincided with the period of what Arthur M. Schlesinger, among others, has referred to as the "imperial presidency," the paucity of attempts from outside the executive branch to reduce the strain on the monetary system by redefining foreign policy is not difficult to understand.[31]

Thus, in 1969, the Volcker Group could give free expression to its conviction that preserving the Bretton Woods system was an objective distinctly subordinate to that of maximizing U.S. autonomy in foreign security policy. Supported by the president's similar evaluation of the place of international monetary policy in the larger scheme of American foreign policy, the Volcker Group's agreement was not disturbed by what was in any case minimal evidence of societal dissent from its own and the administration's conception of the appropriate relationship between foreign policy and international monetary policy. As a result, the option of reshaping American foreign policy to resolve the immediate and foreseeable difficulties of both the U.S. payments accounts and the Bretton Woods system remained outside what Harold and Margaret Sprout have referred to as the "milieu" of the Nixon administration's subcabinet-level officials.[32]

---

[30]See, for example, the debate in Congress on Johnson's 1968 payments initiatives, recounted in the *Congressional Quarterly Almanac* (1968), pp. 717-28.

[31]Arthur M. Schlesinger, *The Imperial Presidency* (Boston: Houghton Mifflin, 1973).

[32]Harold and Margaret Sprout, "Environmental Factors in the Study of International Politics," in *International Politics and Foreign Policy*, ed. James Rosenau (New York: Free, 1969), pp. 41-56.

The Volcker Group would recommend no more than an effort to cut the foreign-exchange costs of U.S. defense expenditures, despite the fact that government spending abroad in support of foreign-policy objectives was a major contributing factor to the persistence and magnitude of U.S. balance-of-payments deficits. As the White House itself noted in 1973, "net foreign aid and military-related outflows have amounted to $7 billion annually since 1967," while averaging about $5 billion annually in the decade before 1967.[33] A high percentage of foreign aid was tied to the purchase of American goods and services, and any attempt to reduce the deficit by cutting military expenditures abroad would have involved some feedback effects.[34] These calculations, however, do not appear to have influenced an administration whose stance on the relationship between foreign policy and the international monetary regime was premised on absolute immunity for the conduct of foreign policy; low politics was simply not to intrude on high politics.

The Fate of Devaluation

The effects of the hierarchy of priorities maintained by the Nixon administration's officials with respect to domestic economic, foreign security, and international monetary policy were not limited to the reflex exclusion of a reduced U.S. payments deficit through restraint on either the level of domestic economic activity or American foreign policy, or both. That ranking of values also relegated to the realm of nondecisions the option of a unilateral devaluation of the dollar. Although that possibility was one of the three that actually appeared in the paper prepared by the Volcker Group and presented to the president, the accompanying discussion and recommendations reduced it to a straw man. As a consequence of the image of the international economic system dominant within it, the Volcker Group treated devaluation in the options paper in so wholly derisory a fashion that no otherwise uninformed decision maker could be expected to advocate its adoption.

[33]*International Economic Report of the President* (1973), p. 19.

[34]Bergsten, for example, estimates that the feedback effects of cutting military expenditures abroad would reduce the balance-of-payments gain by approximately 50 percent (see Bergsten, *The Dilemmas of the Dollar*, p. 294).

When the Volcker Group considered the alternative of devaluing the dollar by raising the price of gold, its members advanced a variety of technical, as well as essentially philosophical, objections. If the U.S. government tried to change the price of the dollar in terms of gold in an effort to alter the dollar's exchange rate vis-à-vis other currencies, it might, for example, abort the creation of the special drawing right, which the international community had just agreed was a more rational instrument for creating liquidity than gold. If the dollar value of gold were increased, foreign central bankers and finance ministers might well lose interest in special drawing rights and all the advantages of these reserves would be lost. The Nixon administration's policy makers at the subcabinet level also feared that the increase in reserves incident upon a rise in the gold price would free other countries to stimulate their domestic economies, exacerbating world inflation. An increase in the price of gold would also result in an arbitrary pattern of rewards, conferring great advantages on the two primary gold producers, South Africa and the Soviet Union, and on countries holding a large proportion of their reserves in gold, such as France. While countries had earned interest on their dollar balances, it remained nonetheless true, concluded Volcker Group members, that "politically, the direct benefits, while limited in amounts, would still be inequitably distributed, favoring a small group of European gold holders at the expense of those who have cooperated by holding dollars in the past."[35]

There was also a consensus that the gold price could not be increased without precipitating a run on U.S. gold stocks of sufficient magnitude to threaten either a suspension or a depletion of stocks. Given the imprecision of administratively determined exchange rates, markets and central bankers were very likely to anticipate a second devaluation of the dollar. Even if this possibility were assessed as remote, the conservatism of foreign central bankers could cause them to hedge against such a contingency by converting their dollar liabilities into gold at the U.S. Treasury. In a situation in which dollar liabilities exceeded gold reserves, conversion on a large scale would eventually force the United States to float the dollar while, in the interim, exerting deflationary pressures

---

[35]"Basic Options in International Monetary Affairs," p. 36.

on the world economy and creating great uncertainty in exchange markets.

But interviews suggest that the most fundamental objection to a unilateral devaluation was the conviction shared by members of the Volcker Group that it simply would not work; that a U.S. devaluation would not achieve its goal of depreciating the dollar. Most members of the group expected that other countries would simply devalue their currencies against the dollar in response to a rise in the price of gold. The ultimate alignment of exchange rates would not appreciably differ from the prevailing pattern. The United States would have succeeded only in writing up the dollar price of gold, at some cost to stable international monetary arrangements. "Certainly the belief at the time," recalls a staff member of the Council of Economic Advisers, "was that we did not have any clear sense of what a gold devaluation would do to exchange rates. That was an uncertainty. We thought the French would be very reluctant to accept any appreciation of the franc, for example, and if they didn't that would pose serious problems for the Germans. And that the Japanese were extremely reluctant to see any appreciation of the yen. So there was very genuine skepticism about how we could effectively depreciate the dollar against other currencies. . . . There was a danger that you would end up only with a higher gold price."[36] While Germany and Switzerland might " 'stand still' if the United States devalued by no more than 10 percent," concluded the Volcker Group, "for the foreseeable future, nearly all other countries—including all the large ones—would be expected to follow the dollar, or to devalue by even more."[37]

Underlying this pessimistic evaluation of the response of other states to an attempted devaluation of the dollar was a perspective on international economic relations that was widely shared by members of the Volcker Group. A logical extension of their own emphasis on the primacy of national objectives over the maintenance of international regimes, that perspective attributed to other states an equally thin veneer of commitment to the survival of the postwar networks of trade and monetary relations. Members believed that this veneer, when subjected to pressure, would quickly vanish to

[36]Interview.
[37]"Basic Options in International Monetary Affairs," p. 35.

74

reveal the much more profound commitment of those states to the achievement of narrowly nationalistic goals.

Were the United States to devalue the dollar in an effort to reduce its deficit and the strain imposed by that deficit on the international monetary system, the Volcker Group calculated that other states would refuse to accept a lower value for the dollar in exchange for an extension of the Bretton Woods system's life span. Group members estimated that most states would instead act to negate the impact of a dollar devaluation on their competitive positions in world markets, effectively rendering the initiative null and void. Projecting its own outlook onto other states in the system, the Volcker Group recommended to the president that he not even attempt a unilateral devaluation of the dollar. As I show later, President Nixon was all too happy to concur, albeit largely for domestic political reasons. Thus devaluation became yet another victim of the value that the Nixon administration's officials placed on autonomy.

It is appropriate to ask, of course, whether the expectations of Volcker Group officials about other states' reactions to a U.S. devaluation were well founded; whether, in other words, their expectations were less a projection of their own perspectives than an empirical reality. Given the nature of the question, only a speculative response is possible. It is, however, interesting to note that not all observers shared the group's pessimistic forecast of reactions to a unilateral dollar devaluation.

Many did; among them was Charles P. Kindleberger, a highly respected American economist who observed in an article originally published in 1970 that "it is widely recognized that if the U.S.A. were to try to devalue it would have to raise the price of gold; and that virtually every other country would follow it, so that it would succeed in changing the price of gold but not altering the value of the dollar."[38] Kindleberger's—and the Volcker Group's—expectations were also supported by the sustained resistance to exchange-rate changes exhibited by many industrialized countries, particularly in the mid-1960s.

Among countervailing arguments from equally well-respected

---

[38]Charles P. Kindleberger, "The Price of Gold and the $n - 1$ Problem," in *International Money: A Collection of Essays*, ed. Kindleberger (London: George Allen & Unwin, 1981), p. 81.

sources was a dissent from the Bank for International Settlements. In a 1972 report, the bank, as Andrew Shonfield notes, "made the point that the accepted line among American officials and commentators . . . to the effect that it was impossible for the dollar to move without precipitating a wave of competitive devaluations by other nations . . . was never very plausible, in view of the opposite experience of 1961 when the D-mark and Dutch guilder did manage to increase their value, modestly, vis-à-vis the dollar." Shonfield adds his own observation that it seemed almost "as if the United States authorities were so eager to believe in the impossibility of a dollar devaluation that they avoided trying to discover whether such a move would have been accepted . . . and if so on what terms."[39] The skepticism of the Bank for International Settlements, Shonfield, and others is supported by the fact that two devaluations of the dollar, in 1971 and 1973, were accepted by other countries.[40] It is, of course, also true that by that time—particularly in 1971— the need for a dollar devaluation was much clearer and less ambiguous than it was as the Volcker Group deliberated in 1969, when the U.S. current account was in surplus, albeit by a relatively small amount.[41]

The Fate of an Immediate Suspension

That its own emphasis on national goals influenced the Nixon administration's evaluation of immediately closing the gold window is also apparent, although more subtly and to a lesser degree than in instances recounted above. The Nixon administration was not persuaded that ending convertibility was intrinsically undesirable or unthinkable as a solution to obvious problems in the monetary system. But it also calculated that, if other states in the system were to respond positively or even neutrally to a suspension, the U.S.

[39]Andrew Shonfield, "International Economic Relations of the Western World: An Overall View," in *International Economic Relations of the Western World, 1959-1971*, ed. Shonfield (London: Oxford University Press, 1976), 1: 58.

[40]Among the skeptics, one in-house dissenter to the opinion prevalent within the Volcker Group was Arthur Burns (see Chapter Five).

[41]The current account surplus was $1.2 billion in 1968 and $0.6 billion in 1969, compared with current account surpluses of, for example, $7.7 billion in 1964, $6.1 billion in 1965, and $4.2 billion in 1966 (*International Economic Report of the President* [1973], p. 81).

action had to appear to be an involuntary response by Washington to conditions of international financial chaos. If the United States were to avoid an automatic, nationalistic response by other countries to its closing of the gold window, in other words, that closing had to appear to be the only course open to the United States.

In part, therefore, to defer the decision until it seemed unavoidable was yet one more projection by the Nixon administration of its own priorities onto other states participating in the international monetary regime. In part, too, however, that deferral reflected the genuine uncertainty that gripped members of the Volcker Group as they contemplated the option of correcting the overvaluation of the dollar and the problems afflicting the monetary regime by suspending immediately the dollar's convertibility into gold in an effort to let the dollar float to a new, lower exchange rate.

The Volcker Group was well aware that an immediate suspension might not have any effect whatsoever on the value of the dollar in exchange markets; countries might simply accept its inconvertible status and continue to peg their currencies to the dollar, in effect acknowledging explicitly the dollar standard that they previously had only acknowledged tacitly. The Volcker Group assessed this outcome as a remote possibility, however. They calculated that exchange markets would interpret suspension as an expression of intent by the United States to depreciate the dollar and would react accordingly, inundating foreign governments with inconvertible, soon-to-be depreciated dollars unless they either revalued their currencies or allowed them to float.

Unlike raising the price of gold, then, an immediate suspension of convertibility was perceived by group members as likely to result ultimately in a lower exchange rate for the dollar. Despite this assessment, however, no one advocated immediate suspension; without exception, every member of the Volcker Group agreed that what many conceived of as the ultimate weapon in the arsenal of options for U.S. international monetary policy ought not to be used except when the situation became untenable.

Despite the strength of this conviction, however, the reasons for its existence were elusive, even to the policy makers themselves. It is quite clear that most American officials thought of suspension in apocalyptic terms, although they could not, for the most part, specify precisely the nature of the catastrophe they feared. "There was enormous uncertainty," recalls a Volcker Group member, "just fear of the unknown. We just didn't know what would happen if the United States announced one day that the dollar was no longer convertible into gold."[42]

Many of the administration's policy makers were extremely apprehensive about possible outcomes of a suspension other than a dollar depreciation. Their fears were exacerbated because they were unable to assess the probability that any particular outcome or outcomes would in fact develop. A Treasury official recalls that he and others considered that

> there was always the question of what would happen to world financial relations if the United States were to close the gold window. Who would do what to whom and how? And just as when Penn Central was about to go under, would United States financial markets collapse, whatever that means? Or wouldn't they?
>
> Because we had no example. We were guessing as to what would happen. . . . But there was a definite fear that closing the gold window . . . would start massive flows of funds. . . . [That prospect] warranted the kind of concern and caution about stepping off the edge of the cliff . . . not knowing how you would land or where you would land.[43]

There are no identifiable distinctions among the various members of the Volcker Group as to the consequences they thought might result from suspension. Some officials spontaneously included repercussions on political relationships within U.S. alliances among its possible effects; none of these, however, was an official of either the State Department or the National Security Council staff. No one in any agency regarded suspension with quite the degree of equanimity with which the Haberler task force contemplated it; most officials were much closer to the opposite end of the spectrum, where it was believed, as a State Department official stated, that the "consequences were so unknowable that it was a last resort."[44]

While no one could predict with any high degree of certainty the effects on the international monetary system of a suspension,

[42]Interview.
[43]Interview.
[44]Interview.

the possibilities foreseen ranged from a benign outcome supporting a liberal international economic order, through the construction of currency blocs, to a fearsome spiral of controls over trade and capital flows. To advocates of fixed rates, the best imaginable outcome of suspension would be a realignment of exchange rates that achieved a lower, more realistic value for the dollar than had previously existed; established the presumption that the dollar would no longer be overvalued as a matter of course; and thereby put the international monetary system on a more stable foundation, albeit different from that of Bretton Woods. To would-be floaters, the best outcome would be the elimination of government interference with the market's determination of exchange rates and a decisive end to the era of the adjustable peg. To everyone concerned, including advocates of limited flexibility, the worst outcome would be a proliferation of exchange controls as countries attempted to retain the competitive advantages of undervalued rates. Protectionism could then reach dangerously destructive heights, trade and capital flows decline precipitously, and international tensions intensify to an uncomfortable degree.

Despite marked divergences between sympathizers of floating and fixed rates on the long-range goals of a suspension, the Volcker Group easily achieved agreement on the wisdom of deferring suspension until what it labeled a "multilateral" approach had been tried and had failed. Agreement was predicated on an assumption universally held within the group, that a suspension that appeared to be the government's calculated decision rather than its involuntary response to a crisis would in all probability result in the worst-case outcome. If it appeared as though the United States were, at its discretion, abrogating one of the basic tenets of a multilateral system to gain some improvement in its balance of payments, other countries could hardly be expected to restrain themselves from protecting their own export sectors in response. International constraints on state action in the international economic arena might as a result fatally weaken. If, however, the U.S. government was seen to be resorting involuntarily to suspension only to avert total chaos in exchange markets and exhaustion of its reserves, foreign reactions might well be constructive. Indeed, they could eventually increase the stability of the international monetary system. As a Federal Reserve Board staff report stated in mid-1969,

> an early United States decision to suspend convertibility, especially if prior to suspension the dollar was under no pressure in exchange markets and no central banks were purchasing gold in significant amounts, would seem to foreign countries to be a throwing down of the gauntlet in a grand manner. In these circumstances it would be natural for the rest of the world to label the United States as the progenitor of the ensuing crisis, and it would probably be easy to make the label stick. There seems little doubt that the governments of the major foreign countries would be less cooperative after a suspension "unprovoked" by an exchange crisis than [otherwise]. . . .[45]

Among themselves, Volcker Group members tacitly agreed that a suspension would be desirable and appropriate if the U.S. gold stock declined to roughly $10 billion in the absence of perceptible improvements in the system. That figure was not selected because it signified a particular ratio of assets to outstanding liabilities or because it represented a statutory minimum of gold holdings.[46] Discussing the focus in the Haberler report on the $10 billion figure, one administration official recalls that "it was just a psychological figure. I don't think [they] . . . made any calculations."[47] Government officials converged on the figure in the same way: a State Department official states that the $10 billion figure appeared as a "watershed" yet had no intrinsic validity; it was simply "a round number . . . [that] we were pretty close to . . . and [that] began to stick in people's minds as the last line of defense."[48]

The consequences for policy of the hierarchy of values that prevailed within the Nixon administration were substantial. The hierarchy removed summarily from serious consideration several policy options that could have served, to different degrees and with varying costs, to alleviate the stresses then affecting the Bretton Woods regime. While the dollar was not under severe market pres-

---

[45]"Balance-of-Payments and International Financial Policies," p. 179.

[46]Until the statutory requirement for gold backing of U.S. currency notes was ended by Congress, in a close vote, in response to Johnson's request in March 1968, however, the $10 billion did represent a legally defined limit to the depletion of United States gold stocks (see Strange, *International Monetary Relations*, p. 289).

[47]Interview.

[48]Interview.

sure when the Nixon administration assumed office, because the U.S. balance-of-payments record for 1968 appeared relatively favorable, it was eminently predictable that a U.S. deficit of substantial magnitude would soon reemerge to threaten the survival of the Bretton Woods system.

The profound commitment of the Nixon administration's officials to the goal of autonomy in domestic economic and foreign security policy, however, precluded serious thought about restraints on domestic economic activity or foreign security expenditures that could have kept future U.S. deficits to proportions more manageable within the regime. Less directly, that commitment also encouraged the Nixon administration's officials to perceive other countries in a way that led them to predict that devaluation of the dollar, either by a rise in the gold price or by an immediate suspension of convertibility, would also fail to resolve the problems plaguing the monetary system.

The consequence of this perspective on relations between states and the international economic system was, in terms of the policy process itself, to narrow the universe of options theoretically open to the U.S. government as it contemplated the probable collapse of the postwar monetary regime. That perspective in and of itself is not sufficient, however, to explain the further narrowing of that universe to exclude capital controls as a feasible policy. Since the option was excluded by consensus, but by consensus of a different kind, it deserves separate treatment.

The Fate of Capital Controls

The Volcker Group gave an intensification of controls such short shrift that it, too, can be accurately called a "nonoption." The view of the Nixon administration's officials, recalls an official of the Council of Economic Advisers, was "that the game was up. . . . [That] means when you get into . . . [a difficult] situation, you're going to suspend gold rather than talking about curbing tourist expenditures, the way the Johnson administration did. . . . The discussion in the Volcker Group was a discussion about whether you should suspend out of a blue sky or not. The implicit assumption was that once we have the next round of problems there will be some changes made."[49] Underlying the relegation of capital

[49]Interview.

controls and other correctives to the realm of nonoptions were a variety of considerations.

Among these was the belief among members of the Volcker Group that the very idea of capital controls and the other restrictions on trade and payments the United States had used in the 1960s was antithetical to the idea of a liberal international economic order.[50] While committed to the principle that national autonomy in domestic economic and foreign security policy should be no more than marginally vulnerable to international financial concerns, the Volcker Group was also committed to the principle that, within those constraints, market forces were to prevail. In the group's view, the Bretton Woods system of freely convertible currencies and the accompanying trade regime symbolized by the General Agreement on Tariffs and Trade were intended to allow maximum freedom of action to market forces, which would determine the direction of trade flows. The controls that had been devised in an effort to preserve the Bretton Woods system, therefore, actually represented an erosion of the foundation on which the system was constructed. As the mixture of corrective measures expanded and threatened to become a permanent fixture in the United States, it became increasingly unattractive to those policy makers committed, for either economic or political reasons, to the concept of an open international economic order.

The law of anticipated reaction also contributed to the Volcker Group's refusal to consider seriously a tightened system of controls as a realistic possibility for U.S. policy. President Nixon's personal antipathy to controls and the concomitant likelihood that he would reject any option that intensified existing controls, or even involved a long-run reliance on the existing system, inhibited the Volcker Group from focusing on any option based on correctives. The group did believe, however, that controls would continue to be necessary in the short run.

That U.S. policy regarding controls might be subject to change under a Nixon presidency became evident during the 1968 campaign, when the Republican candidate declared his intention to dismantle the system of controls. While campaign pledges do not

[50]Interview.

always become administration policy, there were early indications that Nixon's stance on controls was a particularly good candidate for such a transformation.

The Haberler task force report, for example, arguing that selective correctives are "wasteful, inefficient, and undermine our free enterprise system," urged Nixon to dismantle the controls that had been applied and tightened by successive administrations when the balance of payments failed to improve. The controls policy was a "failure" in the eyes of the task force because "the promised restoration of balance in the international accounts has not been achieved and 'temporary' controls had to be multiplied, tightened, and extended." The decade-long U.S. experience with trade and capital controls, the report contended, had only served to demonstrate the "truth of two general principles . . . the 'fungibility' of money which enables it to flow around road blocks set up by artificial restrictions and, second, the tendency of specific and temporary controls to spread, expand, multiply, tighten and become permanent" unless supplemented by more fundamental techniques of adjustment.[51]

In addition, the international economics section of Arthur Burns's transitional report to the president-elect began with the assertion that "the broad objective of the new administration must be to move away from the system of controls over foreign lending and investing."[52] Moreover, President Nixon ordered cabinet officers attending the very first meeting of his Cabinet Committee on Economic Policy, a subcommittee of the cabinet he established to formulate broad economic policy, to develop a specific program to demonstrate his commitment to the elimination of capital controls. He said that he wanted "something to show we're trying to get rid of the damn controls"; and he wanted it soon.[53]

Despite its potential impact on balance-of-payments policy and the future of the international monetary system, the president's opposition to capital controls really had very little to do with either. Nixon's determination to eliminate the controls developed in iso-

[51]"Report of the [Haberler] Task Force," p. 15.

[52]"International Economic Relations," *Transitional Report* (n.d.), pp. 107-17, document in the files of Martin Anderson, San Marino, Calif., p. 107.

[53]"Report on the Cabinet Committee on Economic Policy," January 28, 1969, p. 6, document in the files of William Safire, Chevy Chase, Md.

lation from considerations about their impact on the balance of payments; it manifested itself long before Nixon would have been privy to forecasts about the U.S. international payments accounts. It was rooted instead in pragmatic political concerns and somewhat abstract convictions about the nature of a desirable economic order.

Secretary of Commerce Maurice H. Stans raised the subject of lifting controls in that first cabinet committee meeting.[54] This suggests that an element of the president's interest in relaxing controls stemmed from his desire to placate business interests, which opposed the continuation of capital controls. Countervailing political pressure to retain controls was nonexistent, domestic interest-rate levels were not favorably influenced by the restraints on capital outflow, and no sector of the financial community perceived their continuation as in its interests. Thus the president could easily afford to give a sympathetic reception to complaints that the controls inequitably affected those small banks and corporations that could not operate as easily in Eurodollar markets as could their larger rivals.

But there was also a powerful impetus behind Nixon's desire to remove the controls independent of industry pressure: the president's innate preference for market-determined solutions to economic problems.[55] His 1971 imposition of wage and price controls notwithstanding, Nixon remains, in his own words, "thoroughly persuaded of the superior merits of a free economy" over a managed economy.[56] He is also persuaded "that, as imperfect as it is— the market system is the best mechanism for pricing."[57]

Why he is so persuaded—apart from his World War II service in the Office of Price Administration (which may have been enough)—is less clear than is his conviction itself. Available evidence on President Nixon's thinking about the issue of free versus managed economies does not demonstrate a high degree of sophisti-

[54]Ibid.

[55]Jonathan David Aronson argues that this preference was more important than were business pressures (see his *Money and Power: Banks and the World Monetary System* [Beverly Hills, Calif.: Sage, 1977], p. 90).

[56]Richard Nixon, *RN: The Memoirs of Richard Nixon* (New York: Grosset & Dunlap, 1978), p. 19.

[57]"Report on the Cabinet Committee on Economic Policy," November 13, 1969, p. 4, document in the files of William Safire, Chevy Chase, Md.

cation. The divergence between private and social costs and the concentrations of market power that argue against the unbridled pursuit of a free market do not, for example, seem to have impressed Nixon. If he objected to reductions of government involvement in the private sector at all, he tended to do so in order to take into consideration what he called the "sociological" consequences of unrestricted competition. These sociological exceptions appear arbitrary: when the Department of Justice pursued the repeal of various free trade acts, for example, Nixon suggested that the department be mindful of the effects of its efforts on the survival of "mom and pop" grocery stores.[58] In the case of capital controls, such considerations did not impede but rather intensified the president's determination to let market forces work freely, because the burden of the controls had been borne by smaller institutions that lacked a well-established tradition of participation in international trade and investment.

Economic analysis, however, did not support the president's belief that capital controls interfered with the efficient allocation of resources. There is no well-developed theory on the efficiency consequences of restraints on capital flow; "when one makes a case for complete freedom of capital movement," as Robert Solomon observes, "one is probably assuming a set of nation states endowed with fairly similar institutions, capital markets, banking systems, and monetary policies; there are all sorts of assumptions one may have to make before one is sure about the efficiency effects of unfettered capital flow."[59]

The president's economic advisers nonetheless concurred in Nixon's judgment that the controls ought to be relaxed, although they took balance-of-payments considerations much more explicitly into

---

[58] In his discussion with cabinet officials of the fair trade acts, Nixon expressed concern over what he perceived as the Justice Department's overly enthusiastic advocacy of their repeal. The president asked whether the repeal would "mean that mom and pop stores are on the way out—and supermarkets are all we'll have. There is a sociological problem here. We may be helping consumers, but we don't help the character of our people. . . . Supermarkets may be able to sell Wheaties at a cent less, but I don't think we want to be a nation of supermarkets" ("Report on the Committee on Economic Policy," April 10, 1969, p. 4, document in the files of William Safire, Chevy Chase, Md.)

[59] Robert Solomon, in *The Economics of International Adjustment*, ed. Randall Hinshaw (Baltimore, Md.: Johns Hopkins Press, 1971), pp. 120-21.

account. Aware that the payments accounts were in a very unsteady state and that the capital controls had been effective in restraining the deficit, they also knew that the controls were unlikely to remain effective. A system of controls eventually develops leaks; it has, as a Council of Economic Advisers official said, "a fading effect. . . . [When] regulations are laid down, these tend to thwart the plans a company has. So the next question is, are there any ways we can go ahead and finance our subsidiary abroad? And . . . increasingly these questions got answered in the affirmative."[60] Moreover, as another high-level member of the Nixon administration remarked, "we were not controls-minded."[61]

The anticontrols sentiment clearly evident at the top levels of the Nixon administration, the inherent contradiction between controls and the principle on which the postwar international economic order had been established, and the increasing ineffectiveness of the controls thus inhibited the Volcker Group from sustained consideration of controls as a long-run response to continuing problems in the Bretton Woods system. Capital controls thus became yet another item on the nonagenda of the Volcker Group's deliberations about long-range U.S. strategy vis-à-vis the difficulties of the dollar and the postwar international monetary regime.

In sum, that the U.S. government took few unilateral initiatives in a period in which the breakdown of the Bretton Woods system seemed much more than a remote possibility is explained in part by the consensus that united the Nixon administration's officials on issues of central importance to the future of the system. A coincidence of perspectives, images, and beliefs prevented the administration from advocating or adopting any of a number of alternatives to the status quo that might have prolonged the existence of the Bretton Woods regime: it precluded serious consideration of deflation, constraints on foreign policy, a rise in the gold price of the dollar, and an extension of capital controls. It also persuaded the administration to defer a decision on ending convertibility, an option that might ultimately have provided a more secure foundation for an international monetary regime or, con-

[60]Interview.
[61]Interview.

versely, might have undermined any prospects for international financial cooperation.

In any case, the consequences for policy of the unanimity that characterized the Nixon administration were profound, narrowing significantly the range of options open, not in theory but in reality, in the dying days of the Bretton Woods regime. Further restricting the Nixon administration's ability to endorse any vigorous initiatives were the structure and the process of Nixon administration international monetary policy making. They are the subjects of the next chapter.

CHAPTER FOUR

The Role of Structure and Process

That the Nixon administration did not vigorously pursue international monetary reform was the consequence of the structure and process of its international monetary policy making. In stark contrast to the virtual unanimity that enabled officials to dismiss quickly a series of other policy alternatives, a heated debate erupted on the issue of international monetary reform. This debate bore many of the imprints considered by bureaucratic politics analysts to be characteristic of the way American foreign-policy decisions are made. It was marked by intense pulling and hauling, divisions among officials from different agencies, and maneuvers to influence outcomes in directions that particular officials favored.

In this chapter I argue that the structure within which the Nixon administration made policy on international monetary affairs—the distribution of power among the agencies involved in administration policy making in this area—is the single most important factor explaining the outcome of that administration's debate on international monetary reform, an outcome that represented the defeat of those advocating reform. I argue that the distribution of power over the making of international monetary policy within the Nixon administration was extraordinarily asymmetrical, closely resembling a unipolar system. Within that structure, preeminence belonged unmistakably to the Department of the Treasury, a department whose attachment to the status quo on issues of international monetary policy was unrivaled within the executive branch.[1] In the setting of Nixon administration policy with respect to the issue of international monetary reform, structure determined outcomes; power determined policy; and Treasury skepticism regarding monetary reform ultimately became U.S. government policy.

The contemporary literature on foreign-policy decision making would hold that this conclusion is anomalous. As bureaucratic politics analysts have persuasively argued, structure, while important, is not an infallible guide to policy outcomes; variables intervening between structure and outcome—what may be labeled "process-level variables"—can overwhelm the influence of structure or what Halperin refers to as "the rules of the game." In Halperin's words, "rules do not dominate the process [of foreign-policy decision making], although they do make a difference to the extent that they structure the game. This still leaves considerable flexibility for participants to maneuver . . . to get the decisions they want."[2]

Nixon administration officials dissatisfied with the implications for policy outcomes of the rules of the game were, however, largely unable to counter the influence of those rules. For a variety of reasons recounted below, individual officials who were restive in a Treasury-dominated game could not use the levers of power available to them to upset that game. They were unable to enhance their influence over the disposition of the issue of monetary reform. That structure proved to be the dominant influence on the outcome

---

[1] That the Department of the Treasury tends to lag behind other agencies with respect to significant departures from prevailing practices is demonstrated not only by the instance of the Nixon administration's policy making recounted here but also by the experience of the Kennedy administration. Then, the Department of the Treasury lagged considerably behind the Council of Economic Advisers, the National Security Council staff, and the Department of State in endorsing proposals for international monetary—specifically, liquidity—reform then current in international and domestic circles. Although Treasury did issue a reform proposal in 1972, that proposal, envisioning a return to a modified par value system, was not a far-reaching departure from the status quo. The comment of an unidentified "non-governmental adviser," reported by Sorensen, seems apt: the Treasury, said the individual quoted, " 'is subject to the banker syndrome, which is to foresee disaster but prefer inaction' " (Sorensen, *Kennedy*, p. 408). For a detailed and perceptive discussion of the division on monetary reform in the Kennedy administration, see Odell, *U.S. International Monetary Policy*, chap. 3. For a discussion of the Treasury's 1972 proposal, see Solomon, *The International Monetary System*, pp. 226-27.

[2] Halperin, *Bureaucratic Politics and Foreign Policy*, p. 115.

of the reform debate, then, can only be understood if the negligible influence of process is also understood.

In this chapter, therefore, I describe in detail the structure and process that produced U.S. international monetary policy during the first two years of the Nixon administration. The interplay of agencies and individuals secured rather than challenged Treasury's dominance of the process and, as a consequence, the Nixon administration did not pursue vigorously the option of international monetary reform. Before doing so, however, I outline the substance of the debate on reform itself, as well as the positions taken by various participants. The profound impact of structure can only be adequately appreciated if the extent and depth of conflict characterizing the administration's discussion of reform are clear.

THE ISSUE UNDER DEBATE

By 1969, systemic reform had begun to appeal to many academic economists, and to some bank and government officials, as a more efficient and sustainable remedy for the evident difficulties of the Bretton Woods system than were what they perceived as the patchwork responses of earlier U.S. administrations.[3] Advocates of reform believed that if the premises of the Bretton Woods system were changed to permit, encourage, and perhaps even require a certain degree of exchange-rate flexibility, other rates would move up, thus alleviating pressure on the U.S. balance of payments. Moreover, in the longer run, a system incorporating greater flexibility could better accommodate different national economic trends than did the adjustable peg.

Academic economists were suggesting several proposals that might relieve the rigidities manifest in the exchange-rate structure, reverse the increasing tendencies to resort to piecemeal trade and capital controls, and preempt a cataclysmic termination of the Bretton Woods system. All the proposals current in the academic com-

---

[3]Writing in 1969, Okun observed that "research economists and academic experts today agree broadly, although not unanimously, that a greater degree of flexibility in exchange rates would be a desirable innovation" (Okun, *The Political Economy of Prosperity*, p. 15).

munity incorporated a greater degree of market participation and a lesser degree of government intervention in the determination of parities. Apart from those who advocated freely floating exchange rates, academic economists tended to focus on limited flexibility variants of the adjustable peg mechanism. They suggested three possible alternatives: a wider band, a crawling peg, and a combination of a crawling peg with a wider band.[4] The Volcker Group examined each of these basic proposals.

Conceptually the simplest, the wider band would have extended the 1 percent margin on either side of parity within which rates could fluctuate under the Bretton Woods system to between 3 and 5 percent on either side. The margins varied according to the preferences of the individual economist. Advocates of a wider band believed that it would deter speculation by increasing the potential for losses should speculators wrongly anticipate that a rate was about to be changed. They also believed that the larger margin of fluctuation would permit markets to transmit a clearer signal to governments that adjustment was necessary while simultaneously facilitating that adjustment. As the width of the band increased, the role of the exchange rate in the adjustment process would expand and the system would move closer to floating rates.

The crawling, sliding, or gliding peg proposals provided for frequent, very small changes in exchange rates to a maximum of 2 or 3 percent per year. Williamson suggested, for example, that parities under a crawling peg change by one-twentysixth of one percent each week.[5] Economists such as James E. Meade, J. Carter Murphy, and William Fellner, who advocated a crawling peg, agreed on the desirable magnitude of rate changes but differed as to the procedures for actually changing the rate. Some thought that specified market indicators should alone determine the decision; others were inclined to allow governments a measure of discretion over the timing of a rate change. Replacing what some began to call the "jumping peg" of the Bretton Woods system with the crawling peg would reduce speculation, advocates believed, because the amount

[4]For a comprehensive review of limited flexibility alternatives, see George N. Halm, ed., *Approaches to Greater Flexibility of Exchange Rates: The Burgenstock Papers* (Princeton: Princeton University Press, 1970).

[5]John H. Williamson, *The Crawling Peg*, Essays in International Finance, no. 50 (Princeton: Princeton University, International Finance Section, December 1965).

of gain on a single rate change would be much reduced if the rate were permitted to change by only a fraction of a point instead of the 9 to 10 percent changes characteristic of the Bretton Woods system. The band around the established parity could either be limited to the traditional 2 percent or, as economists supporting the alternative of a crawling peg cum wider band desired, be extended to perhaps 10 percent.

Whether any of these limited flexibility proposals could be successfully negotiated and implemented was uncertain. It was that uncertainty which provided part of the animus for the debate on reform that occurred within the Nixon administration. Advocates of vigorous U.S. initiatives for reform tended to believe that, given certain conditions, the reforms under consideration would be both acceptable to other governments and successful in resolving the adjustment problems plaguing the Bretton Woods regime.[6] Opponents, conversely, were skeptical of the negotiability and the prospects for success of those same proposals.

In retrospect, as Williamson observed in 1977, given "the magnitude of capital outflows from the United States and the time taken for the dollar devaluation to make an impact on the U.S. payments position . . . it must be judged highly doubtful whether a downward crawl of the dollar initiated as late as 1970 or 1971 would in fact have averted the crisis of August 1971." But, as Williamson himself added, had the crawl "been accompanied by a renunciation of 'benign neglect' and the dollar standard, which would have implied a more cautious monetary policy than that actually adopted by the United States and perhaps an earlier initiative on the incomes policy front, it might have induced the Europeans to continue holding the fort a good bit longer, and this might have enabled a sufficiently forceful initiative to succeed in securing the orderly evolution to the gold/SDR exchange standard that was once hoped for."[7]

Whether vigorous U.S. advocacy of multilateral reform during

---

[6] Robert Solomon, for example, believed that a crawling peg would "probably work well only if it were introduced at a time of general balance-of-payments equilibrium," requiring, therefore, a prior realignment of exchange rates among the major countries. Even then, Solomon saw "significant political obstacles to a system of greater flexibility in which the dollar would not flex" (see Solomon, *The International Monetary System*, pp. 170, 175).

[7] Williamson, *The Failure of World Monetary Reform*, pp. 41-42.

the Nixon administration would have been persuasive to other governments and successful in resolving the adjustment problems of the Bretton Woods regime remains uncertain even today. The conditions required for success on both counts, it is true, were sufficiently stringent as to make the skeptics' case even in 1969 somewhat stronger than that of the proponents of reform.[8] That some uncertainty existed, however, was sufficient to fuel a heated debate among officials of the Nixon administration regarding the merits, or lack thereof, of proposals for reform.

The Debate on Reform and the Nixon Administration

During the first several months of the Nixon administration, Volcker Group members considered all three limited flexibility proposals. Intragovernmental examination of these alternatives to the adjustable peg had actually begun during the last year of the previous administration, but President Johnson had not committed the U.S. government to either the general idea or any specific variant of limited flexibility by the time he left office.[9] The work was pursued in the Nixon administration by a working group of the Volcker Group, as well as by the group as a whole.

William B. Dale, U.S. executive director of the International Monetary Fund, chaired the working group, which, according to one of its participants, included representatives of the Federal Reserve Bank of New York, the staff of the Federal Reserve Board of Governors, and the White House.[10] Designed to present a report

[8]Most governments—with the exceptions of the British, German, and Dutch—were not very receptive to greater exchange-rate flexibility. Moreover, a crawling peg system presumed that other exchange rates would move while the dollar would not—a system that, to be acceptable to other countries, required that the United States keel its economy to a steady, noninflationary course. Given the U.S. economy's previous performance and the country's strong preference for domestic economic autonomy, it was improbable that other countries could be convinced that the United States would not abuse its position at the center of a reformed system.

[9]Fowler apparently considered publicly advocating limited flexibility at the annual meeting of the International Monetary Fund in September 1968 but decided that a public stance would better be left to whatever administration replaced Johnson's (interview).

[10]Interview.

to its parent body, the group never succeeded in doing so. Substantial differences among its members prevented consensus—opinions ranged from intractable opposition to any limited flexibility scheme to enthusiastic advocacy of systemic reform.

It is possible to discern in the arguments advanced for and against limited exchange-rate flexibility the hopes and fears of the participants with regard to fixed versus floating rates. That individuals not paralyzed with fright at the idea of floating rates should be more sympathetic to limited flexibility schemes than were wholehearted advocates of fixed rates is not surprising, since it was possible that relaxing the Bretton Woods system to incorporate limited flexibility would eventually lead to the abandonment of all but the shadow of fixed rates. Thus the Federal Reserve Bank of New York, to whom floating rates were anathema because of its preoccupation with the restraint on inflation it perceived in a fixed parity, staunchly opposed even the principle of limited flexibility. To an extent that was unusual within the government, the Federal Reserve Bank of New York maintained that change was unnecessary, because nothing was really wrong with either the structure of the Bretton Woods system or the techniques that had been devised to bolster it. With a judicious exchange-rate change here and there and the continued, efficient cooperation of central bankers, the system could endure indefinitely.

The position of the New York bank with respect to limited flexibility resulted from its particular responsibilities, which led it to place an extraordinarily high value on stability and gave it a perspective on the Bretton Woods system different from that of most other government agencies. The bank is the operating arm of the U.S. government in the management of the public debt and in the conclusion of swaps and exchange-market intervention; stability is a prerequisite of the former and a goal of the latter task. Thus the New York bank assigned a very high priority to stability as an ultimate goal. It aimed for minimal disruption of established procedures, and limited flexibility schemes did not conform to that goal.

Nor, from the perspective of the New York bank, were such reforms necessary. In a more technical sense than was true even of Treasury, the bank managed the Bretton Woods system and it was convinced that the system functioned reasonably well. Because of its responsibilities, the New York bank was accustomed to looking at the Bretton Woods system from the bottom up; it knew the nuts and bolts of the system because it not only managed them but in some cases had designed them. It had successfully countered increasing assaults on the fixed-rate system and could continue to do so; there was no need to scrap the entire machinery when a few extra nuts and bolts would do.

With distinctly different responsibilities and a diametrically opposed perspective on the Bretton Woods system, C. Fred Bergsten, the member of Henry Kissinger's White House staff specifically charged with responsibility for international monetary policy, came to a correspondingly different conclusion. The interests of the United States, Bergsten thought, would best be served by systemic reform in the direction of greater flexibility of exchange rates. The "quadruple bias" against the United States displayed in the Bretton Woods system would be removed if the premises of the Bretton Woods system were revised so that rates would change more readily. After such revision, deficit countries would no longer be subjected to greater pressure than surplus countries experienced; revaluations would not be smaller than required to restore payments equilibrium; devaluations would not be larger than necessary because of the need to deter speculation on a possible further change; and chain-reaction devaluations would no longer be the system's modus operandi.[11] The interests of the United States and those of international traders and investors could be met simultaneously by an ambitious reform of the adjustable-peg mechanism. The particular variant of limited flexibility that Bergsten favored was the combination of crawling peg and wider band.[12]

Unlike officials of the Federal Reserve Bank of New York, Bergsten's primary responsibility was policy. He did not get involved in the intricacies and manifold technicalities of managing the dollar. Instead, he perceived swaps, for example, in the context of the

[11]C. Fred Bergsten, "The United States and Greater Flexibility of Exchange Rates," in Halm, *Approaches to Greater Flexibility*, p. 68.
[12]See Bergsten's discussion of limited flexibility in his *Dilemmas of the Dollar*, pp. 431-74.

operation of the entire system and categorized them as funda-
mentally antithetical to the system's overall goals of efficiency and
maximization of international trade and financial flows. Bergsten
had assumed his policy responsibilities after a three-year stint at
the Council on Foreign Relations, where he had spent a good deal
of time examining alternatives to the adjustable peg as a remedy
for the increasingly untenable position of the dollar.[13] He was an
early convert to exchange-rate reform and its enthusiastic sup-
porter within U.S. policy councils.

Ralph C. Bryant represented the Federal Reserve within the
working group that examined limited flexibility. A staff member
of the Federal Reserve Board's Division of International Finance
who would later succeed Solomon as the division's chief, he was an
ardent advocate within the Federal Reserve system of international
monetary reform. Like Bergsten, Bryant was persuaded that the
techniques that had been devised to keep the Bretton Woods system
alive were only stopgap measures. He believed that a longer-term
solution to the problems of the dollar, and of the system as a whole,
was essential.

By mid-1969, Bryant had analyzed in great detail and at great
length the balance-of-payments options available to the United
States. He concluded that a rise in the gold price, further controls,
and deflation were not desirable choices. He suggested instead that
the United States look toward a reform of the international monetary system with a particular focus on the exchange-rate mechanism. Arguing strongly against the assumption of fixed rates, Bryant
contended that "any set of fixed rates can, and probably will, become inappropriate with the passage of time . . . in the sense that
one or more countries will ultimately choose or be forced to change
their exchange rate rather than deal with a payments imbalance"
using any combination of demand management policies, controls,
or extensive financing.[14] The greater uncertainties of freely floating
rates left Bryant "strongly" inclined toward limited flexibility as "in
the best interest of the United States and of the world payments
system as a whole," although he cautioned that intensive study by

---

[13]For the result, which was much delayed by Bergsten's acceptance of the National
Security Council post, see ibid.

[14]"Balance-of-Payments and International Financial Policies," p. 132.

the government was necessary before a firm conclusion could be reached.[15]

Within the Federal Reserve, Bryant's interest in international monetary reform was unusual. The Board of Governors as a unit did not hold a formal position on the desirability of limited flexibility. This conformed with its general lack of interest in international monetary policy issues. The New York bank fervently opposed any tampering with the adjustable peg mechanism but Bryant took a more liberal position on the issue of reform, a position characteristic, according to administration officials, of other members of the Board staff including its chief, Solomon.[16]

Bryant's academic background and professional interests inclined him toward a comprehensive solution to what he perceived as the Bretton Woods system's problems, in much the same way that Bergsten's did. Bryant had first come to the Federal Reserve in 1965 to do research for his doctoral thesis. After completing the thesis he joined the Board staff and began to work with others in the government on the negotiations that culminated in the creation of the special drawing right. He later headed a small staff within the Division of International Finance that concentrated on interpreting contemporary problems of international monetary policy within the context of a larger analytical framework. Given his academic training and professional experience, it is not surprising that Bryant's diagnosis of and prescription for the ills of the dollar and the Bretton Woods system included a dose of reform that was very similar to that being recommended by many within the academic community.

In a stance that was uncharacteristic of Treasury officials, William Dale, who chaired the working group of the Volcker Group, also believed that the international monetary system needed an exchange-rate mechanism more flexible than the adjustable peg. A long-time member of the higher echelons of the Treasury bureaucracy, Dale's views on limited flexibility were more compatible with those of officials in other agencies than of those in his own.

Dale's responsibilities, however, were not typical of most other

[15]Ibid., p. 175.
[16]Interviews.

officials in the Department of the Treasury at his level.[17] Dale had been U.S. executive director of the International Monetary Fund since 1962 and would leave Treasury in 1974 to become deputy managing director of the Fund. As the U.S. director, Dale conveyed U.S. policy to and participated in discussions among members of the Fund's Executive Board, one of its two main policy-making bodies. Because of his position, Dale was much more heavily exposed to the perspectives of foreign officials and to issues of peculiar importance to the intrnational monetary system than were his colleagues at Treasury. That Dale would be particularly sensitive to the system's needs and receptive to systemic solutions to obvious problems was a logical consequence of his professional responsibilities.

The deadlock in the working group meant that the entire issue was shifted back to the full Volcker Group. There, primarily because the New York bank did not ordinarily participate in Volcker Group meetings, the idea of injecting greater flexibility into the exchange-rate mechanism received a more sympathetic reception. None of the State, Federal Reserve, Treasury, or White House representatives who regularly attended Volcker Group meetings agreed with the bank's adamant opposition to reform. Discussion, therefore, took place within a consensus that the idea of greater exchange-rate flexibility was worth exploring and was punctuated by Bergsten's and Council of Economic Advisers member Hendrik S. Houthakker's marked enthusiasm for not only talking about but actually moving toward a crawling peg system.

Scornful of the methods employed by previous administrations to shore up the dollar and the system, Houthakker believed that they had put the system in a situation he would later compare to that of "a boat that is attempting to pass down a river with many sand banks and other obstacles. Rather than adjusting the rudder, it was decided to pump more water into the river so that the boat would not run aground so often."[18] Houthakker's sympathy lay

---

[17]With respect to issues that arise in international lending, the U.S. executive director of the World Bank, also a Treasury post, is in a similar position.

[18]Hendrik S. Houthakker, "The Breakdown of Bretton Woods," in *Economic Advice and Economic Policy: Recommendations from Past Members of the Council of Economic Advisers*, ed. Werner Sichel (New York: Praeger, 1978), p. 47.

instead with a reform of what he perceived as the system's rudder: the exchange-rate mechanism.

Houthakker believed that revaluations by other countries were a useful and desirable short-term solution to the difficulties of the dollar. In the longer run, however, the Bretton Woods system could survive only if it were reformed in such a way as to incorporate greater flexibility. For both the short and the long term, Houthakker subscribed wholeheartedly to the strategy of benign neglect that the Haberler task force, of which he had been an active member, had advocated. The United States, according to Houthakker and the task force as a whole, should relax controls, inhibit gold conversions, and await the responses abroad of inflation or appreciation. In the meantime, the United States ought to press other countries to consider reforming the Bretton Woods system. Houthakker was persuaded by his own talks with foreign officials that the Treasury had underestimated their receptivity to reform.

Unlike most of his colleagues, Houthakker tended to attribute to foreign officials a profound commitment to the good of the monetary system, a commitment at least equal to if not stronger than their commitment to more narrowly defined national interests. As early as 1962 Houthakker had been convinced, he would later recall, that the United States could successfully achieve a much-needed devaluation of the dollar; he was confident that other countries would not respond with devaluations of their own because such responses would have violated the Bretton Woods agreement, which forbids competitive devaluation.[19] Given his assessment of other countries and his belief that a crawling peg system provided a theoretically apt solution to overly rigid exchange rates, Houthakker concluded that only the absence of an earnest effort by the U.S. government stood between the illness and the cure of the Bretton Woods system.

The counterweight to Houthakker's and Bergsten's enthusiasm for a crawling peg and to whatever other sympathy existed for more flexible exchange rates was Treasury. This conclusion has basically to be inferred, because Paul Volcker, who for all practical purposes *was* Treasury, reportedly never expressed an opinion

---

[19]Houthakker would later come to believe that other countries would act to vitiate a dollar devaluation. See his discussion in ibid.

within the Volcker Group about which exchange-rate mechanism he considered most desirable.

Appointed to chair the Federal Reserve Board of Governors in 1979, Volcker assumed the position of under secretary of the Treasury for monetary affairs in early 1969, and he remained in that post until 1974. The recipient of graduate degrees from the London School of Economics and Harvard University, Volcker spent his entire career prior to 1969 either in government or in banking. From his first professional position as a junior management assistant at Treasury, Volcker moved to the Federal Reserve Bank of New York in 1953 and to Chase Manhattan Bank in 1957. He returned to Treasury in 1962, first to head the Office of Financial Analysis and later to become deputy under secretary for monetary affairs. He served his two-year stint as deputy under secretary under Roosa, the originator of the Roosa bonds and the advocate of numerous other techniques to maintain the Bretton Woods system. When he left Treasury in late 1965 to return to Chase Manhattan, Volcker continued his involvement in government by participating in the Balance of Payments Advisory Committee of the Department of Commerce. His stint in the Nixon administration Treasury would be followed by a one-year sabbatical at Princeton University and then, in 1975, by the assumption of the presidency of the Federal Reserve Bank of New York. From that post he would be promoted by President Jimmy Carter to chair the Federal Reserve.[20]

Within the constraints established by the imperatives of foreign and domestic economic policy, the policy preferences of the under secretary can largely determine the course of international monetary policy, particularly when, as was true at the outset of the Nixon administration, the Treasury secretary is content to play a largely passive role. Volcker's preferences during his tenure as under secretary were difficult to discern at the time, however, despite the fact that he and other Nixon administration officials confronted policy problems that tapped basic beliefs about the nature of a desirable international monetary order. Questions about the optimal role of the dollar in the international system, the degree

[20]The data on Volcker's career are drawn largely from *Current Biography Yearbook, 1973*, ed. Charles Moritz (New York: H. W. Wilson, 1973), pp. 425-28.

of flexibility that the system should incorporate, and the appropriate extent, if any, of governmental intervention in the setting of exchange rates inevitably arose. Never, however, was it clear, even to Volcker's Treasury colleagues, where he stood on any of these issues. "Having worked with him," reflected one Treasury official in 1979, "I could not tell you . . . whether he [Volcker] would have advocated fixed or floating rates. I would guess, and it would be a pure guess, an imputation" that he would have preferred fixed rates if he thought they were feasible.[21]

Lack of interaction with the under secretary does not explain the inability of most policy makers to identify Volcker's preferences. Within the Department of the Treasury itself, there were extended and frequent staff meetings to discuss policy issues and ensure the adequacy of contingency planning for any international monetary crisis that might develop. The same type of contact occurred regularly between Volcker and all other subcabinet-level officials engaged in issues of international monetary policy. In both forums, however, Volcker's style obscured his policy views. He customarily assumed the role of devil's advocate, challenging, criticizing, and encouraging other views but never advancing his own views forcefully. It is very frequently said of Volcker's style during his tenure as under secretary that he "played his cards close to his vest." Volcker, said one Nixon administration official, "is a man who never shows his hand. I worked closely with him . . . and was on very good terms with him, but I think it's fair to say I never knew what he was doing. That didn't become clear to me until long afterward."[22]

The explanation for Volcker's style is both role-related and idiosyncratic. The sensitivity of foreign-exchange markets constrains officials of any government from freely discussing exchange-rate policy, for fear of upsetting the established parity of their country's currency. In the case of the United States, this sensitivity about exchange rates extends to discussions of the international monetary system as well, because the United States, unlike any other country, could move unilaterally to implement a new system and thereby upset several important parities simultaneously. This constraint applies with particular severity to the under secretary, who is crucial

[21] Interview.
[22] Interview.

to the direction U.S. policy will eventually assume. Any leaks of the under secretary's comments to the media could devastate the stability of foreign-exchange markets. As a consequence, caution is the byword for the office's incumbent.

The role of under secretary for monetary affairs can also be interpreted by its occupant as prohibiting even a guarded expression of individual policy preferences. The under secretary technically functions as an adviser to the secretary; the secretary may reasonably expect advocacy to be subordinated to a comprehensive and objective analysis of policy problems and potential solutions. In trying to present the secretary with the best available information and options, the under secretary draws on a number of officials in other agencies; a strong statement of individual preference in that capacity might well serve to deter free expression of contradictory opinions.

Modifying and, in Volcker's case, intensifying the role-related constraints on the under secretary are the attributes of the incumbent. The absence of any substantial evidence of Volcker's own views has been interpreted by several of his colleagues in government as evidence that they simply did not exist. A State Department official, for example, discussing the absence of any forceful advocacy by the U.S. government of international monetary reform in the two years prior to the August 1971 decision, attributed that absence in part to Volcker's indecisiveness: Volcker, he reflects, "would always keep his views very close to his chest. Never came down one way or the other. . . . I used to think that he was very clever in how he dealt with things, but then I realized that Paul wasn't sure."[23]

Volcker's predominant attitude with respect to international monetary reform appears to have been one of profound skepticism. Some of his colleagues in the Volcker Group perceived such an attitude at the time and he himself expressed it in contemporary conversations with foreign officials.[24] Moreover, had he been free to choose between systems of fixed and flexible rates, available

[23]Interview.
[24]Interviews; U.S., Department of the Treasury, "Memorandum of Conversation," April 21, 1969, p. 13, document released by the Department of the Treasury under an FOIA request.

evidence suggests that he would have chosen fixed rates. That choice would lend further credence to the admittedly speculative evidence that Volcker was, at best, ambivalent about the option of international monetary reform advocated by some of his colleagues in government.

That he preferred fixed to floating rates, where feasible, is apparent in Treasury statements that Volcker authored while under secretary, as well as in his own statements after he left the department. In a 1978 speech, Volcker reviewed the world's five-year experience with floating rates and concluded that the monetary system "had begun to reveal some potential difficulties more reminiscent of the flavor of the 1930s than of much of the theorizing about floating rates."[25] Secretary of the Treasury George P. Shultz's speech to the International Monetary Fund in September 1972, which Volcker drafted, called for a presumption in favor of what was called "central values," with "provision" for countries desiring to float their currencies.[26] When pressed, a Treasury official ascribes to Volcker his own views about a desirable exchange-rate mechanism. "I think," he states,

> that it would be very nice to live in a fixed rate world. I still think that's true. But I think the world we were then in and that we were moving toward was not one which would permit the luxury of a fixed rate system. And, just as for political reasons we had to be forced off a fixed rate system, I think that we needed to do everything we could to make the old system hold together. But that raises the question of what reasonably you should do. Do you put on controls, interest equalization taxes—do you wreck the system just trying to preserve a fixed rate system?
>
> I don't think Volcker would have been an advocate of flexible rates as a system but neither was he opposed to them, in a sense. He was looking for a system that would work. And as the fixed rate system became increasingly unworkable, he was being pushed, not by theology but by events, toward accepting and trying to make work a flexible system.[27]

[25]Paul A. Volcker, "The Political Economy of the Dollar," The Fred Hirsch Lecture, Warwick University (Coventry, England, November 9, 1978), p. 28.

[26]For a text of the speech, see Gerald M. Meier, *Problems of a World Monetary Order* (New York: Oxford University Press, 1974), pp. 263-66.

[27]Interview.

Moreover, as Treasury officials Volcker and his deputy, Bruce K. MacLaury, were much more oriented toward the short term than were academic economists such as Houthakker or even policy-oriented economists such as Bergsten. Before joining the Nixon administration's Treasury, both had had experience on the ground floor of the Bretton Woods system at the Federal Reserve Bank of New York. MacLaury had spent seven years in its foreign-exchange operations department and Volcker had spent part of his time there preparing memoranda on foreign financial problems.[28] As Treasury's highest officials responsible for international monetary affairs, both MacLaury and Volcker were heavily involved in the management of the Bretton Woods system. Because management involved responding to the inevitable crises of the Bretton Woods system that, as they accumulated, suggested that the system itself might be in crisis, the under secretary and his deputy also became heavily involved in more abstract questions about the international monetary system than their focus on management might suggest. In doing so, however, they were especially sensitive to the divergences between theory and practice that had characterized the adjustable peg; they had no confidence that a crawling peg or any other limited flexibility system would work in practice as it did in theory; and they knew that the adjustable peg mechanism could at least be managed.

THE RESOLUTION OF THE REFORM DEBATE

Thus, the debate within the Nixon administration on a U.S. advocacy of international monetary reform displayed the disagreements familiar to those conversant with bureaucratic politics analyses of U.S. decision making in the field of foreign policy. With their perspectives on international monetary reform apparently influenced by their professional backgrounds as well as by their agency affiliations, officials in the Nixon administration assumed positions

---

[28]In 1953-55, part of Volcker's responsibilities as an assistant in the domestic research division of the New York bank involved preparing reports on foreign financial problems; many of his responsibilities, however, had much more to do with domestic than international financial markets (see the description of Volcker's career in Moritz, *Current Biography Yearbook, 1973*, pp. 425-28).

on reform that rational analysis alone could not hope to reconcile.

Thus the debate on reform became a good candidate for a resolution based to a large extent on the balance of power that prevailed within the administration—susceptible, in short, to a political rather than an analytical solution. Politics did in fact determine the outcome of this particular aspect of the Nixon administration's international monetary policy-making process: a combination of structural and process-level variables extended to Treasury the power necessary to translate its skepticism about the viability of international monetary reform into official U.S. government policy.

The outcome of the Nixon administration's debate on the reform of the Bretton Woods system reflects above all else the influence of the structure within which the debate occurred. The Department of the Treasury held virtually hegemonic power over the determination of U.S. international monetary policy—yet, as Halperin's comment quoted at the outset of this chapter suggests, the fact that structural variables were translated so directly into policy outcomes is somewhat surprising. Given that Treasury officials apparently did not strongly oppose and officials in other agencies were fervently committed to international monetary reform, the task of overwhelming the influence of the rules of the game to shift the United States toward strong advocacy of international monetary reform should not have presented insuperable difficulties.

That it did so indicates the interaction between particular officials and their parent agencies, which rendered almost all efforts to influence the course of policy futile. Those officials of the Council of Economic Advisers, the White House, and the Federal Reserve Board who were particularly interested in reform as an alternative for U.S. policy could not overcome Treasury's tendency toward stasis because they were, for the most part, handicapped by their agency affiliations and by their own inabilities to mobilize their individual talents effectively.

Agency affiliations adversely affected advocates of international monetary reform in two ways. The more clearcut handicap was the inability of most subcabinet-level agency officials—who were those most intimately involved in the process—to gain the support of their agency heads for their proposed initiatives in international monetary policy. Most cabinet-level officials were unwilling to spend their scarce time with the president on issues that were peripheral to their (and his) central concerns. Thus the subcabinet-level officials most actively engaged in making international monetary policy, largely by the default of the president and his senior advisers, could not budge Treasury by threatening to move disputed issues to a higher level.

The second way in which agency affiliations handicapped individual officials is more amorphous. It is not only less easily defined but it is also less easily supported by evidence than is the disadvantage inflicted by the unwillingness of agency heads to support their subordinates. Nonetheless, agency "reputations" exerted a palpably negative effect on the efforts of officials from various agencies to influence policy. Composed of the ways officials elsewhere in government perceive a particular agency's overall competence and traditional stands on policy questions, agency reputations can either diminish or enhance the power exerted by particular individuals by the force of their own personalities.[29] For officials from the Council of Economic Advisers and the Federal Reserve, the reputations of their agencies tended generally to dilute their power, although the relationship between individuals and their agency's reputation is, of course, complex.

It would be inaccurate, however, to attribute wholly to agency affiliations the inability of particular officials to counter successfully the structural advantages possessed by Treasury. In the dynamics of interagency policy making, individuals themselves, as many government officials attest, can influence policy through their own innate bargaining abilities.[30] With one exception, however, the Nixon administration's international monetary policy makers were not, for a variety of reasons, effective in the exercise of that influence which relies on individual attributes.

The interplay of these structural and process-level variables relegated systemic reform to a low-level priority in U.S. international monetary policy during the early years of the first Nixon admin-

[29]Thus, officials throughout the government speak of the Treasury as staid and mired in detail; the Council of Economic Advisers as excessively abstract and intellectual; the Federal Reserve as overly preoccupied with price stability; and the Department of State as simply ineffective (interviews).

[30]See Halperin, *Bureaucratic Politics and Foreign Policy*, pp. 222-25.

istration. The handicaps that afflicted advocates of reform help to explain why structure exerted such a strong impact on the course of this particular debate.

The Influence of Structure on Policy

A clearly visible, starkly hierarchical order regulated the interactions of the five agencies involved in making international monetary policy. At the pinnacle of power in the administration's hierarchy stood the Department of the Treasury, initially under Secretary David M. Kennedy. In the Nixon administration, as in previous administrations, Treasury's power to shape the relationship of the United States to the Bretton Woods system far surpassed that of any other government agency.

Why the Treasury was assigned the task of overseeing the relationship between the United States and the Bretton Woods regime, first by Franklin Roosevelt and subsequently, formally or informally, by succeeding presidents, is not an uncomplicated question.[31] The extent to which international financial relations implicate questions more generally relevant to foreign policy suggests the Department of State as an equally plausible candidate to control U.S. policy in the area. Nor can the dominance of Treasury be adequately explained by its officials' monopoly in expertise on broadly defined issues of relations between the United States and the Bretton Woods system. Economists and political scientists well-versed in such questions are deployed throughout the government, not only in Treasury but also in the Department of State, the staff of the National Security Council, and the Council of Economic Advisers, among others. While the Treasury does have an advan-

[31]Kennedy, for example, charged Treasury Secretary C. Douglas Dillon with chairing the newly created Cabinet Committee on the Balance of Payments (Roger S. Porter, "Economic Advice to the President: Eisenhower to Reagan," paper prepared for delivery at the 1981 annual meeting of the American Political Science Association, New York, September 3-6, 1981, p. 9); Johnson charged Secretary of the Treasury Henry H. Fowler with chairing the Volcker Group's predecessor, the Deming Group, which Johnson formally created in 1965 to work in "strictest secrecy" to develop both long-range policies with respect to liquidity provision and shorter-term options for dealing with the British payments problem ("Memorandum from the President to the Secretary of the Treasury, June 16, 1965," in Lyndon Baines Johnson, *The Vantage Point: Perspectives of the Presidency, 1963-1965* [New York: Holt, Rinehart, & Winston, 1971], pp. 597-98).

tage over other departments and agencies in terms of the number of its officials technically equipped to handle the intricacies of U.S. involvement in international financial relations on a day-to-day basis, any claim to a similar advantage on questions related to the structure of the system itself or to significant reforms of that system would be ill-founded. Neither substantive relevance nor a monopoly of technical expertise, therefore, adequately explains Treasury's commanding position.

The weight of history and tradition more satisfactorily explains Treasury's leading role. According to Alfred Eckes, Treasury's power can be traced to Roosevelt's appointment of Henry Morgenthau as Secretary of the Treasury in 1934. The president appointed Morgenthau less on the basis of his inherent qualifications for the post, which were notably lacking, than on the basis of Morgenthau's known sympathy for Roosevelt's domestic and international financial policies. Morgenthau, adds Eckes, "had a reputation as a bureaucratic empire builder, and after he became Secretary in 1934 the Treasury quickly established jurisdiction over international monetary matters."[32]

A particularly intense bureaucratic battle in 1942 and 1943 for control over the formulation of U.S. international monetary policy served to confirm Treasury's power. It erupted during the Roosevelt administration, over the question of control over postwar international economic planning. To Secretary of State Cordell Hull, the primacy of the Department of State was a perfectly natural consequence of security considerations being paramount in U.S. international economic policy. Faulty international economic arrangements, he argued, had contributed to the outbreak of one world war and would do so again unless there were an intimate, unbreakable link between security policy and foreign economic policy.

While Hull's intellectual premises were indisputable, their translation into facts of bureaucratic life were not: the Departments of Treasury, Agriculture, and Commerce, as well as the Board of Economic Warfare, raised the predictable objections to the secretary of state. Again for reasons related to the philosophical and personal compatibility of Roosevelt and Morgenthau, Roosevelt authorized Treasury to lead government planning on postwar in-

[32]Eckes, *A Search for Solvency*, p. 42.

ternational monetary policy. As a result, Treasury, in the person of Harry Dexter White, chaired the American Technical Committee that developed the U.S. proposals for an international stabilization fund and bank. The committee paralleled the advisory committee structure for postwar foreign policy planning controlled by the Department of State.[33]

Only if bureaucratic inertia is very heavily weighted, however, can tradition alone serve to explain Treasury's position at about 1970 in the formulation of U.S. international monetary policy. That other agencies seeking greater control in the field have consistently been thwarted suggests that more than the weight of history is responsible for the skewed pattern of bureaucratic power that persists in the issue area. It suggests that Treasury's conduct of international monetary policy over the years has been such as to earn it powerful allies, inside and outside the executive branch, in its struggle to retain its dominant position.

From the somewhat different perspectives of both the president and domestic economic interest groups, Treasury's conduct of U.S. international monetary policy has been guided by an "appropriate" ordering of priorities—that is, an ordering that subordinates the demands of the international monetary order to the imperatives of domestic economic policy and foreign security policy. Reinforcing the political support that its implicit hierarchy of priorities generates has been Treasury's ability to forestall the collapse of the international financial system by its energetic and often ingenious efforts to plug leaks without impinging more than marginally on the conduct of either fiscal and monetary policy or what has been defined as "high" foreign policy.

Treasury had avoided fundamental reforms of the Bretton Woods system and responded to the problems of the dollar glut by a series of ad hoc tactical maneuvers rather than by vigorously advocating the suppression of U.S. official spending abroad or a recessionary policy at home. In doing so, it had earned itself the support of the president. The Council of Economic Advisers and the Department of State have on occasion been more preoccupied with the unstable foundations of the Bretton Woods regime and correspondingly less

[33]U.S., Department of State, *Postwar Foreign Policy Preparation, 1939-1945* (Washington, D.C., 1949), p. 142.

impressed with the disadvantages of negotiating from a position of evident weakness. The Treasury's perspective on U.S. policy toward the international monetary system has coincided more closely with that of postwar presidents.

Treasury's conduct of international monetary policy also served to earn it the political support of groups outside the executive branch. Treasury has refused to subordinate domestic economic policy to the needs of the international monetary regime while simultaneously trying to preserve the Bretton Woods system. This strategy was well-suited to its domestic political constituencies. The contrast between the U.S. and British treasuries in this respect is dramatic: the stop-go macroeconomic policies that so damaged the British economy were rooted in the British Treasury's efforts to preserve sterling's role as a reserve currency. That the American economy should be sacrificed to preserve the international role of the dollar and the Bretton Woods regime was anathema to the U.S. Treasury.

Instead, the U.S. Treasury simultaneously attempted to maintain autonomy in domestic economic policy, the reserve role of the dollar, and an international monetary regime that supported a liberal international economic order. In doing so it placated international banks, multinational corporations, and import or import-dependent industries, on the one hand, and predominantly domestic producers and American consumers at large, on the other. It is true that, insofar as Treasury's conduct of international monetary policy perpetuated an overvaluation of the dollar that injured American export and import-competing industries, it threatened to arouse political opposition to its continued control of that policy. Until the early 1970s, however, the exchange rate of the dollar was not clearly identified as the locus of these industries' difficulties and opposition to Treasury's policies vis-à-vis the international monetary system was muted—and countered, in any case, by the diverse interests that were well-served by those policies.

The proven ability of Treasury to respond effectively in its conduct of international monetary policy to the conditions set from above by the president and from below by domestic economic interest groups combines with the weight of bureaucratic inertia and Treasury's own interest in the existing distribution of power to explain why Treasury has been able to retain its position at the peak of the hierarchy of power over U.S. international monetary policy. That this dominance translated into policy in the case of international monetary reform during the Nixon administration also implies (within the bureaucratic politics framework of analysis), however, a failure of participants to maneuver successfully around the given rules of the game. It implies, in short, a failure of process to overwhelm structure. |

The Failure of Process

Volcker's apparent indecisiveness and Treasury's unfavorable reputation as an agency mired in detail—as an agency that couldn't see "the Bretton Woods for the Bretton trees"[34]—opened the way, at least theoretically, for other participants in the Volcker Group to exert an influence on policy out of proportion to their parent agencies' position in the structure of international monetary policy making. Given Volcker's seeming ambivalence on critical issues, strong personal preferences, a capacity to mobilize more powerful allies, and an ability to rely on a positive agency reputation could have overwhelmed the edge Treasury possessed by virtue of its structural advantages in this area of policy.

The dynamics of the Volcker Group during this period, in which it debated options for long-range U.S. international monetary policy, do not, however, demonstrate that the combined force of agency affiliations and individual talents accomplished any significant adjustments in the distribution of power. Indeed, what is most impressive is the extent to which agency and individual variables tended to reinforce rather than to alter the formal distribution of power. A case-by-case analysis of the forces that worked to dilute the power of members of the Volcker Group who advocated international monetary reform vividly illustrates why structure emerged triumphant in the resolution of the group's debate on monetary reform.

The Defeat of the Federal Reserve

During the Nixon administration the Federal Reserve was usually represented in the Volcker Group by J. Dewey Daane, the Federal

---

[34]As Houthakker commented with respect to International Monetary Fund officials (see "The Breakdown of Bretton Woods," p. 61).

Reserve Board governor charged specifically with attending to international monetary policy issues, and by Robert Solomon, head of the Federal Reserve Board's Division of International Finance. On rare occasions officials of the Federal Reserve Bank of New York also participated in the group's discussions.

The Federal Reserve is perceived within the government as the American species of the genus central bank. It conjures up, as a consequence, the images of conservatism and exceptional caution that most observers attribute to all central banks. The Federal Reserve, said one Volcker Group member, for example, "was the voice of conservatism. The Federal Reserve was the voice of maintaining convertibility, of maintaining the system, of doing whatever had to be done domestically to maintain external equilibrium. And there are times when that message is well-received and there are other times when it isn't. To put it mildly, that was a period when . . . we were moving away from that."[35]

The Federal Reserve system has to be disaggregated, however, if its power and orientation are to be accurately portrayed, the dynamics of the Federal Reserve's participation in the Volcker Group are to be understood, and Solomon's failure to gain support for reform is to be explained. On matters of international monetary policy there are three analytically distinct units of the system: the Board of Governors, its staff, and the regional bank in New York. The most conservative of the three units is the Federal Reserve Bank of New York. It is the single most important of the twelve regional banks of the Federal Reserve system because it is headquartered in the nation's largest financial market and it conducts both foreign-exchange operations and open-market transactions for the system as a whole. In the 1960s, it was known as a staunch defender of the Bretton Woods system, more inclined than other Federal Reserve units to key domestic policy to the requirements of the balance of payments. In the middle of the spectrum stood the Federal Reserve Board itself, which, in the 1960s and early 1970s, tended not to have strong views on international monetary policy and seemed content to let the moderate views of the chairman represent its own. The board under Burns, therefore, was less

[35]Interview. As this quotation and later analysis suggest, agency reputations can deviate considerably from reality.

antagonistic to exchange-rate changes, for example, than the New York bank but not as interested as its staff was in systemic alternatives to the adjustable peg. The gap between the policy views of the board's staff and the New York bank, therefore, could be quite wide.

The global reputation of the Federal Reserve as a bastion of conservatism vitiated the effectiveness of its representatives to different degrees. Most severely affected were the representatives of the New York bank, who were excluded from almost all policy discussions within the Nixon administration because of the reputation of the institution with which they were associated. Charles A. Coombs personified the Federal Reserve Bank of New York during his years there as senior vice-president; he charges that the Nixon administration totally ignored the bank in making its decisions about international monetary policy.[36] When asked about this point, a high Treasury official pointed to the "substantial differences of view" between the Treasury and the bank. The Federal Reserve Bank of New York, he stated, "was much more strongly in favor of fixed rates, seeming to Treasury not to appreciate the constraints on Treasury policies in the domestic market. In other words, not appreciating that there were constraints, at least as the Treasury perceived it, to fiscal measures that would be consistent with holding fixed rates and, therefore, increasingly unrealistic if not irrelevant."[37] The inability of representatives of the New York bank to influence policy, therefore, was largely attributable to the reputation of their parent agency.

However, primary responsibility for the ineffectiveness of the Federal Reserve Board's representative at the subcabinet level lay not in the system's conservative reputation but elsewhere. It was a consequence partly of the particular individual who occupied the board's seat in the Volcker Group and partly a consequence of the board itself. In the early years of the Nixon administration, Governor Daane represented the board not only at Volcker Group meetings but also at the Bank for International Settlements. Both

[36]Coombs states that "as the Nixon administration took office in January 1969, the Federal Reserve Bank of New York was abruptly cut off from Washington discussions of foreign financial policy" (see his *The Arena of International Finance*, p. 204).

[37]Interview.

in frequency and perspicacity, however, Daane's contributions to Volcker Group discussions reportedly were minimal. Daane, said one of his colleagues in the Volcker Group, "was not a very strong or active participant in the Group. And that explains a lot about why the Fed was rather silent."[38]

To attribute the ineffectiveness of the Federal Reserve Board in the Volcker Group wholly to the individual governor assigned to the group would be to misconceive the larger significance of Daane's assignment, however. That the board selected an individual as passive as Daane to represent it is both a symbol of its lack of interest in international monetary policy and an expression of its determination not to allow balance-of-payments considerations to influence its conduct of domestic monetary policy. The board lacked power in the Volcker Group not only because of its reputation or because of the characteristics of its representative, or even because its formal responsibilities in the area were minimal; more importantly, it lacked power because it did not want power. Daane's assignment to the Volcker Group and his limited influence there reflect the board's decision, conscious or unconscious, not to seek or accept a significant amount of influence over the Volcker Group's deliberations.

The third constituent unit of the Federal Reserve system relevant to the Volcker Group is its research staff, specifically its Division of International Finance. Unlike Governor Daane, Solomon, the Federal Reserve's staff representative, actively engaged in Volcker Group discussions and supported a change in U.S. international monetary policy in the direction of reform of the monetary system itself. The recipient of a doctorate in economics from Harvard University and a long-time member of the professional staff of the Federal Reserve Board, Solomon seems to have been well-regarded by other members of the Volcker Group.

The extent to which Solomon was effective within the group was almost entirely a function of the respect that he himself commanded. While the board's research staff does not seem to have been tainted by the relatively unfavorable reputation of the Federal Reserve considered as an undifferentiated whole, its influence on international monetary policy making was limited by its known lack

[38]Interview.

of influence with the Federal Reserve Board. As a staff member of the Board of Governors, Solomon had to gain the acquiescence of both Daane and the chairman before he could represent his views as those of the board itself and thus invoke its power, however limited, in trying to affect the course of U.S. international monetary policy. And while Solomon apparently did not shrink from attempts to persuade his superiors to change their views, on the whole he does not appear to have been terribly successful.

He was not successful in large part for the same reason that explains Daane's assignment to the Volcker Group: the distinct lack of interest in international monetary policy shown by the Federal Reserve Board. Much like the Nixon administration's Council of Economic Advisers, and for similar reasons, the board exhibited little jealousy of the Treasury's dominant role in making international monetary policy. Indeed, it seems to have considered any time expended by its employees on the issue of international monetary policy a frivolous diversion.

It did so for reasons related to its conception of its mission and its view of the U.S. economy. Created by Congress in 1913 as an institution formally independent of executive branch control and charged with the management of the domestic monetary supply, the Federal Reserve has sought to keep the domestic economy on an even keel; it has tended to consider the resolution (or irresolution) of international economic policy issues of marginal relevance to that quest. Although the Federal Reserve Board has always assigned one governor specific responsibility for attending to international monetary policy issues, in the overall hierarchy of the agency those issues do not rank very high.

That ranking reflects above all else the fact that the United States is a relatively closed economy, although it is less closed now than it was prior to and during the Nixon administration's tenure in office. By definition a closed economy is one in which the proportion of the gross national product represented by the traded goods sector is relatively low; in 1970, as noted earlier, that sector represented only 9 percent of U.S. gross national product. Open economies, by contrast, sometimes rely on their traded goods sector for 20, 30, or even 40 percent of total gross national product. That the United States is a relatively closed economy implies, in turn, that events in the international economic sphere exercise a relatively insignificant influence on the overall course of the domestic economy, although they can, of course, reward or destroy particular industries.

As a result of the nature of the U.S. economy, most members of the Federal Open Market Committee—the monetary policy-making unit of the Federal Reserve system comprised of all seven Federal Reserve Board governors, the president of the New York Federal Reserve Bank, and four presidents representing the other eleven regional Federal Reserve Banks—have not allowed balance-of-payments considerations to govern their decisions on monetary policy.[39] Nor, therefore, have they been particularly concerned with the course of the government's international monetary policy or the fate of the dollar, even in the period immediately preceding the suspension of gold convertibility. Discussions of top Federal Reserve officials and testimony of Federal Reserve Board staff members indicate that most, albeit not all, governors and other members of the Federal Open Market Committee did not feel compelled to become intensely involved in issues of international monetary policy.[40]

Instead, the board remained content with the minimal responsibilities it was given in international monetary policy: it participated in interagency discussions on policy formulation and implementation; it administered, through the New York bank, the swap network; and it acted, again via the New York bank, as the agent of the Treasury in the foreign-exchange markets. A representative of the Federal Reserve system also is a member of or leads the U.S. delegation to meetings of Working Party Three of the Organization for Economic Cooperation and Development (an OECD subcommittee charged with examining balance-of-payments prospects);

[39]As Sherman J. Maisel, a former Federal Reserve Board governor, commented, "throughout my tenure [1965-72], a majority of the Board was unwilling to change domestic policy much, if at all, for international reasons. The result was that only a small number of decisions taken by the Board were significantly influenced by the balance of payments." Maisel estimates that international concerns caused a change in Federal Open Market Committee targets "in only eight out of more than one hundred directives" (See Maisel, *Managing the Dollar* [New York: W. W. Norton, 1973], pp. 224, 221). Maisel's observations are supported both by interviews and by a review of the 1968 *Minutes of the Federal Open Market Committee (FOMC)*, an important year in international monetary relations.

[40]Interviews and *Minutes of the FOMC.*

the Group of Ten; and the central bankers' meetings at the Bank for International Settlements.

Solomon was unable to increase his leverage within the Volcker Group by persuading the Federal Reserve as a whole to champion the cause of international monetary reform. Nor was he aided in his effort to influence the course of U.S. government policy by the reputation of the Federal Reserve as an institution wedded to conservatism, although he seems to have been considered less an emissary of the Federal Reserve per se than of its Division of International Finance, which enjoyed a more favorable reputation than its parent agency. Solomon's attributes as an individual, while apparently impressive, were not sufficient to overcome the handicap of affiliation with an agency known to be satisfied with impotence in international monetary policy. Thus, one of the more vigorous advocates of international monetary reform possessed only limited power within the Nixon administration's policy-making councils.

The Defeat of the Council of Economic Advisers

Hendrik Houthakker's influence on the course of U.S. policy with respect to international monetary reform was even more limited than Solomon's, despite the fact that his enthusiasm for reform seems to have exceeded that of the Federal Reserve staff member. In Houthakker's case, his influence was restricted not only by virtue of his parent agency's lack of interest in the area, and its unfavorable reputation more generally, but also because Houthakker himself was ineffective in arguing his brief for reform.

Like Solomon, Houthakker could not mobilize his agency, the Council of Economic Advisers, to take an active interest in international monetary reform—in effect to challenge the Treasury's monopoly over the issue area. Established by the Employment Act of 1946, the Council's task is to provide the White House with the advice that will enable the country to pursue maximum employment and economic growth while maintaining stable price levels. Its focus on the management of a relatively closed economy has dictated that its members, like those of the Federal Reserve, consider international monetary issues relatively unimportant. Under the chairmanship of Paul W. McCracken, an economist from the

University of Michigan, Nixon's council did not seek to expand its limited role in international monetary policy, which included chairing the U.S. delegation to meetings of the Economic Policy Committee of the Organization for Economic Cooperation and Development and dispatching one member and one senior staff member to Volcker Group meetings. There was little, in short, to suggest that Houthakker would be able to persuade McCracken to do battle with the Treasury on the issue of international monetary reform.

Houthakker's role within the Volcker Group was also handicapped by the reputation of the Council of Economic Advisers. Although Solomon, as do others, describes the council as "normally . . . somewhat more adventurous than other government agencies in international matters," it is difficult to attribute an enduring institutional reputation to an agency in which the three principals rotate regularly every two years and the international staff changes even more frequently.[41] As a small bureaucratic entity employing approximately twenty professional economists, the council assumes the coloration of its three ever-changing principals. As such, it is difficult to describe the agency's reputation as anything less amorphous than "intellectualism," analogous to the association of the Federal Reserve with "conservatism."

These reputations arise, in part, as a consequence of assumptions about the orientations of the professional pools from which the agencies draw their members: in the case of the Federal Reserve Board the pool has only recently been expanded beyond bankers, while the council has been populated almost exclusively by economists on academic leaves of absence. As a consequence, observes Roger B. Porter, "executive departments and agencies view the CEA as an advocate. . . . It is viewed not as an advocate for a constituency such as farmers or labor unions, but as an advocate

---

[41]Solomon, *The International Monetary System*, p. 59. Edward S. Flash, Jr., comments: "In effecting differences, the Council has been, not always but usually, on the side of promotion rather than restraint. Distinct from the Budget Bureau's traditional 'No,' its reaction has typically been 'Go.' Its successes have derived from getting things started or changed, and its failures from being unable to prevent things from being undone or delayed or stopped" (Flash, *Economic Advice and Presidential Leadership: The Council of Economic Advisers* [New York: Columbia University Press, 1965], p. 279).

for the view of professional economists—usually favoring markets and opposing subsidies."[42] That council members are academic economists is apparently due to the provision of the Employment Act of 1946 that requires every council member to "be a person who, as a result of his training, experience, and attainments is exceptionally qualified to analyze and interpret economic developments. . . ."[43]

In a policy setting, the suggestion that an agency is a fount of intellectualism is actually an indictment alleging that the agency is irrelevant, if not actually an impediment, to policy making. Thus to state that the Council of Economic Advisers is the preserve of academics is not merely to state fact; it is to suggest that its members are plagued by the ethereal concerns peculiar to academics whom the grind of daily life has not honed to the sharp-edged realism essential to effective policy making.

In practice, council members do tend to approach questions of international monetary policy from a more abstract perspective than do, for example, Treasury officials. The context in which Treasury officials operate and frequently their backgrounds as well predispose them to think more about managing the existing system than about whether that system has crossed some threshold beyond which it can no longer be managed without sacrificing the goals it was originally designed to achieve. At a certain point, of course, and earlier for some than for others, the pressure of events would make it apparent to Treasury officials that the system itself was not worth saving. Until they began to think intensively about an alternative system, however, Treasury officials were preoccupied with attempts to resolve and foresee problems in the operation of the Bretton Woods system. It was their job to attend to the nuts and bolts of the system: particular International Monetary Fund drawings, special issues of U.S. securities abroad, the maturation of a swap agreement, and so on. "The council is paid to think about systems as systems," observes one of the Nixon administration's Treasury officials, "and the Treasury has a heck of a lot of . . .

---

[42]Roger B. Porter, "The President and Economic Policy: Problems, Patterns, and Alternatives," in *The Illusion of Presidential Government*, ed. Hugh Hecclo and Lester M. Salamon (Boulder, Col.: Westview, 1981), p. 209.
[43]15 United States Code Sections 1021-1024.

operational responsibilities that doesn't [*sic*] allow it the luxury of looking for a theoretically elegant answer to the problems."[44]

The line between operational issues and policy questions was, of course, often very thin and Treasury officials, including those in the Office of the Assistant Secretary for International Affairs at the senior civil servant level, frequently crossed it. If a swap, for example, was about to mature, was it to be paid off in gold? If so, how many more swaps could be concluded before the drain on the U.S. gold stock became intolerable? What consequence would that hold for the Bretton Woods system? While higher-level Treasury officials, particularly the under secretary, concentrated as much energy on strictly policy issues as members of the Council of Economic Advisers did, their backgrounds still gave them the distinctive cast of management: Roosa, Deming, and Volcker, for example, came to the Treasury not from academia but from the Federal Reserve or private banking; Dillon, Fowler, Kennedy, and Connally came from government, banking, or politics.[45]

Council members, conversely, frequently crossed the line between operational and policy issues in the other direction, submerging themselves in detailed problems that could not be resolved by appeals to the solutions dictated by economic theory. In an academic setting, as a council official observes,

> it would be very easy . . . to say the fixed rate system is at an end, so we'll go on to a floating rate system. But you get down here [to Washington], and you suddenly start to face operational questions. . . . How do you do it? What kinds of panic movements of funds might you get? How were you going to handle them? You don't know; you're unsure. . . .
>
> You suddenly see that this isn't an advanced seminar in international finance where you debate the merits of floating versus fixed rates. You've got a hell of a lot of tactical, important questions that you've got to have answers to.[46]

Council members are forced by events to moderate their emphasis

[44]Interview.

[45]Deming was under secretary for monetary affairs, 1965-1969; Dillon was secretary of the treasury, 1961-1965.

[46]Interview.

on the abstract to attend to the concrete; Treasury officials, on the other hand, are forced by events to shift their attention to the systemic implications of specific events.

The views of the Council of Economic Advisers and those of other agencies converge as a result of council officials' immersion in the daily press of government business, somewhat alleviating, as a consequence, the handicap of a reputation as the preserve of academicians. But the fact that the council is populated by university economists nonetheless impedes its officials' effective exercise of power in at least one other way: their tenure in office is more limited than that of other Volcker Group members because they are generally restricted to two-year leaves of absence from their academic commitments. Representatives from the Treasury, Federal Reserve, White House, and Department of State sometimes endure years beyond their council colleagues in the making of international monetary policy. The senior staff economist from the council who participates in the Volcker Group can, in fact, change every year. Marina v. N. Whitman replaced G. Paul Wonnacott in that slot in mid-1970, and she herself left the council staff less than a year later. Four weeks before Whitman returned to the University of Pittsburgh to resume teaching, Houthakker vacated the other council slot on the Volcker Group to return to Harvard University. Replacing Houthakker as the council member with particular responsibility for international trade and investment issues was Ezra Solomon, who also assumed Houthakker's responsibilities in the Volcker Group.

Thus, representatives of the Council of Economic Advisers have less opportunity to acquit themselves of the charge of "ivory-towerism" than other officials have to clear themselves of comparable charges. How well they can do so is, again, a function of their individual traits. Houthakker, who was the more important of the two council representatives on the Volcker Group, apparently did more to reinforce the council's image and its impotence than to overcome either. Houthakker tended to be inattentive to the practical and political problems of implementing changes that were appealing in theory. His influence over policy making was correspondingly small: he has been referred to as simply " 'the cannonball on the deck' " of the Nixon administration's apparatus for making international monetary policy.[47] Thus, a combination of agency and individual factors undercut the power of a second advocate of monetary reform.

The Defeat of the National Security Council Staff

Equally ardent in his advocacy of international monetary reform, Bergsten was defeated by factors similar to those that defeated Houthakker: he could not gain his superior's support for his initiatives and he was an ineffective proponent of his own views on policy. He was not affected, either positively or negatively, by the reputation of the National Security Council itself, primarily because no such reputation seems to have existed. Since its initiation in 1947, the National Security Council and its staff have been used in such diverse ways by different presidents that no enduring perspective on it has developed in the other agencies of government; each is considered sui generis.[48]

In President Nixon's administration, of course, Henry Kissinger's National Security Council staff developed a reputation for influence with the president that theoretically should have provided Bergsten with enormously effective leverage in the Volcker Group, despite the fact that the staff lacked any sizable formal responsibility for making international monetary policy. Kissinger and his staff had succeeded in totally eclipsing the Department of State and had emerged as the dominant foreign-policy actor in the Nixon administration. As I. M. Destler observes, "though never really saying so publicly, Nixon had chosen—apparently quite consciously—to build an organizational system which would give his Assistant for National Security Affairs the central responsibility for foreign affairs short of the president. . . . Immediately after his inauguration he established a policy-making system providing unprecedented White House staff authority, all the while reaffirming 'the position of the Secretary of State as his principal foreign policy adviser.' "[49]

---

[47]Quoted in Mayer, *The Fate of the Dollar*, p. 172.

[48]For a discussion of the roles played by the National Security Council and its staff in different administrations, see I. M. Destler, *Presidents, Bureaucrats and Foreign Policy: The Politics of Organizational Reform* (Princeton: Princeton University Press, 1974).

[49]Ibid., pp. 1-3.

But Kissinger's influence in the Nixon administration did not increase Bergsten's leverage within the group because the national security assistant was obviously unwilling to dispute Treasury's dominance over international monetary policy. At the outset of the Nixon administration, it did in fact appear as if Kissinger were prepared to challenge the existing order in the international monetary policy process in an effort to supplant Treasury's predominance. On January 21, 1969, Kissinger issued a National Security Study Memorandum—the seventh in a long series of what would become known as NSSMs within the bureaucracy—which notified agency heads that "the President has directed the creation of a permanent Working Group to make recommendations on U.S. international monetary policy to the NSC. . . ." NSSM 7 also ordered the newly created Working Group to "prepare a paper on U.S. international monetary policy for early consideration by the National Security Council. It should consider our policy alternatives with regard to the U.S. balance of payments, the functioning of the international monetary system, and contingency plans for response to potential currency crises such as a franc devaluation and/or British resort to a freely flexible exchange rate for the pound." The completed paper, the memorandum added, was to "be forwarded to the NSC Review Group," which Kissinger chaired.[50]

As John Newhouse has observed, these study memoranda and their counterparts, the National Security Decision Memoranda, were integral elements of Kissinger's plan to establish "nothing less than an entirely new national security system," a system that

> would be invincibly White House controlled. Other agencies and institutions—the Departments of State and Defense, the Joint Chiefs of Staff—would be held strictly subordinate to the President and his senior adviser. A number of devices would clip bureaucracy's wings, not least the NSSM-NSDM innovation. Both are written in the White House and signed by the President, which means only he (and his staff) can assign the issues to be studied and frame the questions to which bureaucracy must respond. Thus, the NSSM allows him to monopolize initiative, while the NSDM, the decision memorandum,

[50]U.S., White House, National Security Study Memorandum 7, January 21, 1969, p. 1, document released by the National Security Council under an FOIA request.

becomes a kind of executive order. Bureaucrats may appeal a NSDM, but only with great difficulty can they undercut it or work around it.[51]

Thus the original design of Kissinger and his staff apparently was to deprive the Treasury of its role and to subordinate the department to the national security staff; international monetary policy, as all else, was to become the province of the White House.

Yet the grand design faltered: there was no change in the long-established pattern of Treasury control. Instead, as soon as Treasury objected to NSSM 7, resisting the obvious attempt to usurp its control over U.S. international monetary policy, Kissinger relented. Preferring to build his bureaucratic empire on turf that he considered to be far more consequential for the future of U.S. foreign policy, Kissinger was not interested in making enemies at Treasury by seriously challenging the department's traditional dominance in international monetary policy. "From the start," as Kissinger notes in his memoirs, he "had not expected to play a major role in international economics, which—to put it mildly—had not been a central field of study for me. . . . I did not seek to manage, much less dominate, the process of policy formulation as I did in other areas of national security."[52] Kissinger would not again attempt to influence U.S. international monetary policy until after the gold window had been closed.

Thus Bergsten, as was true of his colleagues Solomon and Houthakker, could not enhance his influence over policy by trading on the power of his parent agency. Moreover, because it was Bergsten who had originally urged Kissinger to issue NSSM 7, it was Bergsten whom Kissinger in effect deserted when the national security assistant so quickly retreated from the skirmish with Treasury he had initiated with the memorandum. As a consequence of his superior's obvious reluctance to challenge Treasury and Kissinger's equally obvious lack of knowledge of and interest in international economic issues, Bergsten's power in the Volcker Group was circumscribed despite the preeminence of the national security assistant and his staff in other areas of foreign policy. Had Kissinger been willing

[51]John Newhouse, *Cold Dawn: The Study of SALT* (New York: Holt, Rinehart, & Winston, 1973), p. 146.
[52]Henry Kissinger, *White House Years* (Boston: Little, Brown, 1979), pp. 950-51.

to delegate authority to his staff in this area, some of his personal power would have benefited Bergsten.[53] Frustrated by Kissinger's unwillingness to do so, Bergsten eventually resigned.[54]

Bergsten's influence in the Volcker Group was also circumscribed because of the antagonism he aroused in other members of the group. Bergsten was perceived by his colleagues in the making of international monetary policy as more than willing to violate the implicit rules of the game of bureaucratic politics in an attempt to advance his own preferences and position.[55] The resentment that Bergsten's style evoked in his colleagues, therefore, reinforced the lack of power that resulted from his agency affiliation.

In sum, the process by which international monetary policy was made could not overwhelm the influence exerted on policy outcomes by the structure of power within which that process occurred. The dominant position of Treasury remained undisturbed by influences at work within the established order of policy making. The consequences of this combination of structure and process were twofold. Treasury's preferences became those most completely and faithfully reflected in actual U.S. international monetary policy. And vigorous advocacy by the U.S. government of international monetary reform was nowhere to be seen.

[53]For a discussion of Kissinger's relationships with his staff, see Destler, *Presidents, Bureaucrats and Foreign Policy*, pp. 142-44.

[54]"Working as an economist for Kissinger," Bergsten later commented, "was comparable to being in charge of the military for the Pope" (*New York Times*, September 30, 1982).

[55]Interviews.

CHAPTER FIVE

The President, Policy Implementation, and the Short Road to Camp David

President Nixon only now enters the analysis to any great extent. His belated appearance accurately reflects the argument of the study in general and of this chapter in particular that the major variables explaining the decision to close the gold window lay not in the Oval Office but elsewhere. The president, for a variety of reasons, did no more than rubber-stamp the recommendation of the decision paper formally presented to him by the Volcker Group in June 1969. The dominant influences on his administration's policy remain the consensus uniting administration officials on the primacy of national autonomy and the structure and process of the administration's policy making.

Moreover, the president's endorsement of the Volcker Group's recommendation accomplished less in terms of establishing actual U.S. policy than it might at first appear. The group recommended that the United States adopt what it labeled an approach of "negotiated multilateral evolution" vis-à-vis the Bretton Woods regime. But this did not represent a coherent approach to policy; instead, it reflected the efforts of the Volcker group to meld disparate policy initiatives. The recommendation's predominant appeal lay in its ability to command the support of a variety of officials whose interests were incompletely congruent.

Actual U.S. international monetary policy between 1969 and 1971, therefore, was set not by presidential decision but to a large extent during the implementation of policy—a process dominated by the Department of the Treasury. In practice, the Nixon administration's policy on the position of the dollar and the survival of the Bretton Woods regime became one of "muddling through," a policy that, given concurrent developments in international financial markets and in the U.S. economy, was to prove viable for two years. When both the international and the domestic economy unraveled in 1971, however, muddling through was doomed to a rapid demise, as was the postwar monetary regime itself.

In this chapter I trace the course of U.S. international monetary policy from the formal presentation of the Volcker Group's recommendations in the Oval Office in mid-1969 to the opening of the Camp David meeting in mid-1971. That course demonstrates the illusory nature of presidential choice, confirms the power of the Department of the Treasury over the making of international monetary policy, and makes clear the emerging clash between the demands of regime maintenance and those of domestic economic autonomy—a clash that would eventually lead the United States to close the gold window.

THE VOLCKER GROUP IN THE OVAL OFFICE

On June 23, 1969, the president, his top economic advisers, and members of the Volcker Group met in the president's office to discuss the decision paper that the group had spent several months preparing. Informing the president that "basic policy decisions in the international monetary area" were "urgent," the paper emphasized the risks to U.S. freedom of decision making in domestic economic and foreign security policy inherent in the ongoing controversy over international monetary arrangements.[1]

That controversy could be interpreted, according to the Volcker Group, "as a struggle over who should assume the main burden for eliminating or adjusting to the excessive U.S. deficit and the form the adjustment should take." Thus the decision paper pointed out to the president that the "outcome will have implications for

---

[1] "Basic Options in International Monetary Affairs," p. 1.

the constraints that may be applied to our foreign and domestic policies; as compared to the substantial degree of freedom we have enjoyed during most of the postwar period."[2] In short, warned the Volcker Group, the stakes involved in the impending presidential decision were substantial.

The decision paper confronted the president with a choice among three courses of action: a unilateral devaluation of the dollar through a rise in the price of gold, an immediate suspension of the convertibility of the dollar into gold, and what was labeled a "multilateral" approach. Despite President Nixon's adamant insistence that such papers contain several different but equally realistic policy options among which he could exercise a genuine choice, the Volcker Group's paper offered the president only the illusion of choice: the three options consisted of two straw men (devaluation and an immediate suspension of convertibility) and one real option (the multilateral approach) designed primarily to enable a bureaucratic consensus to form. Neither domestic deflation nor constraints on foreign policy appear as options in the decision paper, although the paper does observe that "the dominant factor affecting the evolution of the international monetary system (and our success in guiding that evolution) will be our ability to contain domestic inflationary forces."[3]

Convinced that a unilateral dollar devaluation would be vitiated by the reactions of other countries to what they would perceive as an unwarranted attempt by the United States to improve its export performance, the Volcker Group advised the president against an attempt to resolve obvious problems in the Bretton Woods regime by announcing a rise, either small or large, in the dollar price of gold. To strengthen its case against a devaluation, the Volcker Group reminded the president of the significant domestic "legal and political obstacles" to a change in the gold price: "legally, congressional sanction would need to be obtained, and a Republican administration would be forced to seek approval from an opposition Congress with liberal economic leadership strongly against a gold price change. Republican Banking and Currency Committee leadership (e.g., [William B.] Widnall) shares this view. Extended

[2]Ibid., p. 9.
[3]Ibid., p. 19.

emotional debate—even if finally won on the basis of ratifying a 'fait accompli'—would at the least magnify the market uncertainties and tend to exacerbate the intuitive association of devaluation by the man in the street with inflation, broken promises, and monetary instability."[4]

In an equally accurate reflection of its earlier discussion of immediately suspending gold convertibility, the Volcker Group suggested to the president that he also avoid any premature closing of the gold window. The appearance of force majeure in such a decision, warned the Volcker Group, would impede the pursuit by the United States of an improved monetary system which "politically, while definitely implying a gradually increasing participation and responsibility for other countries in the management of the international monetary system commensurate with their growing economic power . . . would retain for an indefinite period a major role for the dollar and monetary leadership for the United States."[5] While the United States was in reality seeking "a substantial element of U.S. control" over the monetary system, its best chance of gaining that control, in the Volcker Group's opinion, was to avoid the appearance of seeking it. Closing the gold window was inconsistent, while a multilateral approach was clearly consonant, with that objective. As the decision paper observed, "in the interest of facilitating international harmony, the appearance of U.S. hegemony should not be sought. In more concrete terms, this tends to point to the desirability of working in a context of multilateral consultation and cooperation, so long as this does not, by reducing progress to the lowest common denominator, frustrate needed change."[6]

Thus the Volcker Group recommended to the president that he adopt its third option, the multilateral approach, adding, however, that "either external developments or a negotiating impasse may at some time, and perhaps soon, justify use of the 'suspension option.' "[7] The recommendation of "negotiated multilateral evolution" included six elements. First, "early and sizeable activation of the Special Drawing Rights scheme. . . . " Second, "some realign-

[4]Ibid., p. 34.
[5]Ibid., p. 26.
[6]Ibid., p. 13.
[7]Ibid., p. 47.

ment of existing exchange rate parities now biased against the U.S.
. . . " Third, following the activation of special drawing rights, "active and sympathetic exploration of the various techniques for in-
troducing a greater degree of exchange rate flexibility into the
monetary system. . . . " Fourth, "expansion of IMF quotas. . . . . "
Fifth, at some stage possibly an exploration of "the feasibility and
desirability of reserve settlement accounts. . . . " And, finally, "continued and strong efforts toward removing structural impediments
to U.S. trade and reducing the balance of payments costs of our
defense efforts. . . . "[8]

THE PRESIDENT'S RESPONSE

That President Nixon essentially rubber-stamped the Volcker
Group's policy paper is congruent with precedents established by
his predecessors in office with respect to the conduct of U.S. international monetary policy. The president nominally occupies the
position of greatest power within the government on international
monetary policy, as he does on all other issues. In practice, however,
most presidents have not been consistently active in efforts to determine the course of the government's policy vis-à-vis the international monetary system.[9] They have, nonetheless, sometimes
exerted a not insignificant influence, in accord with the workings
of the law of anticipated reaction. In President Nixon's case, for
example, his underlings' awareness of his preferences contributed
to, although it did not wholly determine, their refusal to consider
seriously deflation, foreign-policy constraints, and extended capital
controls as potential, partial remedies to the ills of the Bretton
Woods regime.

Systemic constraints, a dearth of domestic incentives and a potential surfeit of domestic costs, and the dissociation between high
and low foreign-policy issues all play a role in explaining the lack

[8]Ibid., pp. 23-25.
[9]See, for example, Porter's observation that organizational "entities established to
address foreign economic policy issues . . . have not succeeded in consistently engaging the President's interest and attention, largely because they have not been
tied to a regular work flow with which he must deal" (in Porter, "The President
and Economic Policy," p. 224).

of active presidential involvement in the making of postwar international monetary policy. Given the structure of the Bretton Woods regime, the relatively low (or, perhaps more accurately, the latent) political salience of international monetary policy issues within the United States—devaluation excepted—and presidential preoccupations with the Cold War, issues related to the postwar monetary regime did not normally engage the sustained interest of U.S. presidents. President Kennedy's reputed preoccupation with the dollar and the monetary regime was an anomaly rather than the norm.

The structure of the Bretton Woods regime itself worked strongly against the president's devoting his scarce time to monetary issues. That structure demanded that the United States conform to a standard of behavior unique within the system, remaining passive with respect to the level of its effective exchange rate. Unless the exchange rate became impossible to sustain, the United States was not to act affirmatively to affect the dollar's value in exchange markets. The passive role that the Bretton Woods regime assigned to the United States, therefore, rendered presidential attentiveness to the dollar and the international financial system as a whole relatively inefficient in the absence of a severe, dollar-centered crisis in the exchange markets.

Because of the structure of the U.S. economy, moreover, presidents could afford to expend relatively little energy on such issues. Heads of state of European countries had more cause to be familiar with and concerned about the setting of international monetary policy. Their countries were proportionately much more heavily engaged in international trade than was the United States and national competitiveness in international markets was for them a much more critical variable in determining aggregate economic activity. Both competitiveness and macroeconomic health, in turn, depended in part on the level of the exchange rate and, because the rate could be altered (at least in theory), it was a powerful policy tool that heads of European governments could not ignore. The structure of the U.S. economy made it much easier for American presidents to neglect Bretton Woods and the dollar.

Nor, structural considerations aside, did most presidents want even to contemplate changing the dollar's exchange rate. Given the U.S. balance-of-payments deficit, any change in the dollar's value would have logically implied a devaluation of the dollar with respect to gold. Most American presidents, Nixon included, considered a devaluation the equivalent of political suicide. Schlesinger's frequently cited recollection of President Kennedy's attitude toward the dollar is a vivid example of the abhorrence with which American presidents regarded the prospect of devaluation. Recalls Schlesinger, "Kennedy . . . used to tell his advisers that the two things which scared him the most were nuclear war and the payments deficit. Once he half-humorously derided the notion that nuclear weapons were essential to international prestige. 'What really matters,' he said, 'is the strength of the currency.' "[10]

The British government's aversion to devaluation of the pound echoes in Schlesinger's recollection, evoking an instinctive association between reserve currency status and world power, and a fear that devaluation would destroy both simultaneously.[11] It is not altogether clear that either American presidents or British prime ministers understood why they mentally linked the two—why, that is, they believed reserve currencies underpinned world power. It is possible, of course, that they were well aware that the exercise of power on a global scale was eased by the use of their national currencies as important elements of other countries' reserves; that they understood that the reserve role of their currencies permitted an expansive foreign policy and the acquisition of corporate empires overseas without an overriding concern for the foreign-exchange costs thereby incurred; that they understood that reserve currency status gave them leverage over states confronting serious balance-of-payments deficits.

The problem with such an explanation is that there is no persuasive evidence that presidents, and perhaps prime ministers as well, thought about the issue in such sophisticated terms. It is clear that presidents on the whole were determined not to allow payments considerations to constrain their grand foreign-policy schemes.[12] It is not clear, however, that they realized it was the

[10]Arthur M. Schlesinger, Jr., *A Thousand Days: John F. Kennedy in the White House* (Boston: Houghton Mifflin, 1965), p. 654.

[11]For perceptive analyses of the importance the British attributed to the reserve role of sterling, see Stephen Blank, "Britain: The Politics of Foreign Economic Policy, the Domestic Economy, and the Problem of Domestic Expansion," in Katzenstein, *Between Power and Plenty*, pp. 89-138, and Strange, *International Monetary Relations*, pp. 153-55.

[12]As amply evidenced by the refusal of presidents to adjust foreign policy to the demands of the U.S. payments accounts.

reserve role of the dollar that enabled them in part to escape that constraint.

Nor is there any evidence that private groups who themselves, for different reasons, were intent on avoiding presidential recourse to a dollar devaluation persuaded presidents to link state power in the international political system to the continuation of the dollar's reserve role. As Stephen Krasner has observed, it does not seem to have occurred to most American elites, including bankers and financiers, that the dollar's value might change.[13] Interest-group pressures therefore do not adequately explain presidential opposition to devaluing the dollar.

The aversion instead may have been instinctive, a product perhaps of presidents' believing that devaluation would so damage their prestige domestically as to undermine seriously their power to act effectively abroad. The $35 per ounce price of gold had been established by Congress in 1934 and, as Susan Strange observes, "much American opinion had come to regard this price as no less sacrosanct than the flag, the Constitution, Thanksgiving and blueberry pie [sic]."[14]

Moreover, American presidents had no significant political incentives on the domestic front to attend to the intricacies of the Bretton Woods system, since the role of the United States in the postwar international monetary system remained an apolitical issue in American politics for a long time. While particular balance-of-payments initiatives by the administration on occasion aroused some political controversy, the monetary system itself for the most part escaped the scrutiny of the public and Congress. With the exception of several hearings and reports by a subcommittee of the Joint Economic Committee, little congressional attention was devoted to issues concerning the Bretton Woods system itself: few Representatives and Senators were equipped to ask, for example, whether the Bretton Woods system itself was responsible for the series of U.S. payments deficits; whether the role of the dollar in the postwar

---

[13]He comments that "until the late 1960s, virtually all sectors of the American elite regarded both the value of the dollar and fixed exchange rates as graven in stone and beyond the tampering of mere mortals" (Krasner, "US Commercial and Monetary Policy: Unravelling the Paradox of External Strength and Internal Weakness," in Katzenstein, *Between Power and Plenty*, pp. 65-66).

[14]Strange, *International Monetary Relations*, p. 42.

monetary system exerted a deleterious effect on domestic industries; or whether the obligation of the United States to convert dollars into gold ought to continue to be U.S. policy. As a result, presidents could afford, at least from a domestic political perspective, to skirt issues related to the monetary system.

Trade issues served as the political surrogate for what might otherwise have become grievances directed at the Bretton Woods system. When special interests lobbied and Congress legislated in the sphere of international economics, they targeted trade much more heavily than they did monetary issues. In part, they were as constrained as the president was from intervening in international monetary issues by the structure of the Bretton Woods system and for a long time they accepted the conventional wisdom that the dollar's exchange rate and its relationship to gold were immutable. Trade issues also proved to be both more susceptible to political influence and more accessible to intuitive understanding than were monetary issues. Every industry that either exported or competed with imported goods knew that reducing foreign trade restrictions or raising U.S. tariff or nontariff barriers directly influenced their balance sheets and, consequently, everyone in Congress knew it too. The history of congressional involvement in the setting of U.S. tariffs, sometimes on an industry-by-industry basis and sometimes by legislating the ground rules for the executive branch's involvement in trade negotiations or adjustment assistance to affected industries, is extensive.[15] Thus, there is a domestic political incentive for presidents to understand and attend to trade issues that does not apply equally to issues in international monetary policy. International trade also involves this political incentive because presidential prestige, at home and abroad, sometimes becomes entangled with the outcome of highly visible international negotiations over tariff levels. The Kennedy Round of negotiations that concluded in 1967, for example, became a symbol of the president's ability to conduct alliance relations while simultaneously promoting his nation's economic interests.

[15]For a history and analysis of tariffs and Congress, see E. E. Schattschneider, *Politics, Pressures and the Tariff* (Englewood Cliffs, N.J.: Prentice-Hall, 1935), and Raymond A. Bauer, Ithiel DeSola Pool, and Lewis Anthony Dexter, *American Business and Public Policy: The Politics of Foreign Trade*, 2d ed. (Chicago: Aldine-Atherton, 1972).

During his administration, President Nixon would conform quite closely to this pattern of skewed attention toward trade and away from money. He had pledged in his 1968 campaign to try to alleviate the plight of southern textile workers; as a result, the Japanese for several years after Nixon's election were the unwilling beneficiaries of a great deal of presidental attention to the issue of trade in textiles. When Congress attended to international economic issues during Nixon's first two years in office it focused on trade, threatening to pass restrictive trade measures such as various proposals to levy surcharges on imports. As the balance of payments deteriorated sharply in 1971, the Subcommittee on International Exchange and Payments of the Joint Economic Committee, chaired by Henry S. Reuss, would begin to press for a fundamental change in basic U.S. international monetary policy; but most congressional energy continued to be expended on trade rather than monetary issues.

On presidents' own foreign-policy agendas, moreover, issues related to the Bretton Woods regime did not rank very highly. Coinciding for the most part with a period of relatively high Soviet-American tensions, the Bretton Woods regime could not compete with, for example, the dispatch of U.S. Marines to Lebanon in 1958, the Congo crisis of 1960, the Cuban missile crisis, Vietnam, or the many other ongoing issues and crises related to the Cold War. In the competition for presidential attention, the appeal of East-West issues was overwhelming; Bretton Woods, while not insignificant, nevertheless achieved nowhere near the salience accorded to traditional security issues by successive American presidents.

As was true of his predecessors then, President Nixon would attend to international monetary issues on an episodic basis. He very plainly did not want to be bothered about the balance of payments: he did not want domestic economic policy restrained by the payments deficit nor did he want the deficit to impinge on his direction of foreign policy.[16] The deficit, he thought, could be best dealt with by forcing the European Community to modify its Com-

---

[16]At an economic policy meeting in his office in November 1970, for example, President Nixon reportedly "exploded" when the balance of payments was "mentioned," stating "I hear all about the balance of payments and nobody worries about 8 percent unemployment!" ("Meeting in Oval Office on Economic Policy," November 30, 1970, document from the files of William Safire, Chevy Chase, Md.)

mon Agricultural Policy or Japan to open its domestic market to American products. It is true that very early in his administration, President Nixon, to the consternation of top Treasury officials, became aware of press reports of unrest in international financial arrangements and expressed to his aides his interest in doing "something short of a summit meeting . . . to show my concern in that area."[17]

But thereafter, until the Camp David meeting in August 1971, Nixon reverted to the more usual pattern of presidential noninvolvement in the conduct of U.S. international monetary policy. Volcker, whose tenure as under secretary coincided with Nixon's presidency, states that "American Presidents . . . have not in my experience wanted to spend much time on the complexities of international finance. But the repeated charge to the negotiators seemed clear, and in a sense ominous: 'I want a system that doesn't have all these crises!' "[18] The fate of H. R. Haldeman's and John Ehrlichman's efforts to engage Nixon's interest in the Italian lira in 1972 is well-known: their attempts evoked the famous, expletive-deleted comment by the president that "I don't give a . . . about the lira." [19] Even before Watergate usurped the president's atten-

[17]"Report on Cabinet Committee on Economic Policy," February 13, 1969, p. 7, document from the files of William Safire, Chevy Chase, Md. Charls E. Walker, the under secretary of the Treasury who was sitting in for Secretary Kennedy at the meeting, was clearly nervous about the president's desire, in Walker's words, not "to be viewed as a 'do-nothing' in international monetary reform" and about the president's expression of intent to discuss international monetary issues in his March 1969 trip to Europe. This, Walker stated in a memorandum to Kennedy relating the events that transpired, "shook me a little" (U.S., Department of the Treasury, "Memorandum for the Secretary," February 13, 1969, pp. 2-3, document released by the Department of the Treasury under an FOIA request).

[18]Volcker, "Political Economy of the Dollar," p. 22.

[19]A larger extract from the June 23, 1972, tape provides further evidence of President Nixon's low-level interest in and understanding of international monetary issues:
Haldeman (H): Did you get the report that the British floated the pound?
President (P): I don't think so.
H: They did.
P: That's devaluation?
H: Yeah. [Peter] Flanigan's got a report on it here.
P: I don't care about it. Nothing we can do about it.
H: You want a run-down?
P: No, I don't.
H: He argues it shows the wisdom of our refusal to consider convertibililty until we get a new monetary system

tion, his advisers had trouble getting Nixon to concentrate on the fate of the international monetary system. During the 1971 meeting with French President Georges Pompidou, at which the United States finally conceded that it would devalue the dollar, Treasury officials competed, not altogether successfully, for the president's time with a televised football game.[20]

The 1969 "Decision": A Presidential Rubber Stamp

In this context of presidential preference for avoiding intimate involvement in issues related to the Bretton Woods regime, it is understandable that President Nixon chose not to deviate from the elaborate rationales and policy recommendations of his experts. His inclination to accept the arguments and options as presented by the Volcker Group was reinforced, moreover, by the fact that, of his cabinet-level aides present at the June 1969 meeting, only one issued a significant dissent. Furthermore, the course of action recommended fitted nicely into his grand scheme of foreign policy.

Among those assembled at the mid-1969 meeting to consider and advise the president on the Volcker Group's recommendations, only Arthur Burns, then serving as counsellor to the president, registered significant dissent.[21] Burns objected to the report's rejection of an immediate devaluation of the dollar by means of a rise in the price of gold and he vigorously attempted to persuade the president of the advantages of the devaluation that the Volcker Group opposed.

Burns expressed his concerns that the dollar was overvalued and that the U.S. balance of payments would continue to threaten the Bretton Woods system unless and until the overvaluation was corrected. Against the consensus prevailing within the Volcker Group, Burns maintained that other countries would not vitiate a unilateral

---

P: Good, I think he's right. It's too complicated for me to get into. (Unintelligible) I understand.

H: Burns expects a 5-day percent (*sic*) devaluation against the dollar.

P: Yeah, O.K. fine.

H: Burns is concerned about speculation about the lira.

P: Well, I don't give a (expletive deleted) about the lira.

(Quoted in Williamson, *The Failure of International Monetary Reform*, p. 175)

[20]Interview.

[21]The following account of Burns's dissent is based on various interviews.

devaluation by reacting with corresponding devaluations of their own currencies. He also argued that because a dollar devaluation was inevitable, it would be to the political advantage of the president to proceed with the devaluation as rapidly as possible. If President Nixon sanctioned the move early in his administration, Burns contended, he could attribute its necessity to the policies and practices of his Democratic predecessors and thereby escape some of the political fallout that was likely to ensue.

The disparity in the forecasts of foreign reactions to a dollar devaluation produced by the members of the Volcker Group and by Burns is not immediately explicable. Burns relied on evidence and analysis markedly similar to those of other policy makers. The foreign officials Burns talked with also talked extensively with other administration officials and Burns was not in 1969 on as intimately familiar terms with other central bankers as he would be later, when he assumed the Federal Reserve Board chairmanship. The history of stubborn resistance by other countries to exchange-rate changes was accessible to all on equal terms, and the 1968 Bonn conference had recently provided a vivid reminder of the rigidity of exchange rates.

The disparity in perspectives had little to do with either evidence or analysis. It was instead a consequence of an underlying dispute between Burns and others on a more fundamental point, the nature of the present and future international monetary systems. Agreement was universal on the goal of a depreciated dollar. The argument over the optimal way to accomplish depreciation, however, reflected a latent but basic conflict over the appropriate role of gold in the future Bretton Woods or any other system, as well as sharply disparate images of international economic relations writ large.

Both opponents and proponents of a unilateral devaluation agreed that one of its effects would be to reinforce the role of gold in the system. They disagreed as to that effect's desirability, however; and it was that disagreement which accounted, in part, for divergent estimates of whether a devaluation would be acceptable to other countries, despite the absence of any logical linkage between the two issues. Most members of the Volcker Group wanted gold demonetized and believed in the greater utility of the special drawing right; they also believed that a rise in the gold price in an effort to realize a dollar devaluation would be self-defeating. Burns, on the other hand, was not particularly enthusiastic about the special drawing right and still believed in gold rather than a paper standard; he believed, accordingly, that a unilateral devaluation would succeed.

Also underlying the disparity in forecasts of foreign countries' reactions to a rise in the dollar price of gold was a disagreement between Burns and most members of the Volcker Group on the nature of the existing international economic system and on the nature of states' participation in that system. As evident in the debate over the closing of the gold window that occurred at the Camp David meeting, Burns did not share the image of the international economic system dominant within the Nixon administration. Unlike most of his colleagues, who themselves accepted and attributed to others a nationalist perspective on the involvement of states in the network of international financial relations, Burns remained convinced that the spirit of internationalism either equaled or exceeded in strength the force of nationalism. He was persuaded, accordingly, that other states would accept a unilateral devaluation of the dollar by the United States and, as a result, he urged President Nixon to raise the price of gold immediately.

The subtleties underlying the dispute over devaluation undoubtedly did not impress Nixon as much as his own conviction that raising the gold price was politically suicidal, to be avoided as long as possible. With the backing of the vast majority of his advisers, therefore, the president decided against an immediate effort to devalue the dollar.

At the same time, the president concurred in the Volcker Group's recommendation that a closing of the gold window ought to be deferred until it appeared that the United States had no alternative but to do so. His concurrence does not appear to have been the result of the Volcker Group's analysis of the impact on the monetary system of an immediate suspension of convertibility but instead seems to have been the product of his own larger foreign-policy design. Intent on gaining Soviet agreement to a strategic arms limitation treaty, stabilizing and expanding Soviet-American detente, and opening contacts with the People's Republic of China, the president had an interest in securing U.S. alliances, in order to bolster his negotiating position with the communist nations and to quell conservative opposition to those moves. To invite conflict within the alliances by suspending gold convertibility before the payments situation degenerated seriously and a crisis in the exchange markets forced such action did not fit in with the president's more broadly conceived plan for American foreign policy.

Against the more certain risk that decisive action involved, a decision to lay international monetary issues aside—to temporize— did not threaten important American interests, at least not in the short term. Even if the deficit were to worsen as predicted, the conduct of domestic economic policy would not be significantly affected given the consensus within and outside the administration that it made little sense to key domestic policy to the course of the balance of payments. Nor was the course of the balance of payments likely to influence foreign policy: if the Nixon administration's foreign policy was to be constrained, it was much more likely to be constrained by public and congressional opposition to the war in Vietnam than by the balance-of-payments deficit.

Furthermore, European objections to the Bretton Woods regime were not expected to pose any serious problems. The only fearsome weapon the Europeans possessed was their de jure right to convert excess dollars into gold at the U.S. Treasury, but it was apparent to them that doing so would only transform that right into a de facto impossibility. When the Nixon administration relaxed capital controls in April 1969, it became unmistakably clear to the Europeans that conversions would precipitate a U.S. float of the dollar. The consequences anticipated from suspension powerfully inhibited European resort to gold, and the Nixon administration knew it. As the Haberler task force ably pointed out, the only viable European responses, were U.S. deficits to reemerge—either appreciation or inflation—would merely provide some relief to the American payments situation. Nothing was to be feared from the European side, therefore, if the president decided to temporize.

That was essentially what the president did when, at the close of the June 1969 meeting, he rejected the options of devaluation and an immediate suspension. Instead, he accepted the Volcker Group's recommendation that the United States adopt a multipronged approach to the problems of the dollar and the Bretton Woods system, an approach that had some small chance of averting their resolution in a suspension of convertibility. Whether he understood the underlying logic of the various components of the policy he sanctioned at that White House meeting is unclear; the president did not modify but simply ratified the strategy favored by the majority of his advisers that had been constructed at the subcabinet level.

It was not until two years later, when he convened his top advisers at Camp David and decided to close the gold window, that the president would again assume a role in determining the course of balance-of-payments strategy and the future of the Bretton Woods system. By that time, however, the president's "choice" would again be largely illusory, decided in advance by a flood of dollars abroad and by the activity and inactivity of those predominantly subcabinet-level officials who had overseen international monetary policy in the interim.

THE IMPLEMENTATION OF POLICY

The Triumph of "Muddle Through"

The multilateral approach that the president approved in 1969 was no more than an agglomeration of various policies to which members of the Volcker Group loaned their support in widely varying degrees. Which components were actually translated into effective policy in the 1969-1971 period, therefore, depended, in the absence of close presidential surveillance, on the distribution of power over the implementation of policy. And since that power belonged largely to Treasury, it was Treasury's preferences rather than the entire multilateral package that became U.S. policy.

That being said, however, it is still difficult to determine what U.S. policy was before the decision of August 1971. It is clear that the desire expressed in the decision paper to activate special drawing rights in sizable amounts was translated into policy; the Treasury did press the Europeans hard on the issue and the first distribution of special drawing rights occurred in 1970. Much of Volcker's energy was expended on this one issue, which proved difficult to consummate because the Europeans were as intent on denying as the United States was on achieving the extra financing for the U.S. deficit that the assets would provide. Volcker was also preoccupied in 1969 by a dispute between the United States and South Africa, as Washington opposed Pretoria's demands regarding gold sales to the International Monetary Fund and foreign central banks.[22]

There was apparent agreement within the Volcker Group that other exchange rates needed revaluation; but whether the United States actually pursued this element of the multilateral approach before it suspended convertibility remains, more than a decade later, a matter of heated controversy. The Johnson administration had begun to move in this direction by late 1968; at the November conference in Bonn of Group of Ten members, for example, Secretary Fowler had urged Germany to revalue the mark. But whether Fowler's successors adhered to the same philosophy is disputed. One vociferous critic of Nixon administration policy, Coombs, charges that the administration never approached Japan, by 1970 one of the two major surplus countries, about its exchange rate. The former Federal Reserve Bank of New York official maintains that "with a sufficiently strong expression of concern, the Japanese government might have been induced [to raise the yen's exchange rate] . . . . Yet no Federal Reserve representative attending the BIS meetings in 1970-1971 was ever asked to urge on senior Bank of Japan officials the importance of revaluing the yen. Nor, as far as I could ascertain, were Nixon officials using other channels for negotiation of a yen revaluation. Senior Japanese financial officials have since confirmed to me that there were no American approaches to them at the time for a revaluation of the yen."[23]

A senior Treasury official rebuts Coombs's allegation as "inconceivable," pointing out that Coombs also complains that he was never privy to Nixon administration policy discussions. He "would have agreed," the Treasury official admits, "that if you could have gotten, at that stage of the game, a small number of countries to substantially revalue . . . their currencies, you could have avoided the trauma of devaluation of the dollar. The question really became one of possibilities: how much leverage did the United States really have to force revaluation of other currencies? And I think the Fed

---

[22]For a discussion of the South African gold dispute, see Solomon, *The International Monetary System*, pp. 125-26.

[23]Coombs, *The Arena of International Finance*, pp. 210-11.

and . . . Coombs felt . . . that the Treasury was not trying hard enough, and if it had only tried a little harder, it could have gotten the job done, and we would have saved ourselves from all this chaos."[24] While clearly believing that the resistance to revaluation was too strong to have been susceptible to persuasion even by Coombs, this Treasury official did not directly participate in discussions of exchange rates with representatives of other countries.

Other U.S. government officials did participate, however, and testify they made it clear that revaluations were essential. During meetings between U.S. and Japanese cabinet members in which he participated, an official of the Council of Economic Advisers states, the Japanese were told "in no uncertain terms" that their exchange rate had to be changed. This council official says he does not "have any sympathy for the idea that if they'd only known they would have cooperated. There wasn't the slightest evidence of that."[25] Moreover, Philip H. Trezise, the State Department's assistant secretary for economic affairs, who frequently conducted negotiations with the Japanese, actually stated publicly in May 1971 that he thought the yen was undervalued.[26] At least one official who himself urged exchange rate changes also believes, however, that the United States did not seriously pressure the Japanese to revalue the yen.[27]

Neither Coombs's charges nor the various rebuttals are precisely accurate, although both contain fragments of the truth. Foreign officials might well have been justifiably confused as to the desires of the U.S. government regarding exchange-rate changes in this period, although some clearly thought that revaluations were a goal of U.S. policy.[28] But many voices spoke in the name of the U.S. government and those voices did not express a consistent, clear-cut policy with regard to exchange-rate changes. Treasury, for example, rebuked Trezise's public call for a revaluation of the yen.[29]

[24]Interview.

[25]Interview.

[26]*New York Times*, May 26, 1971.

[27]Interview.

[28]By late 1969 some European countries, for example, began to ask that swap agreements carry a guarantee of exchange-rate value in case of a revaluation as well as a devaluation (*Minutes of the FOMC*, November 25, 1969).

[29]In May 1971 then Secretary of the Treasury John B. Connally also criticized the upward float of the deutsche mark (see Odell's discussion in *U.S. International Monetary Policy*, chap. 4).

While this might reasonably be attributed to bureaucratic pique or concern for market stability, it instead appears to be consistent with actual policy, at least as Volcker conducted it.

"Appreciation of other currencies," explained Volcker later, "never seemed (to me at least) to provide an answer. It was expecting too much to think then, before inflationary concerns had become so great a consideration in exchange rate policy, that individual countries would voluntarily take the political and economic risks of seeming to write off exports, jobs, and profits so long as they had another alternative."[30] Volcker also apparently adhered to the view that whatever exchange-rate changes might have resulted from American pressure would not have been sufficient to restore global payments equilibrium; but they might have been sufficient to cause the collapse of the entire Bretton Woods system. In this view, any relaxation of exchange-rate rigidity would have created an incentive for holders of dollars to convert their stocks into currencies that they saw as likely candidates for revaluation. As the discarded dollars began to pile up in foreign central banks, pressures to convert those dollars into gold at the U.S. Treasury would have increased, compelling the United States to close the gold window either immediately or when its gold stock had been depleted. The revaluations that some members of the U.S. government were urging as a solution to the problems of the Bretton Woods system appeared instead to the under secretary to threaten its demise.

Whether the option of persuading other countries to revalue their rates actually was adopted as U.S. policy is, therefore, a more complex question than it appears at first glance. The answer depends, in part, on which official of which department the observer perceives to have represented the U.S. government. Volcker, as a representative of the most influential department in U.S. international monetary policy and as the country's chief negotiator abroad, wielded an authority at least equal to that of cabinet officials carrying different messages. To complicate matters further, many subcabinet-level officials in a variety of agencies who had contact with their counterparts in foreign governments plainly thought that U.S. policy was to encourage other countries to revalue in order

[30]Volcker, "Political Economy of the Dollar," p. 15.

to alleviate pressure on the U.S. balance of payments. To observers in finance ministries and central banks abroad, American policy undoubtedly appeared ambivalent and thus justified either revaluing an exchange rate or maintaining a parity unchanged.

Nor was systemic reform in practice a clear priority of the U.S. government, reflecting Treasury's fear that serious discussions of change could cause the collapse of the existing system without providing any reliable replacement. For its part, the Volcker Group apparently never reached a conclusion as to which system of limited flexibility, if any, was most desirable. The Treasury did undertake bilateral discussions with officials of the British Treasury on the technical feasibility of particular limited flexibility systems.[31] Volcker did inform Canadian authorities that the U.S. government intended to study proposals for such systems to determine their feasibility.[32] Furthermore, in the person of William Dale the United States participated in a secret study by the executive directors of the International Monetary Fund that examined limited flexibility in the context of a larger study of the exchange-rate mechanism.[33]

Members of the Volcker Group and other U.S. officials maintain, however, that there was no serious U.S. commitment to reform the existing exchange-rate mechanism. Volcker, said one official of the Council of Economic Advisers, "really wanted no part of any reform, and he just played along . . . but he never had his heart in it."[34] In the opinion of a Federal Reserve official, Volcker's attitude toward reform was "schizophrenic. . . . He could never quite make up his mind what he thought about it until very late in the game. . . . Some days he would lean one way and some days another. . . . " As a consequence, "the government never really put their heart into [achieving systemic reform]. . . . They didn't take it half as seriously as they would have had to . . . to prevent the situation that we got into in 1971. . . . "[35]

---

[31] Interview.

[32] "Memorandum of Conversation," p. 13.

[33] The resulting International Monetary Fund study was published in 1970 (see "The Role of Exchange Rates in the Adjustment of International Payments," in J. Keith Horsefield, ed., *The International Monetary Fund, 1945-1965: Twenty Years of International Monetary Cooperation*, 3 vols. [Washington D.C.: International Monetary Fund, 1969], vol. 3: *Documents*).

[34] Interview.

Indeed, it apparently was the case that systemic reform did not receive high-priority attention from the U.S. Treasury between 1969 and 1971. As a State Department official commented wryly, "during those years when we had those marvelously interesting discussions of how to reform the system . . . the fact is that the action that was taken always went along the traditional line. . . ."[36] "The hope was," a Treasury official confirmed, "that the system could be saved by people accumulating dollars and that the balance of payments of other countries would be reduced, always on the assumption that United States domestic economic policy would be tolerable. . . . The implicit assumption or hope was that we could muddle through."[37]

Volcker's enthusiasm for systemic reform in the direction of more flexible exchange rates proved, in practice, to be limited. He appeared to doubt that such reform would resolve the dollar's problems and to believe that too much experimentation in that direction might precipitate crises. His outlook on the U.S. balance of payments and the monetary system as of 1969 seemed to be that the situation was difficult but perhaps not untenable. If both domestic and international economic trends moved in a favorable direction, it might prove possible to sustain both the dollar and the system via reliance on traditional methods. Reliance on options other than the traditional ones, Volcker feared, would precipitate a run on the dollar and force the closing of the gold window, which he, like other members of the Volcker Group, regarded with some trepidation.[38]

The Treasury also gave apparent credence to the arguments of those who contended that the contemplated reforms would not, in fact, prove acceptable to other governments or workable even if implemented. Most governments were demonstrably antipathetic to more flexible rates; most would not accept a crawling peg system in which the dollar did not flex; and the exchange-rate changes envisioned in the limited flexibility proposals would not suffice to alleviate the U.S. balance-of-payments deficit. Combined with the

[35]Interview.
[36]Interview.
[37]Interview.
[38]Based on various interviews.

fear that vigorous pursuit of any reform initiatives would itself destabilize exchange markets, these arguments apparently persuaded the Treasury to expend relatively little energy on the issue of systemic reform. "Muddle through" remained dominant.

The End of "Muddle Through"

The Treasury, the U.S. government, and the Bretton Woods system were able to muddle through successfully for two years as, contrary to the expectations of the Haberler report, the Nixon administration's first years in office turned out to be placid ones for the dollar. Exchange markets focused on the mark and the franc, which the 1968 Bonn conference had indicated were likely candidates for parity changes. The stringent monetary policy pursued by the Federal Reserve to combat domestic inflation raised interest rates to levels that attracted large inflows of Eurodollars, draining foreign central banks of their dollar reserves, relieving pressures on the U.S. gold stock, and raising European interest rates. In contrast to their earlier complaints about excess dollars, the Europeans began to complain about the dollar drain and the effects of the Federal Reserve's tight money policy on their interest rates. In response to these complaints, and also in an attempt to equalize the competitive positions of domestic banks with foreign branches and those without, the Federal Reserve imposed marginal reserve requirements on Eurodollar deposits, thus raising the cost of borrowing abroad.

In 1970, the tight money policy began to have its intended effect. The domestic economy began to slide into recession, boosting the current account position of the United States but by a perceptibly smaller amount than would have prevailed in the absence of an overvalued dollar. Despite the strains its actions would be likely to impose on the Bretton Woods regime but in accord with its long-standing tradition of awarding precedence to domestic economic policy, the Federal Reserve began to relax monetary policy as the pace of the domestic economy slowed. Interest rates in the United States began to decline and, by early 1971, the flows of funds that had concerned the Europeans in 1969 reversed direction. Massive outflows of funds from the United States moved both the Treasury and the Federal Reserve to distinctly marginal efforts to stem the tide.[39] The probable effects of domestic recovery and capital out-flows on the U.S. balance of payments led market participants to anticipate a change in the dollar's value. By spring 1971, outflows of funds from the United States began to appear not only as a response to interest-rate differentials but also as speculation on a dollar devaluation. Currency flows expanded massively early in May, as four West German research institutes recommended a revaluation of the deutsche mark. After absorbing $1 billion in one hour on May 5, Germany closed its exchange markets. Several days later it let the mark float; the Netherlands followed; and Austria and Switzerland revalued. The current-account position of the United States weakened and in May the United States announced trade figures for April demonstrating that, as Solomon put it, the "now small export surplus had given way to an import surplus. . . ."[40]

Sometime in the spring of 1971, intense contingency planning began within the U.S. government in anticipation of a suspension. Unknown to most Volcker Group members, their earlier deliberations about the desirability of a suspension in the event of a crisis were being translated into reality. Volcker and John R. Petty, the Treasury's assistant secretary for international affairs, began to assemble a "game plan" for the suspension.[41] In their planning, Volcker and Petty considered whether foreign governments ought to be alerted in advance of the suspension, whether Volcker ought to be on his way to Europe as the suspension was being announced, whether the Group of Ten would be an appropriate forum in which to discuss exchange-rate changes after the suspension, and whether a three-day weekend should be the target date for the announcement.

Petty and Volcker were also convinced that a domestic anti-inflationary program had to accompany the suspension, to persuade foreign governments that they were not to bear alone the full burden of correcting the dollar's overvaluation. They recommended wage and price controls and an across-the-board budget cut, which

[39]The Treasury issued several billion dollars' worth of securities abroad to absorb dollars that otherwise might have ended up in foreign central banks and the Federal Reserve decreased the reserve-free base of member banks.

[40]Solomon, *The International Monetary System*, p. 181.

[41]Interview.

then Secretary of the Treasury John B. Connally pressed on the president and George P. Shultz, director of the Office of Management and Budget, and Paul McCracken opposed. Sometime in July the president accepted Connally's recommendation on the domestic economy and possibly on the gold window as well. It was in mid-July, one official of the Council of Economic Advisers recalls, that Volcker confided to him that " 'we were coming to the end of the road [vis-à-vis gold convertibility].' He [Volcker] said, 'we can get through this weekend. I think we can get through next weekend. We might even get through the next. But not much further.' "[42]

In August, pressure on the dollar intensified. Belgium and the Netherlands demanded that the United States pay off their swap obligations, pushing the United States uncomfortably close to the exhaustion of its automatic borrowing rights in the International Monetary Fund. Britain and France converted $800 million into gold at the U.S. Treasury to repay their drawings on the Fund and the U.S. gold stock dropped below the crucial $10 billion mark.[43]

On August 6, 1971, Reuss's Subcommittee on International Exchange and Payments of the Joint Economic Committee issued a report urging that the United States suspend gold payments if it could not otherwise obtain a depreciation of the dollar.[44] On August 13, the British government requested that the United States guarantee a portion of its dollar holdings at the prevailing sterling-dollar parity.[45] Secretary Connally was called back from his Texas vacation and a meeting of the president and his top advisers was convened at Camp David to decide whether the time had come for the U.S. government to close the gold window. "Muddle through" was at an end.

[42]Interview.

[43]Susan Strange, "The Dollar Crisis, 1971," *International Affairs*, 48 (April 1972), p. 203; the Treasury reported on July 26, 1971, that its gold stock stood at $10.507 billion, but that included priority claims against that stock by the International Monetary Fund that reduced its value to $9.979 billion (*New York Times*, July 27, 1971).

[44]*Action Now to Strengthen the U.S. Dollar.*

[45]Exactly what and how much the British requested remains a matter of some controversy (see, for example, Solomon, *The International Monetary System*, p. 185).

CHAPTER SIX

The Camp David Meeting

The denouement of the Camp David convocation would prove to be a presidential address to the nation on Sunday evening, August 15, 1971.[1] That speech announced to the American public and to the world at large the president's decision to close the gold window and to impose a 10 percent surcharge on imports.[2] It also informed the American public of President Nixon's decision to implement a "New Economic Policy," a package of domestic economic initiatives designed to stimulate the domestic economy.

In this chapter's analysis of the process and outcome of the Camp David meeting I reaffirm my earlier observation of the critical role that the Nixon administration's consensus on the primacy of national autonomy played in the decision to close the gold window. Clearly evident at the August meeting, the force of this consensus, buttressed by idiosyncratic and agency-related influences, easily

[1] In attendance at the meeting were the secretary and under secretary of the Treasury, Connally and Volcker; the Council of Economic Advisers chairman and vice-chairman, McCracken and Herbert Stein; the Federal Reserve Board chairman, Burns; the Office of Management and Budget director, Shultz; and the Council on International Economic Policy chairman, Peter G. Peterson; in addition to their top aides. The president's economics speechwriter, William Safire, and Nixon's two assistants, Haldeman and Ehrlichman, also joined the weekend meeting.

[2] Most, although not all, of the administration's economic officials believed that the surcharge coupled with the suspension constituted overkill, dangerous because it invited retaliation by other nations. Camp David participants generally adhere to the view that the surcharge would not have been imposed had Connally not been secretary (Interviews).

defeated the lone dissenter to the proposed suspension of convertibility: Arthur Burns was overwhelmed by a tidal wave of sentiment that favored a clear expression of U.S. determination to maintain its freedom of action at home and abroad.

This reconstruction of the Camp David meeting also yields some important insights into the relationship between politics and economics in the United States. The decisions of elected and appointed political officials, it suggests, are highly responsive to their perceptions of the status of the domestic economy. This responsiveness is attributable less to the power of business than to the relationship incumbent officials perceive to exist between the probability of their reelection and the condition of the domestic economy.[3] President Nixon's preoccupation with that relationship would ultimately resolve his doubts about the potentially adverse domestic political effects of a decision to close the gold window.

Severe constraints on the president's freedom of choice existed as the Camp David meeting began. Despite the intense controversy that erupted at that meeting, there is a sense in which those deliberations can be appropriately considered to be only a play within a play, an act whose outcome was decided by the larger drama in which it was inextricably embedded. The script had been written for the Camp David players, in a sense, long before that weekend in mid-August. It had been dictated in part by the structure and evolution of the Bretton Woods system, in part by the decisions of previous administrations with respect to the relationship between the United States and the international monetary regime, and in part by the earlier decisions of the Nixon administration itself. It was also shaped by the perceived status of international financial markets in August 1971.

The heated debate at Camp David nonetheless serves to illustrate the kinds of considerations that preoccupied the president and his advisers as they contemplated the end of the postwar monetary regime. The dynamics of that meeting, therefore, remain an im-

---

[3]Although the power of business, the state of the economy, and the incumbent's electoral prospects are obviously intertwined. See Chapter Seven for a discussion of the relationships among the three.

portant source of evidence. They are explained in the discussion that follows.

POWER OVER OUTCOMES: THE ROLE OF CONSENSUS

The issue of closing the gold window confronted President Nixon with the need to choose between the U.S. national interest defined in terms of preserving autonomy in decision making and a definition of the national interest that recognized the American stake in the maintenance of international rules for regulating extensive economic interdependence. A decision to follow the latter definition of the national interest would have required the United States to impose restraints on either foreign or domestic economic policy, or both—restraints severe enough to persuade exchange markets of American determination to reduce its payments deficit and maintain the dollar's convertibility into gold. It would have required, in short, a reversal of the priorities that had long governed U.S. international monetary policy. That the decision was to hold to a national autonomy definition of the U.S. national interest was, therefore, not at all surprising.

The conflict between the two definitions of the national interest implicit in the impending decision on the gold window was expressed at the Camp David meeting in the form of a heated argument between Burns and other members of the administration. Burns alone maintained that the debate between the competing definitions ought to be resolved in favor of interest defined as adherence to the rules of the game.

Burns argued vigorously that a suspension of the dollar's convertibility was ill-advised and extremely dangerous because it threatened to cause a wave of economic nationalism that could ultimately inundate the United States, disrupting both the country's markets and its alliances abroad. Burns feared the ramifications for international economic and political relationships not only of the abrogation of dollar convertibility but also of the aggressive way others in the administration were proposing to do it. Arguing that the United States had to gain the cooperation of other states in the international system if it were to achieve its objectives, Burns contended that the tactics advocated by Connally would deprive the United States of any foreign support.[4]

Burns's opposition seems to have derived from his concern over the effects of the proposed tactics on alliance relationships; it was apparently also rooted in his association of floating rates and international conflict. Connally's style sparked the chairman's fears that the end of the adjustable peg would make confrontation the usual mode of interaction among the major countries, returning to the pattern of the interwar years. As Willett observes, "to many the exchange rate procedures adopted at Bretton Woods became a symbol of international financial cooperation, rather than just the form in which such cooperation was initially implemented. For many people pegged exchange rates and the par value system became falsely identified with internationalism, the rule of law and international financial cooperation; while greater exchange rate flexibility became equally falsely associated with isolationism, destructive economic nationalism, international anarchy, and all of the many disorders of the 1930s."[5]

Burns argued accordingly that the gold window did not have to be closed immediately, and perhaps not at all. He contended that other aspects of the president's New Economic Policy—particularly the wage-price controls, the import surcharge, and the cut in government spending—would provide enough evidence of the government's determination to restrain inflation and control the payments deficit to calm foreign-exchange markets. The New Economic Policy, Burns asserted, would " 'electrify the world. The gold outflow will cease.' "[6] If his predictions proved inaccurate, the gold window could be closed later and any interim period could profitably be used to construct a clear U.S. position on how the Bretton Woods system ought to be reformed. Agreeing that the dollar was overvalued, Burns did not think that the most desirable method to achieve its depreciation was the action the president was considering. The United States should instead attempt first to initiate

---

[4]Interview.

[5]Willett, *Floating Exchange Rates*, p. 11.

[6]Quoted in William Safire, *Before the Fall: An Inside View of the Pre-Watergate White House* (New York: Doubleday, 1975), p. 513.

multilateral negotiations to raise U.S. exports and realign exchange rates.[7]

That Burns believed in mid-1971 that there was a reasonable possibility that the United States could achieve its goal of a depreciated dollar largely within the established rules of international monetary relations is consistent with his advocacy earlier in the Nixon administration of a unilateral devaluation of the dollar. Common to both positions was an image of international economic relations that his colleagues in the Nixon administration clearly did not share. Whereas administration officials generally assumed an international economic system in which the force of nationalism greatly exceeded the force exerted by the need to adhere to rules, Burns's image was of a system in which the two opposing forces were more equally balanced. His analysis emphasized the presence of international cooperation and national restraint; his colleagues emphasized expressions of conflict and the pursuit of particular interests.

As in his earlier advocacy of a devaluation, Burns opposed a closing of the gold window not only because of a particular image of the international economic system but also because of his attachment to gold. Ending the dollar's convertibility into gold obviously threatened to diminish the role of gold in the international monetary system, a prospect Burns regarded with antipathy. Although his regard for gold was unusual within the U.S. government, it was not at all unusual among his fellow central bankers, many of whom believed in gold and regarded special drawing rights with suspicion. Gold appealed to the guardians of price stability in a way that special drawing rights could not rival. As Williamson observes, "whatever they may say to the contrary, deep in their hearts central bankers regard the SDR as funny money and gold as real money."[8]

For several reasons, then, Burns argued strenuously that the national interest lay to a greater extent in the observation of the rules of the international monetary regime than in the pursuit of freedom of decision making. That Burns's argument did not prevail was primarily the consequence of the much more impressive influ-

---

[7]Based on ibid. and interviews.
[8]Williamson, *The Failure of World Monetary Reform*, p. 33.

ence wielded by those officials who disagreed with his interpretation of the national interest.

The Defeat of Burns

Preeminent among those who disagreed with Burns was Secretary of the Treasury Connally. A three-time governor of Texas, secretary of the Navy in the Kennedy administration, and a protégé and confidant of Lyndon Johnson, Connally was highly regarded by Nixon, who reportedly thought he was one of the very few people in the country who understood how to use power.[9] Replacing David Kennedy in December 1970 (although not sworn in until February 11, 1971), Connally affirmed the dominance of Treasury in economic policy making within months of assuming the secretaryship. In June, Nixon appointed Connally to be the chief economic spokesman of his administration, signaling Shultz's eclipse as the president's principal economic adviser.

The extent of Connally's influence with the president was extraordinary. Porter maintains that in Connally President Nixon found precisely what he had been seeking: "an economic czar to whom he felt comfortable delegating most economic policy decisions."[10] Connally himself explained his mandate from the president in the following way:

> Most of the meetings that I had with the president were one-on-one. In the economic field, he made it clear that I was his chief economic adviser. Throughout my entire time there, it was a situation in which he clearly delegated the authority to me. I kept in constant contact with George Shultz, with Paul McCracken, with Arthur [Burns]. When we had all these meetings in Rome and London and Washington on the international monetary currency exchange rates, we were the only people who had any authority to do anything. There wasn't a finance minister in the room in any of those meetings, in my judgment, that could commit to anything. But the president had clearly said to me, 'Just go ahead and do what you think you have to do.' He just gave me almost unlimited authority and delegation of authority. Of course, I kept him fully informed all the way along.[11]

[9]Safire, *Before the Fall*, p. 498.
[10]Porter, "Economic Advice to the President," pp. 11-12.
[11]Ibid., p. 27.

In the months preceding the Camp David meeting, Connally had thus become the principal channel between the administration's top economic policy makers and the president. He became a forceful advocate of suspension, arguing strenuously that it was essential to achieve a lower exchange rate for the dollar. That he understood the intricacies of the postwar monetary regime that had led his subordinates in the department to endorse, reluctantly and with some trepidation, a closing of the gold window is unlikely. As Connally himself candidly admits, he "knew nothing about finance when the president asked me [to become secretary of the Treasury]. I was trained as a lawyer."[12]

That he would perceive the U.S. national interest to lie in the perpetuation of an international regime about which he knew little was, as a consequence, unlikely. But his lack of specific information about the rules regulating postwar international monetary relations need not have prevented Connally from interpreting the existence of rules themselves as an overriding U.S. interest. That he did not do so—that his trade-off of competing U.S. interests resulted in a victory for national autonomy—reflects the perspective from which he viewed international economic relations generally. Connally entered office convinced, according to his associates in government, that Western Europe and Japan were exploiting the United States, penetrating American markets with underpriced exports while simultaneously restricting entry to their domestic markets.[13] Suspension would provide a potential lever for the United States to increase its access to foreign markets; it could free the United States from the threat of discipline by surplus countries; and it might possibly increase Washington's ability to extract additional burden sharing from its allies. All of these possibilities appealed to Connally. What seems to have impressed Connally most was the fact that the postwar international monetary system constrained the United States from altering its exchange rate in a way that it constrained no other country.

To constrain U.S. decision making in order to preserve rules that discriminated unfairly against the United States made no sense to the Treasury secretary. Thus the most influential member of the

[12]Quoted in Mayer, *The Fate of the Dollar*, p. 181.
[13]Interviews; see also Solomon, *The International Monetary System*, p. 191.

Nixon administration at the Camp David meeting maintained that closing the gold window was eminently desirable in terms of the country's "national interest," as he argued it ought to be defined.

Tilting the balance further against Burns were the arguments of Peter G. Peterson. Peterson, like Connally, believed that Western Europe and Japan had been derelict in their responsibility to help maintain a liberal international economic order. Appointed in early 1971 as an assistant to the president for international economic policy and as executive director of the newly created Council on International Economic Policy, Peterson had argued this position forcefully and apparently persuasively in his private meetings with Nixon. Peterson's organizational vehicle, the council, was an umbrella group of cabinet members whose departments had some interest in international trade and investment. It explained little of his influence with the president, as it met only three times in its first year of existence and by all accounts failed to exert any influence on the course of international monetary policy.

Peterson himself, however, did command the president's attention. In early April, he briefed the president extensively on international economic trends; a much more elaborate edition of the briefing was published as the Peterson Report the following December. Peterson's report emphasized that times had changed, that "to meet the new relities, not only our policies but our methods of diplomacy will have to be changed. Our international negotiating stance will have to meet its trading partners with a clearer, more assertive version of a new national interest. . . . I believe we must dispel any 'Marshall Plan psychology' or relatively unconstrained generosity that may remain. . . . This is not just a matter of choice but of necessity." Peterson informed the president that "the ghost of seventeenth century mercantilism, which held the accumulation of gold to be the primary purpose of trade, rose again in the postwar period in the policies of the stronger countries."[14]

Enhancing Peterson's and Connally's influence were the president's own inclinations on the subject. Nixon's understanding of the outstanding issues seems to have been congruent with those of

[14]U.S., Council on International Economic Policy, *The United States in the Changing World Economy: A Report to the President*, vol. 1: *A Foreign Economic Perspective* (The Peterson Report) (Washington, D.C., 1971), pp. 49, 17.

Connally and Peterson. The relationship of a closing of the gold window to the international monetary system seems to have been particularly remote from the president's thinking about a suspension of convertibility. Nixon's own version[15] of his decision betrays no understanding or concern for the probable effects on the Bretton Woods system. His remarks indicate that he was aware only of a danger that U.S. gold reserves would be exhausted and that suspension is synonymous with letting the dollar float. He recounts Burns's opposition but offers no substantive reasons for his decision to overrule the Federal Reserve Board chairman. He says only that "this was to be one of the few cases in which I did not follow his recommendations."[16]

Nor does the president appear to have been concerned that his action might have been interpreted abroad as an act of economic nationalism inviting retaliation and threatening the existence of a liberal international economic order. Indeed, the nationalistic aspects of the impending decision seem to have impelled Nixon toward rather than away from a decision to close the gold window. Nixon understood the issue, according to a Camp David participant, "in somewhat nationalistic terms, which is the way I think Connally understood it. That we were hemmed in to a degree that other countries were not [by the gold convertibility requirement]. That our competitive ability was limited by this. That our ability to manage our own affairs was limited by this. That other countries were not limited by this, and that it was a blow for American independence."[17] A State Department official concurs, observing of the president and others that "there was a feeling around that we were unduly constrained, both domestically and internationally, in what we were able to do because of the dollar and our role in the system. And my own belief is that that was the major single factor in the minds of people who made the political decision to do what they did. They thought that they were freeing America from the bondage of the dollar commitment to uphold the Bretton Woods system—a feeling that they needed more room in domestic policy

[15]See Richard Nixon, RN, pp. 512-22.
[16]Ibid., p. 518.
[17]Interview.

to deal with recession, to deal with trade problems, military costs, a whole variety of things."[18]

Thus a coalition of actors was arrayed against Burns's interpretation of the desirable trade-off between autonomy and regime maintenance. It would be strengthened further by the absence from Camp David of those senior administration officials who might have allied themselves with Burns. Those primarily responsible for the status of U.S. relations with other countries, Secretary of State William P. Rogers and National Security Assistant Kissinger, could reasonably have been expected to counsel against the spirit of nationalism that permeated decision making at Camp David. Neither Rogers nor Kissinger, however, was present, although Rogers was consulted by telephone.[19]

The secretary of state's absence from Camp David reflected his negligible involvement in international monetary policy making. Rogers delegated responsibilities in this policy area to his deputy under secretary, and Rogers himself was reportedly "bored stiff" by the area as a whole.[20] Moreover, the secretary and his department played a very limited role in the Nixon administration's making of foreign policy. This tendency to exclude State from inner policy councils as a matter of routine would have been even stronger in the August 15th instance, where the president was not amenable to what he considered the department's exaggerated emphasis on the interests of other countries.[21]

Kissinger's standing with the president would most likely have assured him an effect on the Camp David deliberations had he been at all interested in exerting his influence. At the time of the Camp David talks, however, Kissinger's interest in and knowledge of international monetary policy issues were as limited as Rogers's.[22]

[18]Interview.
[19]Interview.
[20]Interview.
[21]In a meeting of the Cabinet Committee on Economic Policy that was discussing upcoming talks with the European Community, for example, Nixon commented that "State invariably looks at this [trade] from the point of view of other countries." While the Departments of Agriculture and Commerce considered issues from the perspective of the United States, said Nixon, "State traditionally leans the other way" ("Report on Meeting of the Cabinet Committee on Economic Policy," March 7, 1969, p. 7, document in the files of William Safire, Chevy Chase, Md.).
[22]See Chapter Four.

He was much more intensely engaged in traditional security areas—in the ongoing Strategic Arms Limitation Treaty negotiations, in the conduct of the Vietnam war, and in the opening of ties with China. On the August 13-15 weekend he was in Paris, talking with North Vietnamese officials.

In short, the principal factor responsible for Burns's defeat was the momentum that had gathered behind the idea that the Bretton Woods system was encroaching on an objective sacrosanct to the most powerful members of the Nixon administration, including the president himself: the maintenance of U.S. autonomy in decision making. Almost all members of the Nixon administration attached overriding importance to it. But a number of subsidiary factors, related to both personalities and agencies as well as circumstances, also contributed to Burns's defeat.

It indicates Burns's standing with the president in 1971 that his opposition at the Camp David meeting to closing the gold window surprised both the president and his senior advisers. Relations between the administration and Burns in the preceding months had been acrimonious and precluded the communication that would have alerted Nixon and his advisers to Burns's thinking on the issue. In the spring of 1971, Connally, Volcker, Shultz, and McCracken had assembled periodically at Treasury to review the deteriorating international economic situation as well as problems in domestic economic policy. Although the usual forum for discussion among top economic policy makers, the Quadriad, includes the Federal Reserve chairman, Burns was absent from the spring meetings. His absence symbolizes the tensions that had emerged during the previous six months between Burns and the administration, due in part to Burns's public advocacy of wage and price controls. The Nixon administration was then quietly examining wage and price controls; it objected to the Federal Reserve chairman's outspoken campaign and resolved to exclude him from its policy debates.[23]

The tense relationship between Burns and the president also

---

[23]White House hostility to Burns's advocacy had given rise that spring to leaks to the effect that the administration was considering doubling the size of the Federal Reserve Board and that Burns had asked that his salary be doubled despite accelerating inflation (see Safire's account in *Before the Fall*, pp. 591-96).

reflected elements of personal and institutional conflict. In the early years of the Eisenhower administration, when Nixon was vice-president and Burns chaired the Council of Economic Advisers, Burns received much acclaim for engineering recovery from the 1953-54 recession. "Both the president and other observers," says a Treasury and Federal Reserve consultant, "were inclined to give substantial credit to the economists, especially Burns, who had helped lead the way through the dangers of recession. Burns somehow managed to be simultaneously a symbol of recovery, modern economics, fiscal responsibility, and conservatism."[24] When the 1958-59 recession began, Burns, who by that time had returned to Columbia University and the National Bureau of Economic Research, urged the Eisenhower administration to push for a tax cut. Eisenhower administration policy makers refused, however, and, in 1960, John Kennedy defeated Richard Nixon in the presidential race. Burns became Nixon's economic adviser during the 1968 campaign and spent a year in the White House while awaiting his seat on the Federal Reserve Board.

Even in that first year in Nixon's White House, however, Burns was beginning to lose influence with the president. Their early difficulties do not seem to have been related to policy disputes; they stemmed, rather, from contrasts of personal style. Burns failed to engage Nixon's attention for long in contrast, for example, to Daniel P. Moynihan, whom Nixon had appointed as his urban affairs adviser. Between the two personal advisers, as Stephen Hess observed, "Burns should have been the winner. He had rank, the president's trust, and presumably a point of view that was ideologically attuned to Nixon. That it did not work out this way is a commentary on the importance of chemistry in doing business with a president. Burns was ponderous. His long monologues had fascinated Eisenhower; they bored Nixon. In juxtaposition, the glittering style and wit of Moynihan engaged the president and became a weapon of considerable utility. Moreover, Moynihan's proposals were dramatic; they appealed to the president's instincts to 'do something.' "[25]

[24]G. L. Bach, *Making Monetary and Fiscal Policy* (Washington, D.C.: Brookings, 1971), p. 121.
[25]Stephen Hess, *Organizing the Presidency* (Washington, D.C.: Brookings, 1976), p. 121.

When Burns moved to the Federal Reserve post on January 31, 1970, his relationship with Nixon started to become tainted as well by the tensions that frequently mark relationships between an administration and the Federal Reserve. The tensions derive from the fact that, while the president takes political responsibility for the performance of the domestic economy, the Federal Reserve system controls one of the two most important instruments of economic policy making and is insulated by statute and tradition from presidential interference. Because the president's and the Federal Reserve's priorities do not always coincide, the division of responsibilities can be a potent source of friction.

Given these clashes of personality and institutional outlooks, Burns's ability to persuade the president to defer a closing of the gold window was severely handicapped. The circumstances in which the August meeting took place compounded the problem.

Camp David participants agree that, as a Council of Economic Advisers official put it, the "thunderclap" that precipitated the announcement of the package of international and domestic economic policy measures was the disturbed state of international financial markets during the preceding days and weeks.[26] The dollar had been under intense speculative attack in exchange markets, in anticipation of a dollar devaluation, and this created within the Treasury the perception of impending crisis that occasioned the Camp David meeting. And, as the Volcker Group had argued in its recommendations to the president two years earlier, it was under such circumstances that the gold window could be closed with the least chance of provoking undesirable official reactions abroad. Therefore, if the group's calculations were correct, the market conditions prevailing in August 1971 would make it appear that the United States had not freely chosen but instead had been forced to abandon the Bretton Woods regime. Burns's prediction of strongly adverse reactions abroad, therefore, garnered little support from other Camp David participants.

Thus, because of the existence of an overwhelming consensus on autonomy's priority over regime maintenance and because, to a significantly lesser extent, of the various handicaps that afflicted Burns's attempt to influence the president, the debate on closing

[26]Interview.

the gold window, considered in the context of national interest, appeared headed clearly in a direction that would effectively end the postwar monetary regime. Reinforcing that trend was a combination of domestic political and economic factors.

POWER OVER OUTCOMES: THE INFLUENCE OF DOMESTIC POLITICS AND ECONOMICS

According to his own testimony and that of officials present at the Camp David meeting, the president was much more concerned about the domestic political implications of the impending decision than about the ramifications of such an action on the established systems of international politics and economics.[27] He viewed the debate at the Camp David meeting through a lens that focused on the 1972 presidential election, then fifteen months away. Domestic politics, specifically his own electoral prospects, seem to have provided the vantage point from which the president evaluated the arguments of his advisers.

Those prospects dominated, in part, for reasons that were unrelated to the gold window issue itself. The timing of the Camp David meeting was determined by events in foreign-exchange markets and the British demand for a guarantee of their dollar reserves; but it was also the occasion for final consideration of initiatives in domestic economic policy including, most importantly, a mandatory freeze on wages and prices that the president had been considering for several months. Domestic political opposition to his economic policies had persuaded the president that some action was imperative. As he later recalled, "The economy remained sluggish in the early months of 1971. There were signs of improvement ahead, but patience had worn thin, and we ran out of time. Demands for action poured down on the White House from all sides. Media criticism of our policies became intense. Republicans as well as Democrats reflected the pressure they were receiving from their constituents and vociferously called for new policies to deal more positively with unemployment and inflation."[28]

[27]See Nixon, *RN*, pp. 512-17; interview.
[28]Nixon, *RN*, p. 517.

The last straw was apparently a congressional briefing on July 15, 1971, that was intended to provide those assembled with a report on the president's just-announced contacts with the People's Republic of China. The briefing instead turned into a forum in which congressional representatives upbraided the president's performance on domestic economic issues; as Nixon later remarked of the meeting, "I found that for every one who expressed support of that dramatic foreign initiative, at least twice as many used the opportunity to express concern about our domestic economic policies and to urge new actions to deal with the problems of unemployment and inflation. After this meeting Connally and I concluded that the time had come to act."[29]

The president's overriding interests as the Camp David meeting convened, then, were the domestic economy and its effects on domestic politics, not the gold window and its implications for the international system. His preparations for the speech to be delivered on the Sunday evening following the Camp David meeting reflected his interests, as he focused on his decision to change course and adopt wage and price controls. In Nixon's words, "As I worked with Bill Safire on my speech that weekend I wondered how the headlines would read: would it be *Nixon Acts Boldly?* Or would it be *Nixon Changes Mind?* Having talked until only recently about the evils of wage and price controls, I knew I had opened myself to the charges that I had either betrayed my own principles or concealed my real intentions."[30]

Domestic political considerations, however, did not provide the president with a simple means to decide about the prospective closing of the gold window. Domestic political factors argued both for and against a suspension of convertibility, creating a need for the president to trade off between incompatible goals. On the one hand, a closing of the gold window could be expected to hurt the president's domestic prestige, as the action was likely to result ultimately in a devaluation of the dollar. Like his predecessors, President Nixon regarded a dollar devaluation as political anathema: at Camp David, the president anticipated that "the media will be vicious. I can see it now: 'he's devalued the dollar. . . .' "[31]

[29]Ibid., p. 518.
[30]Ibid., p. 520.
[31]Quoted in Safire, *Before the Fall*, p. 514.

On the other hand, however, a dollar devaluation could ultimately yield the president political advantage, if it were to affect positively the U.S. trade balance. An increase in U.S. exports and a decrease in imports could boost employment and offer the president some aid in his bid for reelection. In a period in which the inflationary effects of a depreciated dollar had not yet impressed themselves on U.S. policy makers, the most influential argument, recalls a staff member on the National Security Council, was "50,000 jobs for every percentage point of dollar devaluation."[32]

Ultimately, of course, the conflict over domestic goals implicit in the gold window decision was resolved by weighting the positive impact of devaluation on unemployment more heavily than the anticipated adverse reaction. This resolution reflected the president's own estimates of the political importance of unemployment figures and the preferences of both Connally and McCracken. Notably absent from the president's consideration of the domestic factors involved was the reaction of business interests; the only societal pressure that played a significant role appears to have been public opinion, writ large.

To a president who feared the effects of rising unemployment on the political prospects of the incumbent party, the likelihood that a dollar devaluation would positively affect U.S. employment levels must have given suspension great appeal. Nixon was apparently convinced that joblessness cost him the 1960 presidential election. As he wrote in his *Six Crises*, "Unfortunately, Arthur Burns turned out to be a good prophet. The bottom of the 1960 dip did come in October and the economy started to move up in November—after it was too late to affect the election returns. In October, usually a month of rising employment, the jobless rolls increased by 425,000. All the speeches, television broadcasts, and precinct work in the world could not counteract that one hard fact."[33]

As a consequence, President Nixon would worry a great deal about the level of unemployment. Early in his administration, he

[32]Interview.

[33]Richard M. Nixon, *Six Crises* (Garden City, N.Y.: Doubleday, 1962), p. 309 (cited in Edward R. Tufte, *Political Control of the Economy* [Princeton: Princeton University Press, 1978], p. 6). See also Tufte's general discussion of President Nixon, politics, and economics, pp. 45-55.

made clear his perspective on the differential political impacts of inflation and unemployment. "When you start talking about inflation in the abstract," he told his cabinet, "it is hard to make people understand. But when unemployment goes up one-half of one percent, that's dynamite."[34] Advising McCracken on his forthcoming testimony before the Joint Economic Committee, the president expanded on his view that unemployment was a politically explosive issue. He counseled the chairman of the Council of Economic Advisers not to

> get tied down to any number on unemployment. We cannot even accept the inevitability of unemployment in cooling inflation. Now, sophisticates will say, "who are they kidding?"—but we'll be in real trouble if we make any predictions along those lines. Let's say "our goal is the achievement of more price stability without an increase in unemployment." Is that too dishonest? Let's never get into the position where we accept unemployment as a certainty. I don't go along with the ideas that will see us as heroes on inflation and villains on unemployment. That will take us to the point where no conservative will ever be elected again. I don't want to see any more "hair-curling" eras.[35]

The president was less perturbed about inflation as a political boomerang, apparently not persuaded that any particularly powerful interests were seriously affected by a general rise in the price level. "Hell," the president commented once, inflation "doesn't worry the bankers—they make it both ways."[36] Nor was the president particularly sympathetic to the concerns of financial interests generally, viewing them as antipathetic to him personally and attributing to them the 1959 recession. The president, commented one of his advisers, "had had a bellyful of orthodox finance in 1960."[37]

Thus the president himself gave great weight to unemployment as a determinant of domestic politics. This tended to bias the president toward closing the gold window, although he remained concerned about a general public outcry against a devaluation of the national currency.

[34]"Report on the Meeting of the Cabinet Committee on Economic Policy," February 13, 1969, p. 4, document in the files of William Safire, Chevy Chase, Md.

[35]Ibid., p. 6.

[36]Ibid., p. 3.

[37]Interview.

Nixon's concerns about the potentially undesirable political effects of presiding over a devaluation of the dollar were undoubtedly allayed by the fact that he was being urged to do so by Connally, whom he regarded as a consummate political actor. They were also allayed by the advocacy of Chairman McCracken. He argued that, given the proposals for domestic economic policy under consideration at Camp David, the president had no choice but to ignore the potentially negative effects on public opinion that a closing of the gold window might involve. Any implementation of the contemplated New Economic Policy, McCracken contended, rendered moot the question of whether the president ought to give precedence to the suspension's positive impact on employment or to its negative impact on public opinion; the New Economic Policy, McCracken maintained, made a closing of the gold window mandatory. Once he decided in favor of the Policy, McCracken asserted, the president would in effect have decided to close the gold window.

At the time the Camp David meeting convened, however, McCracken's influence with the president was at a low ebb. McCracken had earned a doctorate in economics from Harvard University in 1948 and was a professor of business administration at the University of Michigan when Nixon, on the recommendation of Burns, appointed him council chairman at the outset of his administration. When Nixon's economic team consisted of McCracken, Shultz as secretary of the Department of Labor, Robert Mayo as director of the Bureau of the Budget, Kennedy as secretary of the Treasury, and Burns as counsellor to the president, McCracken was a very active player, second only, perhaps, to Shultz in the extent to which he intervened in policy debates within the government.[38] After Shultz assumed the top position at the newly created Office of Management and Budget and particularly after Connally became secretary of the Treasury, however, McCracken's influence waned. In the spring of 1971, Nixon ended the Council of Economic Advisers' role as the primary agency responsible for commenting on economic developments.[39] He later overruled

[38]See the various "Reports of the Cabinet Committee on Economic Policy" for 1969, documents in the file of William Safire, Chevy Chase, Md.

[39]"CEA: A Weaker Role for a Former Powerhouse," *Business Week*, January 20, 1973, pp. 76-78.

McCracken's opposition to wage and price controls.[40] In November 1971, McCracken returned to the University of Michigan.

The uneven course of McCracken's relationship with President Nixon was a consequence, in part, of his agency affiliation. Because the council is charged with providing the White House with advice that will enable the country to increase employment and growth while maintaining stable price levels, the political fortunes of its chairman tend to become associated with the state of the domestic economy despite the fact that the council obviously does not control all the forces affecting the economy. Treasury, Congress, and the Federal Reserve all influence the course of fiscal and monetary policy, and that course is sometimes set only after heated inter-agency debate. To achieve success as council chairman in the face of these obstacles, as McCracken says, "a very important require-ment is to play the economic rhythm correctly. This means taking the job when therapy to straighten out an economic problem has been applied but before it has taken hold, or before people perceive that it has taken hold, and to leave before the next mess comes along, which in the ineluctable rhythm of the economic cosmos is apt to occur."[41] Given the state of the economy in mid-1971, the extent to which Connally dominated economic issues at the time, and his agency affiliation, McCracken did not hold overwhelming influence with the president at the Camp David meeting.

Nonetheless, McCracken possessed several assets that contrib-uted to his ability to argue persuasively that the ending of con-vertibility was the only option congruent with the diverse elements composing the New Economic Policy, then also under serious con-sideration. He had a reputation as a competent, pragmatic, profes-sional economist whose advice, unlike Connally's, could be assumed to rest on a profound understanding of international financial is-sues, of the workings of the domestic economy, and of the intricate relationship between the two. When McCracken argued that the New Economic Policy demanded a closing of the gold window regardless of potentially adverse effects on domestic political opin-ion, therefore, he commanded the president's attention.

[40]"Nixon's Quadriad Gets Back in Step," *Business Week*, May 8, 1971, p. 88.
[41]Paul W. McCracken, "An Elder Statesman's Advice to a CEA Chairman," in Sichel, *Economic Advice and Economic Policy*, p. 7.

Precipitated by the politically intolerable combination of what was then an unacceptably high inflation rate of 4 percent and an equally unpalatable unemployment figure of 6 percent, the New Economic Policy had been under consideration by the administration prior to the Camp David meeting.[42] Connally and Burns had been pressing the president to implement an incomes policy, in order to suppress inflation without exacerbating unemployment. Supported by McCracken and Shultz, the president had been resisting their pleas for wage and price controls. He had reaffirmed his preference for a gradualist policy at a meeting with his advisers held at Camp David in late June. In early August, however, the president's resistance was weakening, as steel and railroad workers successfully bargained for large increases in wages, twelve Republican Senators introduced legislation establishing a wage and price board, and wholesale prices increased at an annual rate of more than 8 percent.[43]

As the Camp David meeting convened, the president had essentially approved the constituent elements of the New Economic Policy. Although the Policy was presented so as to emphasize its potential for containing inflation, as a whole it was clearly intended to provide a stimulus to the domestic economy whose benefits in terms of employment and output would be evident before the 1972 election. In addition to a ninety-day freeze on wages and prices, the New Economic Policy promised an imminent request to Congress to accelerate a $50 personal income tax exemption, repeal the 7 percent excise tax on automobiles, authorize a 10 percent tax credit for new industrial investments, postpone revenue sharing for three months and welfare reform for one year, and cut Federal spending by $4.7 billion.[44] The net effect was intended to accelerate, not to repress, the economy.[45]

In terms of the balance-of-payments accounts, McCracken pointed

[42]Leonard Silk, *Nixonomics*, 2d ed. (New York: Praeger, 1972), p. 17.

[43]Ibid., p. 71.

[44]See U.S., Department of the Treasury, "The White House Explanatory Material on the President's Economic Program," August 15, 1971, pp. 1-3, document released by the Department of the Treasury under an FOIA request.

[45]In later congressional testimony, McCracken estimated that the New Economic Policy would add approximately $15 billion to the gross national product during calendar year 1972 (see the *Congressional Quarterly Almanac*, 92d Cong., 1st sess., 1971, vol. 27 [Washington, D.C.: Congressional Quarterly Service, 1972]: 693).

out, the stimulus inherent in the Policy and the temporary nature of the wage and price freeze promised an increase in the U.S. deficit. As a consequence, McCracken contended, the domestic economic program demanded a closing of the gold window. He argued "that if there's one lesson you can draw from history, it's that wage and price controls don't stop inflation. . . . I think we got that message across to the president: all you've done is buy yourself a temporary respite. If you look at the history of wage and price controls, you get a flattening out of the price level and then you get an explosion. And, to pursue that, at that point the dollar would have been scuttled in the worst of all possible circumstances. Then you would have had disorder."[46] The only measure consistent with an expansionary domestic program, in light of the speculative pressures already evident against the dollar, would be to end convertibility. If the president wanted to go ahead with the New Economic Policy, he would simply have to bear whatever domestic political fallout developed as a result of its necessary concomitant, the suspension of convertibility.

That the president ultimately implemented the New Economic Policy and closed the gold window despite potential costs to his domestic prestige confirms again, albeit in a slightly different way, the high priority his administration gave to autonomy in domestic economic management relative to international regime maintenance. It highlights, in particular, the role played by domestic—especially electoral—politics in establishing his order of priorities. Domestic politics determined the Nixon administration's domestic economic course, which, in turn, contributed to the demise of Bretton Woods.

In sum, the course and outcome of the Camp David meeting confirm the importance of the Nixon administration's emphasis on national autonomy in explaining the breakdown of Bretton Woods. The meeting confirms earlier observations about the low level of interest in international monetary policy characteristic of President Nixon. Moreover, it reveals to an extent not previously evident the intricate intertwining of domestic politics and domestic economics that played a role in the decision to end the postwar monetary regime.

[46]Interview (quoted by permission).

CHAPTER SEVEN

Conclusion

In this chapter I consider the dominant domestic political influences that contributed to the Nixon administration's decision to close the gold window. I also respond to the larger questions I raised at the outset and compare my conclusions to those of other studies of the decision to suspend gold convertibility cast at the same level of analysis. Furthermore, I assess the implications of this book for ongoing theoretical debates in the field of international relations concerning the nature of the state, the influence of international regimes on state behavior, and the processes of regime transformation.

U.S. POLITICS: THE DOMINANT INFLUENCES

Writing in 1977, Edward L. Morse succinctly captured the central emphasis of this book. "The basic dilemma posed for governments in making choices about the monetary order," Morse observed, "is that of preserving the economic and political benefits of international interdependence while minimizing costs to national autonomy."[1] Until August 15, 1971, successive U.S. administrations managed that dilemma essentially by refusing to acknowledge it. Determined to sacrifice autonomy no more than marginally in domestic economic and foreign security policy, the Eisenhower, Ken-

---

[1] Edward L. Morse, "Political Choices and Alternative Monetary Regimes," in Hirsch, Doyle, and Morse, *Alternatives to Monetary Disorder*, p. 78.

nedy, and Johnson administrations relied instead on tactical expedients to preserve the postwar monetary order. Among them were the swap agreements, the Roosa bonds, the gold pools, the tying of foreign aid, and the imposition of capital controls.

These measures alone do not explain why the United States was able for more than a decade to avoid a direct confrontation between the demands created by economic interdependence and those arising from national autonomy. That ability also resulted from the benefits the rest of the world derived from a U.S. deficit that, for most (although certainly not all) of the period between 1958 and 1971, was kept to manageable proportions. Those benefits included an injection of international liquidity sufficient to sustain increases in world trade and to reconcile what otherwise would have been inconsistent balance-of-payments targets among the major countries. Moreover, neither the domestic economic policy nor the foreign security policy that stemmed from the American demand for autonomy caused, until the mid-1960s, concern among other states in the Bretton Woods regime.

The ability of the United States to forestall a final trade-off between the competing claims of national autonomy and economic interdependence also derived, however, from the exercise of power. Other states for the most part abstained from making demands on U.S. gold stocks and thus did not force the United States to choose between the two claims. Their abstinence was not only the product of their own preferences, however; it was also a consequence of the U.S. government's clear antipathy to any such attempts. That antipathy, in turn, derived its effectiveness from the underlying political and military power of the United States in a Cold War world—in a world where it was not entirely incredible that a country that provoked Washington's wrath by converting surplus dollars into U.S. gold could find itself standing alone against the U.S.S.R. However remote the prospects of abandonment and subsequent danger might be, they were sufficient to deter most countries from making demands on the U.S. gold stock.

Any effort to discipline the United States risked security consequences; it could also provoke economic consequences of at least equal magnitude. The repertoire of responses that the United States could invoke to meet a run on its gold stock included ending the postwar monetary regime and replacing it with a system of floating exchange rates. Because of its pivotal position within the Bretton Woods system, the United States alone possessed the power to decide unilaterally to undermine the Bretton Woods system by refusing to exchange gold for dollars. A highly probable, though not entirely certain, result of such a refusal would be a floating rate system, anathema to most states participating extensively in international trade and finance. Fluctuating exchange rates, while freeing macroeconomic policy from payments constraints and eliminating the need for reserve assets (at least in theory), also create adjustment costs that increase in proportion to the size of an economy's traded goods sector. Because most small countries' economies are open economies, floating rates hold little attraction for them; the inhibitions on dollar conversions were correspondingly large.

Thus a combination of economic and political factors had deterred raids on the U.S. gold stock and enabled the United States to treat its balance-of-payments and international monetary policy as the residue of domestic economic and foreign security policy. As the character of international politics changed and as the stock of dollars abroad exerted ever-greater strains on the Bretton Woods system, the ability of the United States to protect its gold stock and, in a more general sense, to preserve its freedom of action at home and abroad, deteriorated. The late 1960s witnessed the advent of detente and with it a generalized perception of the Soviet Union as a status quo power, less interested in expanding abroad than in securing its power at home through increased trade with the West. At the same time, the Vietnam war undermined the prestige and power of the United States while weakening its economy. As the payments deficit persisted, the ability of the United States to maintain market confidence in the convertibility of the dollar and discourage the exchange of dollars for gold declined. Only the serendipitously timed French riots in the spring of 1968 permitted the Johnson administration to escape a choice between the Bretton Woods regime and independent decision making.

President Nixon's administration, then, assumed office at a time when conditions at home and abroad were not at all propitious for the simultaneous exercise of autonomy in domestic economic and foreign policy, on the one hand, and the maintenance of the postwar international monetary regime, on the other. It was, indeed, very likely that the Nixon administration would at some point have to confront directly the dilemma its predecessors had managed to avoid. That it would choose to sacrifice the regime on the altar of national autonomy followed logically from the priorities that had long governed the conduct of U.S. international monetary policy.

The reigning hierarchy of objectives held sacrosanct freedom of decision making in both domestic economic and foreign security policy. The preservation of the postwar monetary regime stood much lower in that hierarchy, although it is clear from the many and varied efforts of high-level officials across three administrations that the prospect of the regime's breakdown was not lightly regarded. Were autonomy and interdependence to clash irreconcilably, however, the governing order among priorities nonetheless dictated that the Bretton Woods regime would succumb first.

From one perspective, it can be argued that the influence of this ordering of priorities on the decision to close the gold window is clearest at the Camp David meeting, which saw an unambiguous resolution of an explicit trade-off among goals. In consonance with the most influential of his advisers at the time and with his own beliefs, President Nixon assigned clear priority to the integrity of U.S. decision making; his choice was reinforced by the links the president apparently perceived among the New Economic Policy, the gold window, and the 1972 election.

Conversely, it might be contended that the influence of the alleged hierarchy of objectives on the Camp David decision is more obscure than obvious, its impact clouded by what many thought was the terminal crisis of the Bretton Woods regime. The state of international financial markets, the magnitude of U.S. deficits, and the scale of speculation against the dollar, it could be argued, would have dictated a decision to close the gold window regardless of the Nixon administration's objectives. There is a sense, in other words, in which the Camp David meeting, given not only its circumstances but also its precedents, can be characterized as only a play within a play.

Even in the presence of some doubt about its effect at the Camp David meeting, the hierarchy of U.S. objectives remains central to an explanation of the decision to close the gold window. The uncertainty about the strength of its effect at Camp David serves to focus this analysis on the two years of the Nixon administration's international monetary policy making that preceded the August 1971 meeting. In examining the administration's decisions and nondecisions in its early years, it becomes clear that the desire not to compromise national autonomy played an important role in increasing the probability that, at some time during its tenure, the Nixon administration would find itself at just such a meeting as Camp David.

Its emphasis on autonomy precluded the administration from contemplating constraints either on foreign policy or on the domestic economy beyond what was considered desirable on domestic grounds alone; it also contributed to the administration's refusal to sanction a unilateral devaluation of the dollar. To the extent that these measures would have prevented a reemergence of sizable balance-of-payments deficits later in the administration, and thereby alleviated a potent source of stress on the Bretton Woods regime, their exclusion—attributable largely although not exclusively to the demand for national autonomy—helped produce the climate that compelled the Camp David meeting.

To a lesser extent, the structure and process of the Nixon administration's international monetary policy making also enhanced the prospects for such a meeting. The distribution of power over the making of international monetary policy in the Nixon administration, as in its predecessors and successors, awarded a hegemonic position to the Department of the Treasury. The power structure proved to be invulnerable against challenges from within and precluded a vigorous pursuit by the United States of an effort to reform the Bretton Woods regime. To the extent that reform promised to improve the viability of the postwar monetary regime, the structure and process of the Nixon administration's international monetary policy making also influenced the later decision to close the gold window.

Thus, from the perspective of politics within the key currency state of the Bretton Woods regime, the factors that explain the U.S. decision to close the gold window are the Nixon administration's ranking of the priorities involved in any effort to preserve the regime, and the structure and process of its international monetary policy making. These factors combined to exclude American pursuit of any one of several options that might have alleviated the strains on the Bretton Woods regime clearly evident when the Nixon administration assumed office.

This is not to say, however, that any of the excluded initiatives had a high probability of radically altering the course of the regime itself. Nor do I claim that domestic political influences can be identified as the most important causes of the breakdown of the postwar monetary regime. By 1969, the maladies afflicting the Bretton Woods regime were many and serious; their sources were multiple and not frequently susceptible to remedy by the United States alone. They included a systemic failure to compel adjustment measures, domestic political resistance in many countries to exchange-rate changes or macroeconomic policies responsive to payments imbalances, and short-term capital flows that, in the context of disparate national economic trends, were undermining the premises of what was essentially a fixed-rate system.

The Nixon administration's emphasis on national autonomy and the structure and process of its international monetary policy making do not, in short, explain the whole story of the progressive collapse of the Bretton Woods regime. They explain instead only the domestic political dynamics that contributed to the U.S. decision to abrogate the constraints that the Bretton Woods regime imposed on it and thereby to provoke the regime's breakdown on August 15, 1971.

Contrasts and Similarities: Other Analyses

My findings are most directly at odds with those unit-level analyses that locate the essential causes of the Camp David decision within the cabal of decision makers allegedly responsible for the suspension of convertibility. According to Graham Allison and Peter Szanton, for example, by mid-1971 economic conditions were serious enough that "something had to be done." Yet "the action taken—President Nixon's abrupt and unilateral suspension of the dollar's convertibility into gold and the imposition of a 10 percent surcharge on imports—rocked the international system." The "shortsighted character" of the decision, they contend, "clearly reflected the unbalanced process that produced it. The group President Nixon relied upon to make the decision was dominated by a newly appointed secretary of the Treasury, John Connally. It included the Chairman of the Federal Reserve and of the Council of Economic Advisers, together with the director of the OMB. Domestic perspectives were therefore weighted heavily. But the group contained neither the Secretary of State nor the Assistant for National Security Affairs, nor any senior subordinate of either. Thus, no one was engaged whose job required him to think hard about the consequences of the decisions for larger foreign policy objectives."[2] Stephen D. Cohen's explanation proceeds in similar fashion. Cohen argues that the decision is a "classic example" of the "presidential fiat" model of decision making, in which decisions "reflect the direct intervention and clear dictation of the president. The latter's personality, his operating style, and the attitude of his senior advisers represent in this case the critical determinants of decision making." The "drastic, abrupt shift in economic policy" that occurred on August 15, 1971, states Cohen, "was constructed by the President and a handful of senior advisers during a single fateful August weekend at Camp David."[3]

In the same vein as Allison and Szanton, and Cohen, Wilfred L. Kohl contends that "the August 1971 decision is another example of royal court decision making," defined as foreign-policy making that is "highly centralized in a monarchical mode, dominated by the King or President or Head of Government, and/or his key adviser(s)."[4]

Although these three interpretations do not coincide on all points, they essentially agree that the decision to suspend the dollar's convertibility into gold was the consequence of a closed decision-making process. They agree further that, had that tight circle of decision makers been expanded to include individuals with expertise in either foreign policy or international monetary affairs, or both, the outcome might have been different. If John Connally had not been secretary of the Treasury, had Henry Kissinger not been in Paris, or had William Rogers attended the Camp David meeting, these studies imply, that meeting might not have ended as it did: people and process play important roles for these analysts.

---

[2]Graham Allison and Peter Szanton, *Remaking Foreign Policy: The Organizational Connection* (New York: Basic, 1976), pp. 144, 145.

[3]Cohen, *The Making of U.S. International Economic Policy*, pp. 80, 81.

[4]Kohl, "The Nixon Foreign Policy System," p. 20.

Clearly, I argue against the idea that the major factors explaining the August decision were rooted in the closed process of decision making that immediately preceded it. I argue, rather, that concurrence on the principles that propelled the Nixon administration toward the closing of the gold window, not only at Camp David but long before, was widespread within the administration, across all levels and agencies. If Paul Volcker, the bureaucrat's bureaucrat and a well-respected authority on international monetary matters, had controlled the Camp David meeting—which he did attend— the United States still would have closed the gold window, although the diatribes (and the import surcharge) that accompanied the suspension of convertibility would probably not have ensued. Attributing a decision that was the product of a high degree of consensus within the administration to a few individual members of that administration is, in other words, misplaced.

Less marked disagreements and correspondingly greater congruence exist between my conclusions and those of, for example, John S. Odell, C. Fred Bergsten, and David P. Calleo.[5] Because their analyses differ as to the most important causal factors at work in the 1971 decision, however, the points at which this book and their analyses agree and disagree differ as well.

John Odell's study of the 1971 decision incorporates factors other than unit-level variables, so that a direct comparison with his *U.S. International Monetary Policy* is difficult. In essence, Odell concludes that "market conditions" (that is, supply and demand in foreign-exchange markets) were the "leading source of change in the 1971 decision"; that the "interstate power structure" also played a role; but that "the market and power perspectives are unable to explain why the new external strategy in August took the form of an import surcharge and unilateral demands rather than compromise bargaining, either bilateral or multilateral, such as the U.S. used on other occasions."[6] The choice between a unilateral and a multilateral strategy, Odell contends, can only be explained by a "cognitive perspective," which identifies the attitudes of, in particular, John

---

[5]Odell, *U.S. International Monetary Policy*; C. Fred Bergsten, "The New Economics and U.S. Foreign Policy," *Foreign Affairs* 50 (January 1972): 199-222 (Bergsten's analysis in his later work, *The Dilemmas of the Dollar*, is similar); Calleo, *The Imperious Economy*.

[6]Odell, *U.S. International Monetary Policy*, chap. 4.

Connally and Peter Peterson as the critical determinants of that choice.[7] In Odell's words, "In choosing Peterson and Connally . . . the President was tapping a minority school of thought about foreign economic policy. If he had depended on an appointed representative of a majority school, the United States probably would have acted differently in 1971. Many . . . would have counseled higher priority to preserving the Bretton Woods system."[8] Odell attributes to Connally and Peterson the form the decision assumed rather than the decision itself, which is broadly in accord with my findings. In the absence of Connally and Peterson, however, I would expect the difference in form to have been not a multilateral or bilateral initiative but a less assertive unilateral strategy; few in the administration by August 1971 dissented from the idea that the time for negotiation had passed. Nor do I take strong issue with Odell's conclusions about the power of market forces in bringing about the August decision, although I emphasize much more strongly than he does the domestic factors that contributed to the emergence of exchange-market pressures against the dollar.

I do, however, differ strongly from Odell's conclusion that an understanding of domestic politics contributes little to an understanding of the August decision. The contrast is partly a consequence of the different definitions of domestic politics employed: Odell identifies domestic politics as "public opinion, electoral struggles, and group pressures."[9] In this book, by contrast, domestic politics refers also to the political practices attendant on a relatively closed economy and a liberal democratic regime.[10] While the fate of Bretton Woods did not depend directly on either interest groups or elections, it did hinge on the implications for international monetary policy of the domestic political and economic structure of the United States.

A comparable definitional difference also separates my analysis from that of Bergsten. He maintains that "as usual, it was domestic politics rather than foreign policy which forced dramatic changes in long standing international arrangements" on August 15, 1971.[11]

[7]Ibid., pp. 242-43.
[8]Ibid., p. 244.
[9]Ibid., p. 233; see also pp. 39-50.
[10]See below.
[11]Bergsten, *Dilemmas of the Dollar*, p. 93.

Bergsten argues that President Nixon's desire to reduce unemployment and placate protectionist elements in the United States explains the decision to close the gold window: that decision represented "a straightforward effort to export U.S. unemployment to other countries. . . . "[12]

Again, my findings, particularly that President Nixon would find appealing the positive effects on employment within the United States that could be expected from the devaluation of the dollar, are not wholly at odds with Bergsten's argument. Bergsten's conclusions about domestic politics differ from mine because of the differences in the way we define domestic politics: Bergsten stresses domestic politics proximate to the decision itself where I emphasize the conditioning effects of domestic politics, more broadly defined, on the course of international monetary policy long before August 1971.

A similar emphasis characterizes David Calleo's recent survey of American foreign economic policy from the Kennedy through the Reagan administrations. Although Calleo devotes only a short chapter to the Nixon administration's decision to close the gold window, Calleo's explanation of that decision and his analysis as a whole are compatible with mine: the unwillingness of the United States to adjust its policies to the demands of an integrated world economy.

Calleo emphasizes the contradictions between American domestic economic policy and the Bretton Woods regime. According to Calleo, "in large part it has been the United States itself . . . that has had the greatest trouble fitting within the mutual constraints of an integrated world system. Increasingly, America's domestic aspirations have been in tension with its responsibilities to a liberal international order."[13] The Nixon administration, he states, simply had the misfortune to enter office when the tension between the two was becoming unbearable. "The demands of domestic prosperity and foreign economic obligation seemed in direct opposition. In particular, Nixon's political survival seemed in flat contradiction to the requirements of the Bretton Woods regime. Rather than continue the recession to save the dollar, Nixon let the dollar depreciate and save his Administration."[14]

---

[12]Bergsten, "The New Economics and U.S. Foreign Policy," p. 204.
[13]Calleo, *The Imperious Economy*, p. 3.
[14]Ibid., p. 30.

Calleo's explanation of the genesis of the demand for domestic economic autonomy diverges considerably from mine. In addition, his analysis of the gold window decision attributes, in my view, too much importance to the roles of President Nixon, Secretary Connally, and the appeal of floating.[15] His treatment of the evolution of American international monetary policy, however, is generally congruent with my conclusions.

IMPLICATIONS FOR THEORY

The Nature of the State

It is not a simple task to encapsulate the process that culminated in the August 15, 1971, U.S. decision to close the gold window in concise theoretical terms. In a very broad sense, the Bretton Woods regime broke down on that date because of the hierarchy of priorities that prevailed within its most powerful state, a hierarchy that ranked the health and ultimately the survival of the regime well below the maintenance of state autonomy in the conduct of domestic economic and foreign policy. The structure of power for the conduct of international monetary policy within the American government could be interpreted, at base, as simply reflecting those priorities: thus Treasury, whose primary mission was the condition of the domestic economy, reigned supreme over the process and thus, also, was the Department of State consigned to impotence.

To explain the decision to close the gold window as the product of overarching priorities and a structure of governmental power that accurately reflected those priorities is, however, to beg some fundamental questions about why and how those priorities were established and persisted. It neglects to explain the political and socioeconomic forces that influenced the United States to adopt its particular ranking of objectives. It fails, in short, to identify the determinants of state action in this sphere of foreign policy.

It is easier to reject hypotheses about the critical determinants of state action in this policy area than it is to accept any particular one, at least in unadulterated form. It is clear that pluralism should

[15]Ibid., chap. 4.

remain the straw man in explanations of state action that it has largely become: there is no evidence that in the sphere of U.S. international monetary policy the state was merely an arena for the free play of competing societal interests. There is instead ample evidence that domestic interest groups were largely quiescent on the entire issue. As Keohane observed, "The direct effects of particular trade measures were highly visible and specific, and could be readily perceived by industrialists, union officials, and members of the general public. Unlike international monetary policy, trade was not perceived as an esoteric issue area that had to be interpreted by squabbling bands of arcane economists. Whether for these or other reasons, trade attracted more domestic controversy than issues of exchange rates and the international monetary system even though the latter may have been more important for the economy as a whole."[16] If the state were the cipher of traditional pluralist theories, the United States would not have had an identifiable international monetary policy.

Neither, however, is there evidence that the state acted in international monetary relations generally, or in the decision to close the gold window specifically, in response to its own autonomously defined conception of the national interest. While enjoying some degree of independence from outside pressures in their conduct of U.S. international monetary policy, state officials (that is, executive branch officials) did not possess complete freedom. Rather, their freedom was contingent on their observing the principle that the domestic economy was to take precedence over international monetary policy, a principle of which they were periodically reminded by congressional representatives and private industry. Constraints on the autonomy of state officials did exist; these constraints were deeply embedded in the fabric of domestic society. The United States has not been an unambiguously strong state in the conduct of international monetary policy.

[16]Robert O. Keohane, "U.S. Foreign Policy toward Other Advanced Capitalist States," in *Eagle Entangled: U.S. Foreign Policy in a Complex World*, ed. Kenneth A. Oye et al. (New York: Longman, 1979), p. 110. Obviously, trade was also a better target for particular interest groups since altering trade barriers in one industry did not threaten to arouse those groups content with the status quo in general U.S. trade policy. The same was not true for international monetary policy, where groups were differently affected by the position of the dollar in the monetary system and where policy changes favoring one group could not help but injure others.

Once it is established that intricate ties bind state and society in the arena of international monetary policy, bureaucratic politics and organizational or cybernetic theories of state action also become manifestly inadequate to explain the decision of August 1971.[17] They assume that the determinants of state action are contained within the government itself. They maintain that foreign policy is the product of the balance of power among players with competing conceptions of the national interest and varied personal and agency stakes in the decision at hand, as well as of organizationally or institutionally determined patterns of behavior.

Some aspects of the decision to close the gold window do bear the unmistakable imprints of bureaucratic and organizational politics.[18] The heated struggle over and resolution of the issue of whether the United States should vigorously pursue the reform of the Bretton Woods regime illustrates the utility of bureaucratic politics analyses in the area of international monetary policy making. That its outcome demonstrated the inability of participants to escape the constraints imposed by the rules of the monetary policy-making game does not negate the insights that a bureaucratic politics perspective yields into the struggle. The marks of intragovernmental politics also appear episodically elsewhere: in the desire to please the president evident in the subcabinet-level examination of options; in the gaps between policy decisions and implementation; in the conflict among advisers present at Camp David; and in the president's preoccupation with his domestic political standing.

While illuminating some aspects of the process that led the United States to close the gold window, bureaucratic politics and organizational theories of state action ultimately fail, however, to explain the decision. They fail because they do not explain the confines within which the intragovernmental struggle took place; they do not explain, in bureaucratic politics' own language, the shared im-

---

[17]On bureaucratic politics, see Allison, *Essence of Decision*, and Halperin et al., *Bureaucratic Politics and Foreign Policy*; on cybernetic theory, see John D. Steinbruner, *The Cybernetic Theory of Decision: New Dimensions of Political Analysis* (Princeton: Princeton University Press, 1974).

[18]Critics sometimes charge that there is very little difference between Allison's Model II (Organizational Process) and his Model III (Governmental Politics). Most analyses seem, in fact, to collapse the two into one; Steinbruner's cybernetic variant has not been frequently employed.

ages that dominated the entire process and dictated that domestic economic and foreign policy remain sacrosanct. Those images lie at the core of a domestic political explanation of the decision to end convertibility. Thus the applicability of bureaucratic politics and organizational theories is limited to the margins of the case.

This analysis suggests a more general indictment of intragovernmental explanations of foreign-policy decision making, although caution is obviously indicated because it only draws from a single case. Bureaucratic politics and organizational theories excel at demonstrating that conflicts among principal participants—individual or organizational—in making foreign-policy decisions are resolved not by an analytic but by a political process. That is, the decisive determinant in resolving conflict is not superior wisdom or reason but the distribution of power among the different actors. Such theories work well to explain the resolution of conflict in the making of foreign-policy decisions.[19]

The question that this and other analyses raise for such theories, however, is whether conflict in the foreign-policy process is either as endemic or as significant as they assume.[20] Clearly, I acknowledge in this book that there was heated controversy in the decision making leading to the closing of the gold window. But that controversy was much less portentous than was the depth and breadth of consensus on issues of more fundamental importance than monetary reform. The boundaries of the controversy were, in other words, accepted by virtually all participants; the controversy itself focused on a peripheral issue rather than on one of central importance.

As a result, bureaucratic politics and organizational theories of state action are in this case useful at the margins but not at the core of the explanatory puzzle. To the extent that this case is typical of others, it calls into serious question the utility of these theories as a whole. Recent analyses of the determinants of American foreign-

---

[19]For a particularly good example see Michael H. Armacost, *The Politics of Weapons Innovation: The Thor-Jupiter Controversy* (New York: Columbia University Press, 1969).

[20]See, for examples, the critiques of bureaucratic politics models by Amos Perlmutter, "The Presidential Political Center and Foreign Policy: A Critique of the Revisionist and Bureaucratic Political Orientations," *World Politics* 27 (October 1974): 87-106; Desmond J. Ball, "The Blind Men and the Elephant: A Critique of the Bureaucratic Politics Theory," *Australian Outlook* 28 (1974): 71-92; and Robert J. Art, "Bureaucratic Politics and American Foreign Policy: A Critique," *Policy Sciences* 4 (1973): 467-90.

policy decision making during the Vietnam war offer powerful evidence that this case may be typical.[21] When shared images so limit the importance of issues on which divisions can and do occur, the applicability of intragovernmental models is equally limited.

In such cases, more adequate explanations of the outcomes of foreign-policy decision making may be found if state officials are viewed as only relatively autonomous actors, constrained by the broader socioeconomic and political structures within which they operate.[22] Instead of being considered independent actors, state officials are seen to be powerfully influenced by the political and economic context within which they operate. In the case of the Nixon administration, this context dictated that the response to any fundamental conflict between the preservation of domestic economic policy autonomy and the postwar monetary regime favor autonomy over regime maintenance. Assigning a higher priority to autonomy than to regime maintenance was the only alternative consonant with the relatively closed nature of the U.S. economy and the concomitant pattern of U.S. political opinion.

It was also the only alternative compatible with the more general tendency of elected officials in liberal democratic societies to avoid, where possible, any compromise of domestic economic objectives. Because both their tenure in office and their ability to extract public revenue depend upon the condition of the domestic economy,[23] state officials tend to avoid the subordination of domestic economic objectives to others.[24] In so doing, they inevitably attend closely to business as well as to the electorate's demands;[25] in a market economy, states can not command but must induce business perform-

[21] See Gelb, *The Irony of Vietnam*; also Daniel Ellsberg, *Papers on the War* (New York: Simon & Schuster, 1972).

[22] See, for example, Lindblom, *Politics and Markets*; Fred Block, "The Ruling Class Does Not Rule: Notes on the Marxist Theory of the State," *Socialist Revolution* 7 (May-June 1977): 6-28; and the various essays in Katzenstein, *Between Power and Plenty*.

[23] Elkin, "State and Regime in the American Republic," pp. 12-13.

[24] Obviously, officials do not always assign first priority to the domestic economy. Equally obvious is the fact that the attainment of even high priority domestic economic goals may not be within the reach of state officials.

[25] That state officials attune domestic macroeconomic policy to electoral rhythms is the focus of political-business cycle theory. For an explanation and defense of the theory, see Tufte, *Political Control of the Economy*, particularly chap. 1.

ance.[26] The rank ordering of domestic economic and international regime maintenance goals reflects this responsiveness of state officials in a liberal democracy to the perceived needs of the domestic economy and to the demands of business and the electorate generally.

Emphasizing the constraints on rather than the independence of state officials also helps to explain the second imperative that guided U.S. international monetary policy: the demand for national autonomy in foreign policy. That successive U.S. administrations similarly ranked security and international monetary policy objectives suggests, although not by any means conclusively, that each administration perceived limits to its ability to alter radically the emphasis on Cold War and political-military issues that has characterized postwar American foreign policy. The sustained pursuit of U.S. security interests, expansively defined, was apparently seen as necessary to preclude either an adverse change in the global balance of power[27] or a resurrection of the intense domestic political struggles that marked the opening of the Cold War,[28] or both. Altering U.S. foreign policy to preserve a particular monetary regime was not a choice available to U.S. officials operating within such boundaries.[29]

Shared images—the emphasis on national autonomy in domestic economic and foreign security policy—form the core of this book's explanation of the domestic politics of the decision to close the gold window. Pluralist, bureaucratic politics, and organizational or cybernetic theories are manifestly inadequate to explain those images. Much more useful are theories which emphasize neither the total dependence nor the independence, but rather the limited autonomy, of state officials in setting policy. In the space left for independent action by state officials, bureaucratic politics explanations

---

[26]Block, "The Ruling Class Does Not Rule," pp. 16-19.

[27]This is, of course, the conventional explanation of the general course of American foreign policy since 1945.

[28]For an excellent analysis of the partisan politics that the author contends is an essential element of the explanation for the Cold War, see Richard Freeland, *The Truman Doctrine and the Origins of McCarthyism: Foreign Policy, Domestic Politics, and Internal Security* (New York: Schocken, 1974).

[29]Even had it been, the evidence does not suggest that U.S. presidents would have preferred to do so.

are indeed very helpful; that space in this case, however, proved fairly small.

The Influence of International Regimes on State Behavior

Political scientists hold diverse views, as Krasner points out, on the question of whether—and, if so, how much—the existence of international regimes influences the behavior of states that participate in them.[30] The range of views extends from those who deny that regimes constrain or affect in any way the behavior of states to those who contend that the influence of international regimes on states is pervasive; in between, of course, are those who maintain that regimes are influential but only under certain specified conditions.

Among the "atheists" is Susan Strange, who believes that regime variables are superfluous to explanations of outcomes in international politics; those outcomes can better be understood by relying solely on more traditional concepts of power and interest. Strange asserts that "all those international arrangements dignified by the label regime are only too easily upset when either the balance of bargaining power or the perception of national interest (or both together) change among those states who negotiate them."[31] Regimes are simply not useful independent variables in explaining state behavior.

At the other extreme are, for example, Donald J. Puchala and Raymond F. Hopkins, who contend that there is "a rather broad range of international relations where regimes mediate behavior largely by constraining unilateral adventurousness or obduracy."[32] Although Puchala and Hopkins also maintain that there are instances in which the regime concept is either a subterfuge for interests or an unnecessary addition to "codified international law or morality," they essentially hold that international regimes "do constrain and regularize the behavior of participants, affect which issues among protagonists move on and off agendas, determine

[30]See Krasner, "Structural Causes and Regime Consequences," pp. 189-94.

[31]Susan Strange, "*Cave! Hic Dragones*: A Critique of Regime Analysis," *International Organization* 36 (Spring 1982): 407.

[32]Donald J. Puchala and Raymond F. Hopkins, "International Regimes: Lessons from Inductive Analysis," ibid., p. 271.

which activities are legitimized and condemned, and influence what, when, and how conflicts are resolved."[33]

Between these two extremes are those who adhere to what Krasner describes as a "modified structural view," a view that "suggests that regimes may matter, but only under fairly restrictive conditions."[34] Characterizing both Keohane and Arthur A. Stein as falling within this category, Krasner describes modified structuralists as believing that "for most situations there is a direct link between basic causal variables and related behavior; . . . but under circumstances that are not purely conflictual, where individual decision making leads to suboptimal outcomes, regimes may be significant."[35] Stein contends that two such situations are dilemmas of "common interests"—"in which the actors have a common interest in *insuring* a particular outcome"—and dilemmas of "common aversions"—in which actors "have a common interest in *avoiding* a particular outcome."[36]

Determining whether, in terms of its influence on the United States, the Bretton Woods regime was a strong regime is not easy. Part of the difficulty lies in determining, essentially, "how much is enough?" That is, how constraining must the Bretton Woods or any other regime be seen to be before it can be categorized as a significant independent influence on state behavior?

On this point there are only vague generalities available in the literature. There can be no disputing, for example, Robert Jervis's contention that the regime concept "implies not only norms and expectations that facilitate cooperation, but a form of cooperation that is more than the following of short-run self-interest."[37] Jervis does not, however, provide clear criteria for assessing how much more cooperation there ought to be before we can say that a regime effectively exists. A similar problem besets Nye's eminently reasonable statement that "realistically, an international regime does not need perfect adherence to have a significant constraining effect, any more than deviant behavior means the irrelevance of domestic

[33]Ibid., pp. 270, 246.
[34]Krasner, "Structural Causes and Regime Consequences," p. 190.
[35]Ibid., p. 192.
[36]Arthur A. Stein, "Coordination and Collaboration: Regimes in an Anarchic World," *International Organization* 36 (Spring 1982):309.
[37]Robert Jervis, "Security Regimes," ibid., p. 357.

legal regimes. Nevertheless, there is a tipping point beyond which violation leads to a breakdown of normative constraints."[38] Where that tipping point might be is left as an intriguing, unresolved question. Jock A. Finlayson and Mark W. Zacher have also attempted to define when a regime is really a regime: "If sovereignty norms [those derived from the structure of world politics] clearly dominate in an issue area, then one cannot ascribe a great deal of behavioral impact to the regime—it merely reflects 'politics as usual.' On the other hand, if interdependence norms [those that derive from interdependencies in specific issue areas that encourage states to cooperate to increase welfare] are judged to have a significant impact on the formulation and implementation of rules one can ascribe a certain degree of autonomy to the regime." With an almost audible sigh Finlayson and Zacher add, however, that observers disagree over the degree of constraining effects interdependence norms must have before a regime can be said to exist.[39]

The dearth of clear standards for assessing whether a regime is strong, weak, or somewhere in-between makes any judgment about the influence of the Bretton Woods regime on U.S. behavior problematic. It is undisputably true, for example, that the United States did initiate a series of policy measures that would have been unlikely in the absence of the Bretton Woods regime. This would tend to suggest that the United States was indeed constrained by the existence of the Bretton Woods regime and, in turn, that the Bretton Woods regime can be considered to have had some independent impact on the behavior of at least one, very significant, state.

Conversely and more importantly, however, it is equally obvious that those measures the United States did undertake were not very significant infringements on what the United States considered to be its core interests. For the sake of Bretton Woods, United States foreign policy was altered in several minor ways: the tying of foreign aid, for example, and the attempt to persuade West Germany to offset the costs of U.S. troops stationed there. Similarly, domestic economic policy was adjusted in equally insignificant directions:

[38]Joseph S. Nye, "Maintaining a Nonproliferation Regime," *International Organization* 35 (Winter 1981): 36-37.

[39]Jock A. Finlayson and Mark W. Zacher, "The GATT and the Regulation of Trade Barriers: Regime Dynamics and Functions," *International Organization* 35 (Autumn 1981): 564.

Operation Twist during the Kennedy administration, for example, and capital controls during the Johnson administration. However, neither the core of an expansive foreign policy nor that of a domestic economic policy attuned to the perceived status of the American economy was affected by developments in the international monetary regime. The United States instead encouraged the participant states in the Bretton Woods regime to adjust to its deficits by a variety of largely tactical expedients. Moreover, when push came to shove—or, to use regime language, when sovereignty norms came into direct conflict with interdependence norms—sovereignty norms emerged indisputably triumphant. Thus, to the extent that a regime should be able to influence not only marginal but also core objectives of participating states in order to be considered "strong," the postwar monetary regime cannot be said to have significantly constrained the behavior of the United States; it should not, therefore, be characterized as a "strong" regime.

Lessons for Regime Transformation

This book was designed to complement existing work on regime transformation. Scholars analyzing the processes of regime change at the systems level have concluded that those processes cannot be explained adequately without reference to the domestic politics of states critical to the existence of particular regimes. I therefore examined the internal politics of the center country of the Bretton Woods regime and identified the variables that significantly contributed to the U.S. decision to end convertibility, thereby ending the postwar monetary regime. In so doing, I have substantiated the claims of many political scientists that the force of autonomy remains a powerful determinant of state action.

Any single case, of course, raises the question of the extent to which its conclusions may be generalized. Are the findings of this book wholly idiosyncratic, or might they instead apply to the transformations of regimes more generally? Given the diversity of international regimes, it is highly unlikely that one regime transformation, even when it is studied in the "disciplined-configurative" mode of analysis, will yield insights applicable to every instance of regime transformation.[40] The factors that explain changes in regimes that regulate the hunting of fur seals, for example, are very likely to be irrelevant to changes in regimes that govern activities of profoundly greater concern to most states.[41] The processes of change in what might be called "high politics" regimes, in other words, will in all probability be very different from those occurring in "low politics" regimes. The findings of this book may apply, therefore, only to transformations of other high politics regimes.

It is proper to classify the Bretton Woods regime as a high politics regime since it involved issues of domestic macroeconomic policy and international trade and monetary policy important to all countries. As it aged, moreover, the Bretton Woods regime also became implicated in a more general struggle for national power and prestige. Conclusions about the domestic political causes of Bretton Woods's collapse, then, would logically be more applicable to regimes of comparable political salience—the international trading regime, for example—than they would to regimes regulating relatively insignificant arenas of interstate activity.[42]

High politics regimes raise in dramatic relief the issue that has pervaded this book: the trade-off between national autonomy and the benefits returned by participation in a network of established rules and conventions in a given sphere of international activity. The tension between these two conflicting goals is said to be constant: as Keohane and Nye observe, "interdependent relationships will always involve costs, since interdependence restricts autonomy; but it is impossible to specify *a priori* when the benefits of a relationship will exceed the costs. This will depend on the values of the actors as well as on the nature of the relationships."[43]

[40]For an analysis of the uses and limitations of case studies, see Alexander L. George, "Case Studies and Theory Development: The Method of Structured, Focused Comparison," in *Diplomacy: New Approaches in History, Theory, and Policy*, ed. Paul Lauren (New York: Free, 1979), pp. 43-68; and Harry Eckstein, "Case Study and Theory in Political Science," in *Handbook of Political Science*, vol. 7, ed. Fred I. Greenstein and Nelson W. Polsby (Reading, Mass.: Addison-Wesley, 1975): 79-137.

[41]See Young, "International Regimes," pp. 321-23, for a description of the variety of existing international regimes.

[42]For an analysis of the postwar international trading regime that confirms the primary importance of what the authors label "sovereignty norms," see Finlayson and Zacher, "The GATT."

[43]Keohane and Nye, *Power and Interdependence*, p. 10.

This book suggests that the center state of the Bretton Woods system assigned widely disparate values to the competing interests of regime maintenance and national autonomy. It suggests, in fact, that throughout the history of the Bretton Woods regime there was no contest between the theoretically conflicting interests: the structure of the international political and monetary systems permitted the United States to realize simultaneously the benefits of interdependence and those of virtually absolute integrity in national decision making. Adjustments at the margins of both the monetary regime and decision making allowed logically inconsistent goals to guide U.S. international monetary policy for more than a decade.

When the two imperatives could no longer be pursued simultaneously, the low priority that the United States had long assigned to the international monetary regime was revealed. In terms of international regime persistence and transformation, the lesson of Bretton Woods's collapse is that high politics regimes resting on a hegemonic structure of power are vulnerable to the great powers' determination to maintain the prerogatives of great power: to adjust international to national realities rather than to compromise critical national goals in order to preserve a particular set of international rules. In an age that many allege to be an era of interdependence, states continue to insist, when they are able, that they are the dominant actors.

Interviews

Listed below are the names of the twenty-three officials of the first Nixon administration who granted interviews. Also noted is the government position each held during that administration. All interviews took place in 1979 and were conducted generally on the understanding that comments were not to be individually attributed.

Bergsten, C. Fred. Senior Staff Member, National Security Council.

Bernstein, E. M. Consultant, Department of the Treasury.

Bradfield, Michael. Assistant General Counsel, Department of the Treasury.

Bryant, Ralph C. Staff Member, Division of International Finance, Federal Reserve Board of Governors.

Burns, Arthur F. Counsellor to the President, 1969; Chairman, Federal Reserve Board of Governors, 1970-1978.

Cross, Sam Y. Staff Member, Office of the Assistant Secretary for International Affairs, Department of the Treasury.

Dale, William B. Executive Director, International Monetary Fund, Department of the Treasury.

Hormats, Robert. Senior Staff Member, National Security Council.

Houthakker, Hendrik S. Member, Council of Economic Advisers.

McCracken, Paul W. Chairman, Council of Economic Advisers.

Machlup, Fritz. Consultant, Department of the Treasury.

MacLaury, Bruce K. Deputy Under Secretary for Monetary Affairs, Department of the Treasury.

Petty, John R. Assistant Secretary for International Affairs, Department of the Treasury.

Safire, William. Chief Economics Speechwriter, Office of the President.

Samuels, Nathaniel. Deputy Under Secretary for Economic Affairs, Department of State.

Solomon, Robert. Director, Division of International Finance, Federal Reserve Board of Governors.

Stein, Herbert. Member, Council of Economic Advisers.

Trezise, Philip H. Assistant Secretary for Economic Affairs, Department of State.

Volcker, Paul A. Under Secretary for Monetary Affairs, Department of the Treasury.

Weintraub, Sidney. Deputy Assistant Secretary for International Finance and Development, Department of State.

Whitman, Marina v. N. Senior Staff Member, Council of Economic Advisers.

Willis, George H. Deputy to the Assistant Secretary for International Monetary Affairs, Department of the Treasury.

Wonnacott, G. Paul. Senior Staff Member, Council of Economic Advisers.

Bibliography

Allison, Graham T. *Essence of Decision: Explaining the Cuban Missile Crisis.* Boston: Little, Brown, 1971.

Allison, Graham T., and Peter Szanton. *Remaking Foreign Policy: The Organizational Connection.* New York: Basic, 1976.

Armacost, Michael H. *The Politics of Weapons Innovation: The Thor-Jupiter Controversy.* New York: Columbia University Press, 1969.

Aronson, Jonathan D. *Money and Power: Banks and the World Monetary System.* Beverly Hills, Calif.: Sage, 1977

Art, Robert J. "Bureaucratic Politics and American Foreign Policy: A Critique." *Policy Sciences* 4 (1973): 467-490.

Aubrey, Henry. *Behind the Veil of International Money.* Essays in International Finance, no. 71. Princeton: Princeton University, International Finance Section, 1969.

Bach, G.L. *Making Monetary and Fiscal Policy.* Washington, D.C.: Brookings, 1971.

Baldwin, David A. "International Political Economy and the International Monetary System." *International Organization* 32 (1978): 497-513.

Ball, Desmond J. "The Blind Men and the Elephant: A Critique of Bureaucratic Politics Theory." *Australian Outlook* 28 (1974): 71-92.

Bator, Francis M. "The Political Economics of International Money." *Foreign Affairs* 47 (1968): 51-67.

Bauer, Raymond A., Ithiel DeSola Pool, and Lewis Anthony Dexter. *American Business and Public Policy: The Politics of Foreign Trade.* 2d ed. Chicago: Aldine-Atherton, 1972.

Bergsten, C. Fred. "Crisis in U.S. Trade Policy." *Foreign Affairs* 49 (1971): 619-36.

——. *The Dilemmas of the Dollar*. New York: New York University Press, 1975.

——. "The New Economics and U.S. Foreign Policy." *Foreign Affairs* 50 (1972): 199-222.

——. "New Urgency for International Monetary Reform." *Foreign Policy*, no. 19 (Summer 1975): 79-93.

Blank, Stephen. "Britain: The Politics of Foreign Economic Policy, the Domestic Economy and the Problem of Domestic Expansion." In *Between Power and Plenty: Foreign Economic Policies of Advanced Industrialized States*, edited by Peter J. Katzenstein. Madison: University of Wisconsin Press, 1978.

Block, Fred L. *The Origins of International Economic Disorder: A Study of United States International Monetary Policy from World War II to the Present*. Berkeley: University of California Press, 1977.

——. "The Ruling Class Does Not Rule: Notes on the Marxist Theory of the State." *Socialist Revolution* 7 (1977): 6-28.

Calleo, David P. *The Imperious Economy*. Cambridge: Harvard University Press, 1982.

Calleo, David P., and Benjamin M. Rowland. *America and the World Political Economy: Atlantic Dreams and National Realities*. Bloomington: Indiana University Press, 1973.

"CEA: A Weaker Role for a Former Powerhouse." *Business Week*, January 20, 1973, pp. 76-78.

Cohen, Benjamin J. *Balance-of-Payments Policy*. Baltimore, Md.: Penguin, 1970.

——. *Organizing the World's Money: The Political Economy of International Monetary Relations*. New York: Basic, 1977.

——. "The Revolution in Atlantic Economic Relations: A Bargain Comes Unstuck." In *The United States and Western Europe: Political, Economic and Strategic Perspectives*, edited by Wolfram F. Hanrieder. Cambridge, Mass.: Winthrop, 1974.

——. "United States Monetary Policy and Economic Nationalism." In *The New Economic Nationalism*, edited by Otto Hieronymi. New York: Praeger, 1980.

Cohen, Stephen D. *International Monetary Reform, 1964-69: The Political Dimension*. New York: Praeger, 1970.

——. *The Making of United States International Economic Policy*. New York: Praeger, 1977.

Coombs, Charles A. *The Arena of International Finance*. New York: John Wiley, 1976.

Cooper, Richard N. "Comment." *Journal of Political Economy* 25 (August 1962): 540-43.

——. *The Economics of Interdependence: Economic Policy in the Atlantic Community.* New York: McGraw-Hill, 1968.

——. "The Future of the Dollar." In *A Reordered World: Emerging International Economic Problems*, edited by Richard N. Cooper. Washington, D.C.: Potomac Associates, 1973.

——. "Prolegomena to the Choice of an International Monetary System." In *International Economics and International Politics*, edited by C. Fred Bergsten and Lawrence B. Krause. Washington, D.C.: Brookings, 1975.

——. "Trade Policy Is Foreign Policy." *Foreign Policy*, no. 9 (Winter 1972-73): 18-37.

Destler, I. M. *Presidents, Bureaucrats, and Foreign Policy: The Politics of Organizational Reform.* Princeton: Princeton University Press, 1974.

deVries, Margaret Garritsen. *The International Monetary Fund, 1966-1971: The System under Stress.* 2 vols. Washington, D.C.: International Monetary Fund, 1976.

Dunn, Robert M. *Exchange-Rate Rigidity, Investment Distortions, and the Failure of Bretton Woods.* Essays in International Finance, no. 97. Princeton: Princeton University, International Finance Section, 1973.

Eckes, Alfred E., Jr. *A Search for Solvency.* Austin: University of Texas Press, 1975.

Elkin, Stephen L. "State and Regime in the American Republic." Paper prepared for delivery at the 1981 annual meeting of the American Political Science Association, New York, September 3-6, 1981.

Ellsberg, Daniel. *Papers on the War.* New York: Simon & Schuster, 1972.

Finlayson, Jock A., and Mark W. Zacher. "The GATT and the Regulation of Trade Barriers: Regime Dynamics and Functions." *International Organization* 35 (1981): 561-603.

Flash, Edward S., Jr. *Economic Advice and Presidential Leadership: The Council of Economic Advisers.* New York: Columbia University Press, 1965.

Freeland, Richard. *The Truman Doctrine and the Origins of McCarthyism: Foreign Policy, Domestic Politics, and Internal Security.* New York: Schocken, 1974.

Gardner, Richard N. *Sterling-Dollar Diplomacy: The Origins and Prospects of Our International Economic Order.* Rev. ed. New York: McGraw-Hill, 1969.

Gelb, Leslie H., with Richard K. Betts. *The Irony of Vietnam: The System Worked.* Washington, D.C.: Brookings, 1979.

George, Alexander L. "Case Studies and Theory Development: The Method of Structured, Focused Comparison." In *Diplomacy: New Approaches in History, Theory, and Policy*, edited by Paul Lauren. New York: Free, 1979.

Gilpin, Robert. *War and Change in International Politics.* New York: Cambridge University Press, 1981.

Haberler, Gottfried, and Thomas D. Willett. *A Strategy for U.S. Balance of Payments Policy.* Washington, D.C.: American Enterprise Institute, 1971.

——. *U.S. Balance of Payments Policies and International Monetary Reform: A Critical Analysis*. Washington, D.C.: American Enterprise Institute, 1968.

Halm, George N., ed. *Approaches to Greater Flexibility of Exchange Rates: The Burgenstock Papers*. Princeton: Princeton University Press, 1970.

Halperin, Morton H., et al. *Bureaucratic Politics and Foreign Policy*. Washington, D.C.: Brookings, 1974.

Hecclo, Hugh. *A Government of Strangers: Executive Politics in Washington*. Washington, D.C.: Brookings, 1977.

Hess, Stephen. *Organizing the Presidency*. Washington, D.C.: Brookings, 1976.

Hinshaw, Randall, ed. *The Economics of International Adjustment*. Baltimore, Md.: Johns Hopkins Press, 1971.

Hirsch, Fred, and Michael W. Doyle. "Politicization in the World Economy: Necessary Conditions for an International Economic Order." In *Alternatives to Monetary Disorder*, edited by Hirsch, Doyle, and Edward L. Morse. New York: McGraw-Hill, 1977.

Holsti, K. J. "Change in the International System: Interdependence, Integration, and Fragmentation." In *Change in the International System*, edited by Ole R. Holsti, Randolph M. Siverson, and Alexander L. George. Boulder, Col.: Westview, 1980.

Holsti, Ole R., Randolph M. Siverson, and Alexander L. George, eds. *Change in the International System*. Boulder, Col.: Westview, 1980.

Horsefield, J. Keith, ed. *The International Monetary Fund, 1945-1965: Twenty Years of International Monetary Cooperation*. 3 vols. Washington, D.C.: International Monetary Fund, 1969.

Houthakker, Hendrik S. "The Breakdown of Bretton Woods." In *Economic Advice and Economic Policy: Recommendations from Past Members of the Council of Economic Advisers*, edited by Werner Sichel. New York: Praeger, 1978.

Jervis, Robert. "Security Regimes." *International Organization* 36 (1982): 357-78.

Johnson, Harry G. "The Bretton Woods System, Key Currencies, and the 'Dollar Crisis' of 1971." *Three Banks Review* (1972): 3-22.

——. "The International Monetary Crisis of 1971." *Journal of Business* 46 (1973): 11-23.

Johnson, Lyndon Baines. *The Vantage Point: Perspectives of the Presidency, 1963-1965*. New York: Holt, Rinehart, & Winston, 1971.

Katzenstein, Peter J., ed. *Between Power and Plenty: Foreign Economic Policies of Advanced Industrialized States*. Madison: University of Wisconsin Press, 1978.

Kelly, Janet. "International Monetary Systems and National Security." In *Economic Issues and National Security*, edited by Klaus Knorr and Frank Trager. Lawrence: Regents Press of Kansas, 1977.

Kenen, Peter B. "The International Position of the Dollar in a Changing World." *International Organization* 23 (1969): 705-18.

Keohane, Robert O. "The Study of Transnational Relations Reconsidered." Address to the British International Studies Association, Warwick University, December 1976.

——. "The Theory of Hegemonic Stability and Changes in International Economic Regimes." In *Change in the International System*, edited by Ole R. Holsti, Randolph M. Siverson, and Alexander L. George. Boulder, Col.: Westview, 1980.

—— "Theory of World Politics." Paper prepared for the annual meeting of the American Political Science Association, Denver, Col., September 2-5, 1982.

——. "U.S. Foreign Policy toward Other Advanced Capitalist States." In *Eagle Entangled: U.S. Foreign Policy in a Complex World*, edited by Kenneth A. Oye, Donald Rothschild, and Robert J. Lieber. New York: Longman, 1979.

Keohane, Robert O., and Joseph S. Nye. *Power and Interdependence: World Politics in Transition*. Boston: Little, Brown, 1977.

Kindleberger, Charles P. "The Price of Gold and the $n-1$ Problem." In *International Money: A Collection of Essays*, edited by Charles P. Kindleberger. London: George Allen & Unwin, 1981.

——. *The World in Depression, 1929-1939*. Berkeley: University of California Press, 1973.

Kissinger, Henry. *White House Years*. Boston: Little, Brown, 1979.

Kohl, Wilfrid L. "The Nixon Foreign Policy System and U.S.-European Relations: Patterns of Policy Making." *World Politics* 28 (1975): 1-43.

Krasner, Stephen D. *Defending the National Interest: Raw Materials Investments and U.S. Foreign Policy*. Princeton: Princeton University Press, 1978.

——. "State Power and the Structure of International Trade." *World Politics* 28 (1976): 317-47.

——. "Structural Causes and Regime Consequences." *International Organization* 36 (1982): 185-206.

——. "U.S. Commercial and Monetary Policy: Unravelling the Paradox of External Strength and Internal Weakness." In *Between Power and Plenty: Foreign Economic Policies of Advanced Industrialized States*, edited by Peter J. Katzenstein. Madison: University of Wisconsin Press, 1978.

Krause, Lawrence B. "A Passive Balance of Payments Strategy for the United States." *Brookings Papers on Economic Activity* 3 (1970): 339-60.

——. *Sequel to Bretton Woods: A Proposal to Reform the World Monetary System*. Washington, D.C.: Brookings, 1971.

Lindblom, Charles E. *Politics and Markets: The World's Political-Economic Systems*. New York: Basic, 1977.

McCracken, Paul W. "An Elder Stateman's Advice to a CEA Chairman." In *Economic Advice and Economic Policy: Recommendations from Past Members of the Council of Economic Advisers*, edited by Werner Sichel. New York: Praeger, 1978.

Machlup, Fritz. *The Alignment of Foreign Exchange Rates*. New York: Praeger, 1972.

———. *Remaking the International Monetary System: The Rio Agreement and Beyond*. Baltimore, Md.: Johns Hopkins Press, 1968.

McKinnon, Ronald I. *Money in International Exchange: The Convertible Currency System*. New York: Oxford University Press, 1979.

Maisel, Sherman J. *Managing the Dollar*. New York: W. W. Norton, 1973.

May, Ernest R. *"Lessons" of the Past: The Use and Misuse of History in American Foreign Policy*. New York: Oxford University Press, 1973.

Mayer, Martin. *The Fate of the Dollar*. New York: Truman Talley, 1980.

Meier, Gerald M. *Problems of a World Monetary Order*. New York: Oxford University Press, 1974.

Michaely, Michael. *The Responsiveness of Demand Policies to Balance of Payments*. New York: National Bureau of Economic Research, 1971.

Morse, Edward L. "Political Choices and Alternative Monetary Regimes." In *Alternatives to Monetary Disorder*, edited by Fred Hirsch, Michael W. Doyle, and Morse. New York: McGraw-Hill, 1977.

Nathan, James, and James Oliver. "Bureaucratic Politics: Academic Windfalls and Intellectual Pitfalls." *Journal of Political and Military Sociology* 6 (1978): 81-92.

Newhouse, John. *Cold Dawn: The Study of SALT*. New York: Holt, Rinehart, & Winston, 1973.

Nixon, Richard. *RN: The Memoirs of Richard Nixon*. New York: Grosset & Dunlap, 1978.

———. *Six Crises*. Garden City, N.Y.: Doubleday, 1962.

"Nixon's Quadriad Gets Back in Step." *Business Week*, May 8, 1971, p. 88.

Nye, Joseph S. "Maintaining a Nonproliferation Regime." *International Organization* 35 (1981): 15-38.

Odell, John S. *U.S. International Monetary Policy: Markets, Power, and Ideas as Sources of Change*. Princeton: Princeton University Press, 1982.

Okun, Arthur M. *The Political Economy of Prosperity*. New York: W. W. Norton, 1970.

Perlmutter, Amos. "The Presidential Political Center and Foreign Policy: A Critique of the Revisionist and Bureaucratic Political Orientations." *World Politics* 27 (1974): 87-106.

Porter, Roger B. "Economic Advice to the President: Eisenhower to Reagan." Paper presented at the 1981 annual meeting of the American Political Science Association, New York, September 3-6, 1981.

——. "The President and Economic Policy: Problems, Patterns, and Alternatives." In *The Illusion of the Presidential Government*, edited by Hugh Hecclo and Lester M. Salamon. Boulder, Col.: Westview, 1981.

Puchala, Donald J., and Raymond F. Hopkins. "International Regimes: Lessons from Inductive Analysis." *International Organization* 36 (1982): 245-76.

Ruggie, John Gerard. "International Regimes, Transactions, and Change: Embedded Liberalism in the Postwar Economic Order." *International Organization* 36 (1982): 379-416.

——. "Review." *American Political Science Review* 74 (1980): 296-99.

Russell, Robert. "Crisis Management in the International Monetary System." Paper presented at the International Studies Association meeting, New York, March 1983.

Safire, William. *Before the Fall*. New York: Doubleday, 1975.

Scammell, W. M. *The International Economy since 1945*. New York: St. Martin's, 1980.

Schattschneider, E. E. *Politics, Pressures and the Tariff*. Englewood Cliffs, N.J.: Prentice-Hall, 1935.

Schlesinger, Arthur M. *The Imperial Presidency*. Boston: Houghton Mifflin, 1973.

Shonfield, Andrew. "International Economic Relations of the Western World: An Overall View." In *International Economic Relations of the Western World, 1959-1971*, vol. 1, edited by Shonfield. London: Oxford University Press, 1976.

Shultz, George P., and Kenneth W. Dam. *Economic Policy beyond the Headlines*. New York: W. W. Norton, 1977.

Silk, Leonard. *Nixonomics*. 2d ed. New York: Praeger, 1972.

Solomon, Robert. *The International Monetary System, 1945-1976: An Insider's View*. New York: Harper & Row, 1977.

Sorensen, Theodore C. *Kennedy*. New York: Harper & Row, 1965.

Sprout, Harold and Margaret. "Environmental Factors in the Study of International Politics." In *International Politics and Foreign Policy*, edited by James N. Rosenau. New York: Free, 1969.

Stein, Arthur A. "Coordination and Collaboration: Regimes in an Anarchic World." *International Organization* 36 (1982): 299-324.

Stein, Herbert. *The Fiscal Revolution in America*. Chicago: University of Chicago Press, 1969.

Steinbruner, John. *The Cybernetic Theory of Decision: New Dimensions of Political Analysis*. Princeton: Princeton University Press, 1974.

Strange, Susan. "*Cave! Hic Dragones*: A Critique of Regime Analysis." *International Organization* 36 (1982): 479-96.

——. "The Dollar Crisis, 1971." *International Affairs* (London) 48 (1972): 191-215.

———. *International Monetary Relations. International Economic Relations of the Western World, 1959-1971,* vol. 2. London: Oxford University Press, 1976.

———. *Sterling and British Policy: A Political Study of an International Currency in Decline.* London: Oxford University Press, 1971.

Treverton, Gregory F. *The Dollar Drain and American Forces in Germany: Managing the Political Economies of Alliance.* Athens: Ohio University Press, 1978.

Triffin, Robert. *Gold and the Dollar Crisis: The Future of Convertibility.* New Haven: Yale University Press, 1960.

Tufte, Edward R. *Political Control of the Economy.* Princeton: Princeton University Press, 1978.

U.S., Commission on International Trade and Investment Policy. *United States International Economic Policy in an Interdependent World,* vol. 3. Washington, D.C., 1972.

U.S., Commission on the Organization of the Government for the Conduct of Foreign Policy. *Report,* vol. 3. Washington, D.C., 1975.

U.S., Congress, House, Banking and Currency Committee. *Background Material on Legislation Modifying the Par Value of the Dollar.* 92d Cong., 2d sess., February 15, 1972.

U.S., Congress, House, Banking and Currency Committee. *International Monetary Reform.* 92d Cong., 2d sess., June 22, 1972.

U.S., Congress, House, Committee on Foreign Affairs. *International Implications of the New Economic Policy.* 92d Cong., 1st sess., September 16 and 21, 1971.

U.S., Congress, House, Committee on Foreign Affairs. *U.S. Foreign Economic Policy: Implications for the Organization of the Executive Branch.* 92d Cong., 2d sess., June-September 1972.

U.S., Congress, Joint Economic Committee. *Action Now to Strengthen the U.S. Dollar.* 92d Cong., 1st sess., August 1971.

U.S., Congress, Joint Economic Committee. *The Balance of Payments Mess.* 92d Cong., 1st sess., June 16-17, 21-23, 1971.

U.S., Congress, Joint Economic Committee, Subcommittee on International Exchange and Payments. *Guidelines for Improving the International Monetary System.* 89th Cong., 1st sess., September 9, 1965.

U.S., Congress, Senate, Finance Committee. *International Aspects of the President's New Economic Policies.* 92d Cong., 1st. sess., September 13-14, October 1, 1971.

U.S., Council on International Economic Policy. *The United States in the Changing World Economy: A Report to the President,* vol. 1. Washington, D.C., 1971.

U.S., White House. *Economic Report of the President, Together with the Annual Report of the Council of Economic Advisers.* Washington, D.C., 1971.

U.S., White House. *Economic Report of the President, Together with the Annual Report of the Council of Economic Advisers.* Washington, D.C., 1972.

U.S., White House. *International Economic Report of the President.* Washington, D.C., 1973.

vanBuren Cleveland, Harold. "How the Dollar Standard Died." *Foreign Policy,* no. 8 (Winter 1971-72): 41-51.

Volcker, Paul A. "The Political Economy of the Dollar." The Fred Hirsch Lecture, November 9, 1978, at Warwick University, Coventry, England. Mimeo.

Walker, David A. "Some Underlying Problems for International Monetary Reform." In *The United States and Western Europe: Political, Economic and Strategic Perspectives,* edited by Wolfram F. Hanrieder. Cambridge, Mass.: Winthrop, 1974.

Wallich, Henry C. "Government Action." In *The Dollar in Crisis,* edited by Seymour E. Harris. New York: Harcourt, Brace & World, 1961.

Waltz, Kenneth N. *Theory of International Politics.* Reading, Mass.: Addison-Wesley, 1979.

Whitman, Marina v. N. *Reflections of Interdependence: Issues for Economic Theory and U.S. Policy.* Pittsburgh: University of Pittsburgh Press, 1979.

——. "The Search for the Grail: Economic Policy Issues of the Late 1970s." In *Economic Advice and Economic Policy: Recommendations from Past Members of the Council of Economic Advisers,* edited by Werner Sichel. New York: Praeger, 1978.

Willett, Thomas D. *Floating Exchange Rates and International Monetary Reform.* Washington, D.C.: American Enterprise Institute, 1977.

——. *International Liquidity Issues.* Washington, D.C.: American Enterprise Institute, 1980.

Williamson, John H. *The Crawling Peg.* Essays in International Finance, no. 50. Princeton: Princeton University, International Finance Section, December 1965.

——. *The Failure of World Monetary Reform, 1971-1974.* New York: New York University Press, 1977.

Young, Oran. "International Regimes: Problems of Concept Formation." *World Politics* 32 (1980): 331-54.

——. "Regime Dynamics: The Rise and Fall of International Regimes." *International Organization* 36 (1982): 277-89.

Zinnes, Dina A. "Prerequisites for the Study of System Transformation. " In *Change in the International System,* edited by Ole R. Holsti, Randolph M. Siverson, and Alexander L. George. Boulder, Col.: Westview, 1980.

Index

Library of Congress Cataloging in Publication Data

Gowa, Joanne S.
  Closing the gold window.

  (Cornell studies in political economy)
  Bibliography: p.
  Includes index.
  1. Foreign exchange problem—United States. 2. Dollar, American—Devalua-
    tion. 3. United States—Foreign economic relations—Case studies. 4. United
    States—Politics and Government—1969-1974. 5. International finance.
    I. Title. II. Series.
HG3903.G68 1983   332.4'560973   83-7184
ISBN 0-8014-1622-1